DON'T SHOOT, IT'S ONLY ME

Bob Hope's
Comedy History
of the United States

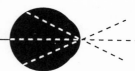

**This Large Print Book carries the
Seal of Approval of N.A.V.H.**

DON'T SHOOT, IT'S ONLY ME

Bob Hope's Comedy History of the United States

BOB HOPE
WITH
MELVILLE SHAVELSON

Thorndike Press • Thorndike, Maine

Library of Congress Cataloging in Publication Data:

Hope, Bob, 1903-
    Don't shoot, it's only me : Bob Hope's comedy
history of the United States / Bob Hope with Melville
Shavelson.
        p. cm.
    ISBN 1-56054-098-2 (alk. paper : lg. print)
    ISBN 1-56054-993-9 (alk. paper : lg. print : pbk.)
    1. Hope, Bob 1903- . 2. United States—Armed
Forces—Recreation. 3. Entertainers—United States—
Biography. 4. Comedians—United States—Biography
5. Large type books. I. Shavelson, Melville, 1917- .
II. Title.
[PN2287.H63A3   1991]   90-24186
792.7'028'092—dc20   CIP
[B]

Thorndike Press Large Print edition published in 1991
by arrangement with G. P. Putnam's Sons.

Cover design by Ralph Lizotte.

The tree indicium is a trademark of Thorndike Press.

This book is printed on acid-free, high opacity paper. ∞

Don't look back.
Somethin' may be gainin' on you.

—SATCHEL PAIGE

To the men and women of the armed forces of the United States and its Allies, the greatest audience a performer ever had; to their families, who also served; to my own family, who waited and sometimes worried; to all the stars and entertainers who willingly went wherever they were needed; to the USO, which extended vaudeville to every corner of the globe; and to the peace that seems finally to have broken out in the hearts of men.

CONTENTS

PREFACE

The terrible thing about growing older is that it lasts so long. You start telling jokes to make a living and one morning you wake up and find you've written the history of half a century. Or your writers have. Accidentally.

I have no regrets. I've known most of the great personalities of our time, in politics, sports, and show business. I've flown a few million miles and been fortunate enough to meet thousands of our men and women in uniform, in war and peace, and have had as guests on my shows some of the most beautiful women in the world.

If I had my life to live over again, I wouldn't have the strength.

But I'd like to try.

Writing this book is as close as I can get to living it all again. Maybe it will help you to remember, too.

As I look back at all the jokes I have told over the years, some good and some that I wrote myself, I realize now that what they are really about is America. They are about what has happened to this country in this critical, tumultuous, crazy, terrible, wonderful half century we've just stumbled through.

I'm only an adopted son. I was born in England and left as soon as I realized I couldn't become king. My mother took all her children on a boat to the New World. It wasn't first class, but we had a lot of fun playing with the cattle. Of course, when we got here, we had to learn the language. And then, in this country, I fell in love. Sometimes I do my best to hide it, but I've got a real crush on America. Nobody ever had a girl like her. Nobody ever gave me as much affection, as much honor, or as much real estate. In a way, in this most democratic of democracies, I sometimes feel like a king.

How did it happen? Why me? I come from a family of seven boys, and the only thing we all had in common was that none of us ever won the Academy Award. Of course, the others weren't really trying.

Did some giant iron claw in the sky drop me into the one place in history where a fellow who barely got out of high school would have a school at Yale named after him? Where three wars in rapid succession would give him a captive audience of fighting men and women who were so glad to be alive they were ready to laugh at anything to prove it?

I'm no philosopher. I'm no historian. Maybe those who are will find some hidden depths in this story I'm going to tell, simply the story of what the United States of America was laughing at in the past fifty or so years, before getting up the next morning and going out to do battle with the enemies all of us have to face: Yesterday, Today, and Tomorrow.

This is a love song to my girl: America, warts and all.

I just read the last few paragraphs over. That's the longest I've ever gone without a laugh . . . on purpose.

That always makes me uncomfortable. Laughter is my business and my life. I need it to feel wanted. I'd feel a lot more secure if I'd looked back at my career in a style audiences have come to expect of me:

"I figure I've spent the last thirty years getting overseas shots. Last week I had acupuncture and all the needles fell out. . . . I can't take a deep breath, there isn't a spot on me that doesn't leak. . . . All those years of eating regular Army food. To this day I still get a little sick anytime I pass a shingle roof. . . . But it's certainly been exciting. I've worked on some stages where, if you made an exit stage left, you were captured. . . ."

There; I feel better now. I've had my fix. I've never gone on the air without asking — begging, sometimes — for laughs. Except for one memorable night, June 6, 1944. That night, D day, I just couldn't do it. I had played for many of the boys who were now making history. Nobody knew if any of them would ever come home. There was no monologue that night. There was no show. Frances Langford sang "Ave Maria," and I signed off by saying, "God bless those kids across the English Channel."

I hope I never have to be that serious again. Like Danny Thomas, when he opened that same June 6 at the Latin Quarter in New York. There he was, frightened to death, his very first appearance in the big time. Milton Berle graciously lent a hand, generously giving Danny a few of his best jokes, and a couple of mine. Then, just before Danny was to go out on the floor and face the tough New York audience and the tough New York critics, he heard on the radio that the invasion had begun. American kids were among those about to land on French beaches in the teeth of the Nazi army. Danny, already well known for his sentimentality (he inspired the line "He's the kind of guy who cries at basketball games") was devastated. He forced himself, shakily, to walk out on that nightclub floor. When the spotlight hit him, he got down on his knees and said, "Ladies and gentlemen, our boys are invading Normandy right now. Let's pray." And right there on the floor of the Latin Quarter he led a Broadway audience in the Lord's Prayer, figuring he had just tossed away his career, but what did it really matter?

Then he got to his feet and went into his nightclub routine, hoping he wouldn't be stoned, like another Fellow from the Middle East.

Hesitantly, Danny started to tell some jokes. Never before or after did he get so many laughs. The audience howled and cheered and gave him a standing ovation when he finally bowed off.

Danny went to his dressing room walking on air, only to be met by Uncle Milty, looking very unhappy.

"What's wrong?" Danny wanted to know. "I thought I did pretty good."

Uncle Milty hesitated. "The act is okay," he finally admitted, "but you're going to have to change that opening."

What bothers me most about these stories is that many kids today don't have any idea of what D day was all about. They are like the young vice president at one of the television networks who was recently asked why he kept turning down wonderful scripts about World War II. And this executive, who had recently learned to shave, said, "Nothing that happened before I was born could possibly have any relevance to my life."

There is an old proverb that those who don't learn from history are destined to repeat its mistakes.

Maybe that applies to that guy's mother.

One of the reasons for writing this book is to tell a whole generation that what happened before they were born does matter. In the modern world, Americans are being outsmarted every day by nations we defeated over forty years ago.

Their kids know exactly what happened.

There are only a few moments when a comedian can get away with being truly serious, and I certainly don't make a habit of it. When you get to a serious subject, comics usually prefer to make fun of it.

I suppose one of the things this book is about is the subject most people prefer to ignore: Age. But you can get loads of laughs out of it. After all, there are a lot worse things than growing older, and I wish I could remember what they were.

It's all relative. When Charles Evans Hughes was chief justice of the Supreme Court and almost ninety years old, a pretty girl passed by wearing a low-cut blouse and a tight skirt. Hughes turned to a friend and sighed, "Oh, to be eighty again."

And then there was the five-year-old boy who said to his father, "Dad, Elaine and I want to get married."

His father smiled and said, "How old is Elaine?"

"Eleven," the kid replied.

"How are you going to live?"

"Well, I get two dollars a week allowance and she gets four dollars. That oughta be enough."

His father smiled again and said, "Yes, but suppose you have children?"

"Don't worry," his son told him, "we've been lucky so far."

So let's forget about age, have a few laughs, and reminisce about something *really* funny . . . the last fifty or so years.

CHAPTER ONE

1938-1940

*"How do you do, ladies and
gentlemen. This is Bob Hope.
(Single laugh from audience)
Not yet, Charlie. But don't leave."
— First "Bob Hope Pepsodent Show,"
September 27, 1938*

I first stepped out on a stage in 1923. It
was in Cleveland, and my dancing partner
was a girl named Mildred Rosequist. She
was all of fifteen years old. We were both
so frightened that we just clung to each other.
Her mother was there and immediately broke
up the act.

I got another partner, and then another,
and then became a single and fought my
way up through the Gus Sun Time vaudeville
circuit in the days when rooming houses
carried signs saying, NO DOGS OR ACTORS
ALLOWED. Since I wasn't considered either
one, I usually got a room. By 1938, I had
left vaudeville and starred on Broadway in

Roberta, Say When, the Ziegfeld Follies, and *Red, Hot and Blue!*

The President of the United States was Franklin Delano Roosevelt, and you could buy a hot dog for a dime. Maybe you couldn't eat it, but you could buy it. Sirloin steak was thirty-five cents a pound and the butcher would deliver. Butter was fifteen cents, and nobody had ever heard of cholesterol. Skirts were getting shorter and women were wearing their hair piled up on top of their heads. Doctors were making house calls for five dollars, and were available twenty-four hours a day. They hadn't learned to play golf yet.

We were just coming out of the Depression and we could finally make jokes about the Communist party, which no longer seemed a threat. I can remember seeing Willie and Eugene Howard (I worked in a couple of Broadway shows with them) doing my favorite routine, the one where Willie played a Communist on a soapbox haranguing a crowd on a New York street corner that included his brother, Eugene.

"Comes the revolution," Willie shouted, hoarsely, "all you downtrodden workers will be driving Packards and eating strawberries and cream!"

And Eugene hollered at him, "I don't like strawberries and cream!"

Willie, a little guy with a pinched face and a large nose, glared at his brother as if he would like to strangle him. "Comes the revolution," hollered Willie, "you'll *eat* strawberries and cream!"

I don't know why that has stuck in my memory, except that it shows how we've come full circle to the age of *glasnost* and *perestroika*. There was a time when I would have been investigated just for knowing how to spell those words.

War clouds were already gathering in Europe in 1938, but war was the last thing on our minds in America then. At least, *my* mind. A new era was beginning in the career of Leslie Townes Hope, sometimes known as Rapid Robert. They could have blown up the Empire State Building and I wouldn't have taken my eyes off the headline in weekly *Variety*, "Paramount Signs Bob Hope." Until then, I had been playing in Broadway musicals and occasionally going back into vaudeville, wherever audiences didn't have a long memory. I had also appeared on the radio on Rudy Vallee's "Fleischmann's Yeast Hour," for which I received a cake of yeast and Rudy's recipe for cupcakes. Video hadn't shown up yet. When it did, I remarked that television was the box they buried vaudeville in.

I had made my first movie, a two-reeler

called *Going Spanish*, which we shot out on Long Island when there was an offshore breeze. After the picture opened, I ran into Walter Winchell and he asked me how the film was. I told him that when the cops caught John Dillinger, they were going to make him sit through it twice.

Winchell printed that line and the producers of the picture promptly dropped my option.

Since by that time I was used to eating, I had to get another job. I hired myself a wonderful agent named Louis Shurr — we called him "Doctor" because of the way he operated. Doc Shurr was short and bald, but he owned an expensive white mink coat he would give to any girl who would go out with him. One look at that mink, and bald became beautiful. At the end of the evening he always took the coat back, but by that time it didn't matter. If things hadn't worked out, Doc could always get another girl, or a toupee.

With that kind of talent, Doc Shurr managed to sell me to Paramount Pictures for a film called *The Big Broadcast of 1938*. I don't know how he did it. The mink didn't fit Adolph Zukor, who made the deal. Zukor was the founder and president emeritus of Paramount. A small, kindly man, he wandered around the lot looking like an elderly kitten, but appearances were deceiving. Zukor was one of the gang of pioneers who had founded the movie industry in Hollywood, a group that included Samuel Goldwyn, Louis B. Mayer, the Warner brothers, and Harry Cohn. The story is that all of them would have sold their mothers, but Cohn would have delivered her.

Zukor was the gambler. He was willing to take a chance on any new experiment — including me.

I talked to him in later years, when he was ninety-eight. He had just come from seeing some new movie, and I asked him how he liked it.

"Too long," Zukor said. "Did you see it?"

"No," I admitted, "I was shooting my television show. Have you seen my show?"

He nodded.

"Too long," he said, but he added, "don't be offended. *Life* is too long."

I was asked to introduce the old boy at some industry function in 1973, and since by that time I felt pretty secure, I wasn't afraid to say:

"Mr. Zukor is from the golden age of films . . . when we were all working. He's been around so long he actually knew some of the people Charlton Heston has played. Mr. Zukor was making movies when *The Ten Commandments* was listed as science fiction."

Adolph Zukor lived to be 103. On his hundredth birthday, Paramount gave him a tremendous party at the Beverly Hilton. They rented a suite for him so Zukor could rest until it was time for him to appear. He sat in the suite, watching the party downstairs on television. Jack Benny was master of ceremonies, reminiscing about Zukor in his usual style, meaning lots of long pauses. Suddenly, Adolph got to his feet and started for the door.

One of the Paramount publicity men jumped to his feet and barred his way.

"Sir, where are you going?" he asked Adolph.

And Adolph said, "Home."

"But it's your hundredth birthday party! You can't walk out on your hundredth birthday!"

"Watch me," said Zukor, and tried to push him aside.

"But why?"

Zukor pointed to the television set.

"Benny," he said. "Too long."

They finally persuaded the feisty old guy to go down and blow out his birthday candles.

It took four Paramount vice presidents to help him complete the job.

He was right about Jack Benny, but that was Jack's style. Too long for anyone else, just right for him. Benny once waited ninety seconds for a single laugh on his radio show. It was the famous scene where the holdup man stuck a gun in Jack's ribs and snarled, "Your money or your life." After ninety seconds of silence, Benny said, "I'm thinking, I'm thinking."

One of the biggest laughs ever heard on radio.

In 1938, Benny had one of the top-rated radio programs in the country. One of the reasons was that he had carefully built up the character of a miser, the tightest man in the world, into one of the most lovable skinflints in show business history, Scrooge with a heart of gold. Benny's method was to take his time, let the character grow at the expense of the easy laugh until it paid off in one final yock that rocked the studio audience.

My method, as it developed in early monologues, was to deliver a series of one-liners, joke joke joke. It was a style similar to Winchell's staccato delivery. I would zing a joke and then start on the next line and wait for the audience to catch up. Then I'd ad-lib, "Laugh first, figure it out later." If someone laughed a little late, I'd ask, "Which one are you working on?"

That style chews up jokes in carload lots. Jack Benny, in over forty years of broadcasting, employed fewer than ten writers. I've given that many heartburn in a week.

Benny and I appeared on each other's shows many times over the years. Jack once said, "Hope and I have an exchange agreement. He appears on my show free and I do his laundry."

I once claimed that I first met Jack on the golf course, when he came up to me and said, "Need a caddy?"

"How can a man with your money be so cheap as to caddy for a few extra bucks?" I asked. What made me so mad is that he didn't say it to me, but to the guy I was caddying for.

Benny had a mincing walk that he was always kidded about. On one show, Phil Harris watched him walk and remarked, "You could put a dress on that guy and take him anywhere."

Once, on the Johnny Carson show, Benny said, "Bob Hope kids me about my walk all the time. He thinks I walk . . . well, *you* know. Now, Bob Hope walks exactly the way I do. But he cups his hands." And he did an imitation of my walk that brought down the house.

If I do walk funny, it's my tailor's fault.

Benny and Fred Allen, the other top radio comedian of that day, had a hilarious running feud for years. Once Jack said, "It's hard getting a Christmas present for Allen. What can you get for a man who has nothing?"

A line Allen used was created by Jack's first writer, Harry Conn. Fred said, "Jack Benny couldn't ad-lib a belch after a Hungarian dinner." Benny himself loved that line, and often repeated it.

Fred Allen, on the other hand, was a superb ad-libber. Fred wrote much of his own material and spent his life at the typewriter. I remember once he invited me up to his apartment in New York. Fred wouldn't have been caught dead in California. He coined the line "California is a great place to live — if you're an orange." I was greeted at the door by his wife, Portland Hoffa — I think Fred wrote that name for her — and as I entered, Fred was hunched over his battered Royal portable. He looked up, said, "Hi, Bob," went back to the typewriter, and I never heard another word from him all evening.

In spite of all the great jokes Fred Allen delivered, he will be remembered most for the time he was upstaged by an eagle. In those days, every radio show was done live, and on this night a guest eagle ad-libbed a response to Fred that was a tribute to the eagle's digestion. The audience howled for five minutes, and for once, Fred was speechless. He thought of lots of things to say, but on a live program he couldn't say any of them.

A lot of Fred's barbs were directed at Jack's violin playing, the world's worst. Yehudi Menuhin once heard him and considered switching to bongo drums. When I made the film *Beau James,* Jack made a guest appearance, unbilled and unpaid for. He didn't utter a line. All he did was play the violin and steal the scene.

The Benny-Allen feud was completely make-believe. The two actually were good friends who admired each other tremendously. Jack was in tears when he heard that Fred had died. And years later, when Jack Benny had played his last false chord, I was asked to deliver the eulogy.

Here's part of it:

"I remember in 1958 when I made my first trip to Moscow and it was announced in all the papers that America's leading comedian was visiting. That night, I went to Ambassador Thompson's home and Mrs.

Thompson met me at the door and said, 'How wonderful you could come. Did you bring your violin?'

"I considered it a compliment."

It's time to meander back to the fall of 1938. *The Big Broadcast* had come out and was a big hit, thanks to a little song number called "Thanks for the Memory," written by Leo Robin and Ralph Rainger. It's the only thing in that picture that may live longer than Adolph Zukor did. Along with Doctor Louis Shurr for my movie deals, I had hired another famous agent to search out work for me in network radio. In fact, I had gone to his office and licked his hand until he agreed to handle me. (I hadn't learned how to act like a big star yet. I was very modest in those days. Of course, as the saying goes, I had a great deal to be modest about.)

Jimmy Saphier was not only smart, he also played a pretty good game of golf. The fact that I could beat him had nothing to do with his getting the job. The fact that he was foolish enough to bet me ten dollars a hole, did.

I needed him then because just about that time, I had been canceled from the "Woodbury Radio Show" and was looking for gainful employment. Fortunately, the advertising executive on the show was a fellow named Ed Lasker, who laughed pretty good at the jokes. When I was canceled, Ed told me I was going to go someplace. I figured he meant the WPA, but Ed said, no, he was going to talk to his father about me. I told him he could talk to his mother, too, if that would do any good. Maybe she'd bake me a cake. But Ed's father happened to be Albert Lasker, who happened to own the Pepsodent Company. I guess they had a good father-and-son talk, because the next thing I knew I was sending Saphier in to make a deal.

Saph negotiated a contract with the Pepsodent Company that gave me my first chance at a radio show all my own. So in 1938, with *The Big Broadcast* already behind me, I went out to Hollywood to make another film and try to knock Benny and Allen out of their top spots in radio. I was the new kid on the block, and even though I loved and admired them both, I preferred for them to love and admire *me*.

About the same time that I was going out to California, England's prime minister, Neville Chamberlain, was clutching his umbrella under his arm and flying to Munich to have tea and crumpets with Adolf Hitler. What Neville didn't know was that *he* was going to be the crumpet.

I suppose, for the benefit of a history like this and students of the bizarre, I should explain just how we started creating the Pepsodent show during those tense days.

I had had my first comedy training in vaudeville, where I would develop a routine and keep the same jokes for at least a season, not daring to change a line for fear all the magic would be lost and I'd have to go back to plucking chickens in my brother Fred's meat market.

But radio was a medium where, every week, more people would hear my jokes than had seen my vaudeville act in ten years on the Gus Sun Time. I had to deliver a new routine every show, or the studio audience would come up and get me. In those days, the radio season ran thirty-nine weeks. That meant I had to tell thirty-nine times as many jokes as I had used in a whole year of vaudeville.

Talented though I was, I knew I couldn't steal that many jokes in one year. I would have to hire the best writers I could find. I realized that would cost a lot of money; but I felt then it was the best investment a young comic could make. Of course, I hadn't learned about real estate yet.

So in the fall of 1938, I hired eight of

the best comedy minds I could find and generously paid them whatever I could get away with. I recently rounded some of them up and asked them to describe our negotiations, for the purpose of this imperishable record. I don't think they knew that I was getting the princely sum of $2,500 a week, and out of that I had to figure out how I was going to pay all of *them*. Eight writers would take a pretty big bite out of it. No comic had ever tried to maintain a staff that size, especially not out of his own end. But I wanted to be Number One, and I knew that jokes were the key; I was willing to pay for it, and I must say, looking back, I got much more than I paid for. Most of that first group went on to fame and fortune; but we were all just starting then, and both the fame and the fortune were in the future. Their recollections of my generosity don't seem to jibe with mine, so I'd better let them tell you in their own words:

MEL SHAVELSON: The late, great Milt Josefsberg (then a Broadway press agent, later, by his own admission, one of the most famous of comedy writers) and I had written some absolutely scintillating material for a new young comic then appearing in vaudeville at Loew's State. The comic had just snared a contract for his first radio show, to be produced in glamorous, glorious Hollywood, and was looking for writers. Since Milt outweighed me by a hundred pounds, most of it ketchup (his favorite food), I appointed him our representative when Robert Hope invited us up to his suite at the Hampshire House to discuss money.

Negotiations proceeded somewhat like this:

> HOPE (*pleasantly, indicating our material*): How much do you guys expect to be paid for writing this junk?
> MILT (*firmly*): A hundred dollars a week.

There was a long pause, and finally Bob asked, "Each?"

> MILT (*his voice breaking*): Each.

There was another long, Jack Benny-ish pause.

Finally, Bob said, "That's a little rich for my blood."

Bob wrestled with his better judgment for three weeks and finally agreed to our price. The contract Saphier drew up, as I dimly recall, required us to write for him exclusively, forever, with options every thirteen weeks. Since I planned to be married as soon as I got my first check, he did give me two hours off for my honeymoon. He was considerate enough, when he phoned during that time to ask for some jokes, to inquire if he was interrupting anything.

According to my bride, not much.

NORMAN PANAMA: Mel Frank and I graduated together from Northwestern University and were doing very well at our chosen profession — starving playwrights — when we heard that Bob was looking for comedy writers. Since we both had to eat — Mel never stopped eating in all the years I knew him — we decided to postpone becoming the Jewish Eugene O'Neills and submitted some jokes. Hope was so overwhelmed by our genius, he immediately offered us eighty dollars a week. For the two of us. Since this was a little better than starving, we agreed.

We stayed with the show for two years before writing a screenplay we called *Snowball in Hell*, about a comic with a penguin in his vaudeville act who becomes an unwitting dupe for a blonde spy in World War II, since he isn't much smarter than the penguin. This seemed like an ideal role for our former employer. Bob made the film with Madeleine Carroll, under the title *My Favorite Blonde*, and Mel and

I were launched on a career in movies.

That was 1941. The rest is history. If only we had remained with Bob, I figure by now we would have been shot at in at least fourteen different countries.

Another missed opportunity.

JACK ROSE: I had been writing jokes for Milton Berle for about thirty dollars a week, and my father was getting suspicious when I brought all that money home. In our Brooklyn family of eleven children, none of my brothers or sisters had ever earned that kind of money. My father asked my brother Ed, later to be an assistant D.A. under Tom Dewey, to investigate me and find out what mob I was with.

I knew then I had to get out of Brooklyn, and submitted some jokes to Mr. Robert Hope. I took as my agent a fellow named Jimmy Saphier. I didn't find out until after he made the deal that he was also Bob Hope's agent.

After what Berle paid me, what Saphier negotiated for me seemed like a real dream deal. I was to be paid a hundred a week, with raises at option time every thirteen weeks. But if Hope didn't pick up my first option, the deal would include a round-trip ticket from New York to Hollywood.

If my option *was* picked up, the deal included only a one-way ticket.

That seemed fair.

SHERWOOD SCHWARTZ: In 1939, my brother Al was the head writer on the new "Bob Hope Pepsodent Show," and so naturally I was living with him. I was finishing my master's thesis at the University of Southern California and planning to go on to medical school. It occurred to me that if my brother could write jokes, it might be an inherited trait in the Schwartz genes. I asked Al if he would show some of the jokes I wrote to Bob, and a lot of them were used.

When the season ended, I got a call from Jimmy Saphier, of whom you have heard. He said Bob wanted me to join the staff of the show the following season.

"Jimmy," I explained to him, "I don't want to join the show! I'm going to be a doctor! But I'll gladly accept a bonus."

Silence from Saphier.

Then I heard that Bob was leaving for England that summer, and I figured that was the last I'd ever hear about a career in show business.

I was wrong. Before he left, Bob prepared a seven-year contract for me — with thirteen-week options — and signed it. He had

Saphier give it to me and tell me that if I didn't get into medical school, I should sign it myself.

Fortunately, hundreds of lives were saved when I failed to get into medical school.

I signed the contract. Hope had held it open for me until the very beginning of the season.

It's a gesture I'll never forget.

Looking back on those tough days, I realize money is relative, and I'm not speaking of Sherwood's brother, Al. When I started playing clubs, I got ten dollars a night for telling jokes, if business was good. A few years ago, I got $100,000 from General Motors just to walk through their exhibit at the Auto Show. They didn't even ask me to tell jokes. I wonder if that meant something?

All of us had money problems back in 1938. None of us knew how long the Pepsodent show would remain on the air. Or if we would remain with it. Pepsodent believed in thirteen-week options, too.

On the Woodbury show, I had worked with a writer named Willkie Mahoney, who also wrote for a highly intellectual publication known as *Uncle Billy's Whiz Bang*. We used to sit up all night writing monologue jokes for the Woodbury program and looking at the pictures of girls in his magazine. But with the responsibility for an entire half hour on my shoulders, I knew I couldn't do that anymore. So I gave up the writing. I decided to hire the best writing staff I could find; actually, I paid them more than any of the other comedians were paying writers at the time. And their jobs were steady. Very steady. Sometimes twenty-four hours a day.

I was damn lucky to get the guys I got; and to get to know them.

I rented a house in North Hollywood on a short-term lease from Walter Lantz, the creator and producer of the Woody Woodpecker cartoons. I guess he wasn't too certain of my chances of becoming a living legend, because whenever the rent was due, I'd get a phone call and that Woody Woodpecker laugh when I said the check was in the mail.

And I'd have to come through with more birdseed.

We held our script meetings at night, in that rented house on Navajo Street. I let a few writers go that first year, but since I had to give them two weeks' notice after I hired their replacements, for a while there were eleven writers writing one half-hour comedy show. When they left the house they looked like Notre Dame coming out for the second half.

All these comedy minds were necessary if I was going to carry out my plan, which was almost unheard of at that time. It was to go on the air every week with topical jokes written right up to airtime. And some even after. Even if they weren't all good, they would give the Pepsodent show an immediacy that I find missing today, when so many shows are taped weeks in advance. And we had no canned laughter then to cover the clinkers. We had to be good, or else. It was life or death, sink or swim, and I knew I needed as many life preservers as possible or we'd all go down with the ship.

With all those mad minds churning out gags, it could have been bedlam if I hadn't figured out a system to select the best material quickly. We all gathered in the den of that house on Navajo Street, most of this great talent sprawled on the floor, still breathing heavily because I had a Great Dane named Red Sun who got his kicks from chasing writers.

My weary geniuses would all read their jokes aloud. If they could get laughs from the other worried gentlemen whose jobs depended upon their keeping a straight face, the joke went into the show. Remember, in 1938 we were just coming out of the Depression. There were still ten million unemployed, most of whom thought they could write. Getting a laugh out of that lineup from murderers' row was like getting a laugh from a guy on the rack during the Spanish Inquisition. It took real talent.

None of us had done a show like this before and we proceeded from ignorance, of which we had an abundance. We had a big blackboard on which we'd write great ideas for next week's show. Then we'd erase it and write great ideas for *last* week's show.

The character that's now known as Bob Hope didn't leap, full-grown, from some writer's typewriter. It developed over several seasons — like a weed, as one of my writers picturesquely described it. He is no longer with me.

The character I played in films at that time had some of the characteristics of the radio personality, but, especially in the "Road" pictures, we put more emphasis on the "boob" aspect.

In 1953, Leo Rosten explained it this way in *The Saturday Evening Post*: "His comic style is ageless. . . . He is the perfect symbol of the man Fate is determined to make a jerk. He brags and blusters, but there isn't a child over five who can't outwit him, disarm him or steal his pants. . . . Single-handed, he took the curse, off being a coward. In fact. he makes cowardice lovable. . . ."

Why did I quote *him?*

Although some of my writers claim they based my radio character on what they observed of me on Navajo Street, don't believe it. In real life I am actually irresistible to women and as strong and tough as Mike Tyson used to be, and I throw my money around like a drunken sailor.

As you can see, they got my character all wrong. What I really am is a liar.

A whole army of untruths grew up about those historic days in that rented house on Navajo Street. First, there was the canard (if that means what I think it means) that at those all-night writing sessions, I would get hungry around midnight and send out the youngest writer (the disappointed medical student, Sherwood Schwartz) to buy a quart of vanilla ice cream. The writers insisted I would then devour it all and scrape the bottom of the carton and never offer them so much as a lick.

I deny this story categorically. If that also means what I think it means. I couldn't have scraped the bottom of the carton — I usually ate it.

Sherwood went into the Army during the war — he says he was drafted as a hostage —

and came back, still in uniform, when it was over three years later. The day he got back, he happened to see me eating in a restaurant, and before I could spot him, he sneaked out, bought a quart of vanilla ice cream, ran back to the restaurant, tapped me on the shoulder, and handed it to me without a word.

I looked up at him and said, "What kept you?"

He also is the one who later had a run-in with a network's Continuity Acceptance Department, a fancy name for censor, when he was writing for a show called "My Favorite Martian." Sherwood got a script back from Continuity Acceptance with much of the dialogue circled in red and a note, penciled in a firm hand, "A Martian wouldn't say this."

Sherwood got his own laugh when he went on to create "Gilligan's Island" and "The Brady Bunch." I could tell you what he called Continuity Acceptance, but a Martian wouldn't say that.

There is another bedtime story about those Navajo Street days. Every Saturday, the tale goes, I would gather the writers at the bottom of the huge circular staircase that led up to the second story. I would stand at the top where my office was, make paper airplanes out of their salary checks, call out their names, sail them down, and let them jump for them.

Well, this one I'll admit to. I was worried about their health. It was the only exercise they got all week, outside of running to escape Red Sun.

They got their own back, though. In those beleaguered days, the competition among the writers was so fierce, each one would try to outdo the other by handing in more jokes. Finally, they realized they were each writing almost twenty pages of comedy a day, a suicidal pace. Workers of Navajo Street, unite! They made a pact to cut down the material. They figured that if they all cut down by the same amount, one page a day, I would never notice what was happening, and soon they all could go to the beach. It worked. They got down to five pages daily and a good tan, and I thought, naturally, they were spending more time on each joke.

The instigator of the Navajo Street revolt became so popular after that success that he was elected three times to the presidency of the Writers Guild of America, and in that office paved the way for the writers' strike of 1987. That called for a response on my TV show.

"Hey, did you all follow the writers' strike . . . or, as it was referred to around my house, 'You took the words right out of my mouth?' I first heard about the strike when my idiot cards went blank. The other day there were three thousand writers picketing. And they all work for me."

Back in 1938, eating was more important than striking, so all my guys stayed at their typewriters. They didn't want to bite the hand that sailed them their paychecks.

Somehow, those beleaguered, leaping gentlemen, worried about their jobs, their families, and their country, managed to produce some of the funniest jokes and sketches broadcast during those early years, and kept a whole nation and its armed forces laughing throughout a time of trial and danger.

Most of them went on to more prestigious work in motion pictures and television, as creators, directors, producers, and Academy Award winners, but I don't think they will ever forget those hectic nights on Navajo Street.

Gentlemen, I'm grateful. And next time you come to visit, I'll tie up the dog.

Now, let's see, we left Neville Chamberlain in Munich, that September of 1938, clutching his ever-present umbrella. After hoisting a few Löwenbraus with Adolf Hitler, Chamberlain happily gave him the store, meaning permission to grab all the available real estate in Western Europe. The Umbrella Man then went home to England, taking bows for achieving what he called "peace in our time." While he was bowing, the German army was marching through the Rhineland and keeping its motors running. Hitler started looking at travel photos of the Eiffel Tower.

At the same time, the first Pepsodent show went on the air September 27, 1938, in front of a large studio audience at Melrose and Gower Street in Hollywood, in the old NBC studios, which have since been torn down in my honor. The reason the studio audience was so large was that I stood out in front of the building and pleaded with them to come in. A few years before, when I started doing the Woodbury show, John Swallow of NBC had been startled when I told him I couldn't work without an audience; I told him I'd faint without encouragement. Swallow thought a minute and then said he'd have ropes put up so that the audience leaving the Edgar Bergen program would have to pass through my studio on their way out. This was ironic, because only a short time before, I had gone into the Ziegfeld Follies just when Bergen got fired. He was a friend of mine, we had played vaudeville together. I used to stand in the wings and fall down with laughter when he'd have Charlie Mc-

Carthy do a couple of asides just for my benefit. Then he got canned from the Follies and I felt so sorry for him, especially when he told me he was going into radio.

"Radio! Nobody will be able to see the dummy on your lap," I told him.

"Yeah," Bergen said, "but nobody will be able to see me moving my lips, either."

Within two years Bergen was the biggest thing that ever hit radio, and I was happy to steal his audience. What else are friends for? All these people would come out of his show following the ropes and looking a little dazed when they found themselves in my studio. I would grab them and say, "Come in! Come in! We're on the air in a few seconds. My name is Bob Hope. Sit right down and laugh and I'll explain all the jokes later."

And someday, I *will* explain them. But in the meantime, I had captured an audience. I have no pride when it comes to laughter.

On the first Pepsodent show, even though it was radio, I insisted on getting into costume, possibly as a disguise. We were going to do a sketch about a popular song called "Ride, Tenderfoot, Ride," and I actually wore a cowboy outfit up to the microphone, complete with ten-gallon hat, boots, and spurs. I also carried a gun, which I felt I might need if the audience realized I was getting paid for this.

These are my opening words, reflecting my concern for a troubled world about to go up in flames:

"How do you do, ladies and gentlemen. This is Bob Hope. (*Single laugh from the audience*) Not yet, Charlie. But don't leave. . . . Well, here we are with a brand-new sponsor, a brand-new program, a brand-new cast, ready to tell some . . . jokes . . ."

War? I did finally get around to it, but it was the wrong one.

"My uncle just left here. He was with the American Legion convention. He was in the Army in 1918 and was one of the first men to go over the top. . . . Somebody pushed him. . . . The Legion held a nice, quiet convention. The second night the boys at the hotel gave the house detective twenty-four hours to leave town."

In those days, war veterans were funny. I hadn't yet been to the hospitals near the battle zone and seen what war did to some of them. Later, when Jerry Colonna and I walked into a ward where guys were lying bandaged to the eyebrows, their arms and legs in plaster casts, I'd say, "Please, don't get up." And they would laugh. They were so grateful to me for coming. *They* were grateful to *me*.

Jerry would start to sing "I Love Life" at the top of his considerable lungs, and we'd jump in bed with some of the guys and then dance with the nurses, anything to make a lot of noise in a place where everybody always spoke in whispers. Then I'd cross to one of the guys and say, "Did you see my last show, or were you sick before?"

And they laughed!

Frances Langford, who sang her way through World War II on the Pepsodent show and in the hospitals, would sing her heart out for those kids. I remember in one hospital, Frances was singing, "Embrace me, my sweet embraceable you — " and she looked down and saw the fellow she was singing to had no arms. She ran out into the hall to cry.

I tried to tell her she had a talent that could make them forget the present and remember a happier past. That cheered her up a bit. But she still cried.

I have no apologies about that first radio show, back there in the ominous days of 1938. We were no different from the rest of the American people, pretending not to hear the distant thunder. We went on with the business of being funny, because that was our life.

Every comedy show then, and now, had to have an announcer to handle the straight lines. We had a great one, Bill Goodwin, who was with us for years until he made a tragic error: He started getting bigger laughs than I did. But on that first show, he was still a straight man, and for the record, these were his first words:

"We have a nice cast on the show, ladies and gentlemen. The topper of the feminine stars in Hollywood, Miss Constance Bennett, Skinnay Ennis and his band, and Jerry Colonna."

Let me run that down, for the benefit of posterity. Connie Bennett was the first of a long line of glamour girls I've had on my shows. She and her sister Joan were among the reigning beauties of Hollywood. If you watch the late show, you may have seen Connie Bennett as a ghost in *Topper* with Cary Grant, who also played a ghost. Connie actually asked me to take Cary's place in her next *Topper* film. Not in those words. I think she said she'd like me to drop dead, but I knew what she meant.

She was very sexy. So we had a lot in common. She was so nervous standing next to a sex symbol like me at the microphone, I dropped my script three times.

Skinnay Ennis. Do you believe that first

name? He said it was a family name, but he must have had a very thin family. One of the lines we used to use about Skinnay was that he was "so thin you could read a newspaper through him."

We were just guessing, of course. In those first days of success, we were all too engrossed in ourselves to read a newspaper. Except for one of the writers named Dave Murray. Late at night he would start yelling, "I have to buy a newspaper! I have to buy a newspaper!"

And we would say, "Why? What's in it?"

And Dave would answer, *"Who knows?"*

He was right. We should have bought one.

And, finally, Colonna. Jerry Colonna, the Mad Professor, who became one of my best friends. One of his greatest hits was his over-operatic thrashing of that old chestnut I mentioned before, "I love life/And I want to live!"

Jerry loved life more than anyone I've ever known, and left it too soon, after a long and tragic illness.

But in those days, none of us thought of life as anything but a roller coaster to a wonderful future. We were all beginning, and so was America as a world power, and nothing was going to stop us. We would all eat strawberries and cream forever.

The character we developed for Colonna was completely zany. I had found Jerry and his oversize moustache hiding behind a trombone in Hal Kemp's orchestra. Something about that moustache and his pop eyes struck me as extremely funny. So did his voice. No one on the show agreed with me, but this was now my show and I was entitled to make my own mistakes. Besides, comedy is a matter of instinct, rather than reason. Funny is funny. If you have to explain it, it isn't funny anymore.

But no one expected the explosions of laughter that Jerry brought to us. He always called everyone "Gate," I suppose because in that era of swing music, if you could swing, you were a gate. "Greetings, Gate," became his standard opening, but it never amounted to much until one of the early shows, when Bing Crosby had opened in a picture called *Dr. Rhythm.* The script ran like this:

> HOPE: Here comes the Doctor now!
> COLONNA: Greetings, Gate. . . . Let's operate!
> HOPE: Who are you, Dr. Rhythm?

My line was supposed to get the laugh. I never got to deliver it. Somehow, Colonna's bulging eyes, his aura of pleasant insanity, and the simple rhyming set the audience to howling the instant Jerry got to "Let's operate!"

We knew a good thing when it hit us in the face. After that, every Colonna appearance was signaled with a rhyming couplet — "Greetings, Gate, let's palpitate!" or something equally intellectual — and we tried to build the foolishness from there.

This being radio, we could go to the outer fringes of the imagination at little expense. In those days, we had a sound man who produced all the sound effects himself, blowing whistles, shooting guns, crackling cellophane to create the sound of a building on fire, and generally running himself ragged in a day when there were no recorded effects. A typical Colonna sound effects joke went like this:

> COLONNA: Hope, I'm calling you from San Francisco. I'm walking on air over the Golden Gate Bridge.
> HOPE: Professor, no human being can walk on air!
> COLONNA: They can't?
> HOPE: No.
> *(Sound effect: slide whistle down . . . loud splash)*

COLONNA: You hadda open your big mouth!

That line became a running gag, along with many others we developed over that first season, like "That's what I keep telling them down at the office," and "All right, so I'm not neat!" When I started hearing kids on the street using these lines, I began paying the Navajo Street rent on time.

Dozens of other Colonna lines still stick in my memory, including the granddaddy of all the idiot jokes.

HOPE: Professor, did you plant the bomb in the embassy, like I told you?
COLONNA: Embassy? Great Scott, I thought you said *NBC!*

This was followed by the biggest onstage explosion that ever got away from our sound man. In the fire and smoke that filled the stage, we ran for our lives. But not all of us. When the smoke had cleared, Jerry was still standing calmly at the microphone, holding his slightly singed script.

"Shall we try that one again?" he asked.

So long, Gate.

While our little show was building its comedy characters and an audience across America, the really Big Show was about to start. The orchestra was already tuning up. The red light was flashing backstage for the stage manager to raise the curtain.

For those of you who weren't around, I'll try to list the cast of characters who walked out on the stage and almost fell into the orchestra pit.

First, Franklin Delano Roosevelt, President of the United States. Again and again. And again. He was a rich man's son who had been governor of New York State and, in 1921, fell victim to polio, which kept him confined to a wheelchair for the rest of his life. With his famous Roosevelt grin and uptilted cigarette holder, he chose to ignore his disability. So, amazingly, did the press. I checked my files, and neither I nor anyone on the program ever mentioned his wheelchair. He *was* our country. Not only that, he was the greatest audience I ever worked for. My biggest thrill the first years of the Pepsodent show was to be invited to Washington to appear before him at the White House correspondents' dinner. This was in 1943, when the United States was in the war all the way. FDR had the affection of the whole nation, not only because of the way he was handling the war, but because we all knew that his wife, Eleanor, was always away from the White House, flying all over the world on some mission or other. Our show was playing an Army camp in Mobile, Alabama, when I got the invitation. I was a little nervous and tried to get out of it by saying I couldn't get airplane reservations. FDR fixed that. He had General Hap Arnold sandwich me onto an Air Force plane. I had to go. It was my first flight as a ham sandwich.

The dinner was held in the ballroom of the Statler Hotel, with Ethel Merman, Ed Gardner of "Duffy's Tavern," and Fred Waring and his orchestra also on the bill. There were some eight hundred correspondents, government officials, ambassadors, and other VIP's in the audience. And Franklin Delano Roosevelt. Someone once asked me, when I was preparing to do a show in front of 100,000 people at the Los Angeles Coliseum, if I ever got nervous facing a large audience. I said, "All the time — until I hear that first laugh." Looking at the President, sitting on a raised dais at the side where everyone could watch him, all the cares of wartime written on that lined face, I didn't think I was ever going to hear a laugh.

But I've never been accused of being bashful. I didn't think he could order me shot, so I plunged right in.

"Good evening, Mr. President. I heard you just had a conference with Winston Churchill on a battleship, about war strategy. War strategy, meaning 'Where will we attack the enemy and how are we going to keep Eleanor out of the crossfire?' "

Roosevelt laughed so loud, I wanted to sign him up for my studio audience. And every time he laughed, he would roar, "Aha ha ha!" and tilt that long cigarette holder upward. The whole audience would turn to watch him. Each time the cigarette holder tilted they laughed automatically, which was all right with me. Franklin was the easiest audience I ever played to. He laughed in all the right places.

One of his greatest enemies was Colonel Bertie McCormick, publisher of the *Chicago Tribune*, which printed daily editorials attacking FDR. Franklin had a Scottie dog named Fala, and I said that Fala was the only canine in history to be housebroken on the *Tribune*. FDR laughed so loud he almost swallowed that cigarette holder. I followed that with another reference to the fact that Franklin's wife was never home. I said he was the first President in history who ate out. FDR slapped the table and laughed so hard I almost voted Democratic.

I hated to leave that audience. If they

didn't laugh, they could be pulled in for being un-American.

It had gone so well, Joe Connelly of King Features came up to me afterward and asked if I'd do a newspaper column for the Hearst newspapers. I told him I was going to the South Pacific and didn't have time, so he said, "Hire a writer who has time."

I hired Roger Price, and the column ran for a few years during the war. Then I decided to stop, but the Boss, William Randolph Hearst, invited me up to his castle at San Simeon to talk me into continuing.

In that tremendous main hall, which looked like Henry VIII's playroom, he introduced me to his girlfriend, Marion Davies, who sat to one side, knitting. She reminded me of Madame Defarge, in *A Tale of Two Cities*, who always knitted before they sent someone to the guillotine. I figured I'd better agree before they threw me into the moat. So I did the column for a couple of more years. Then Marion stopped knitting and it was safe for me to quit.

To get back to FDR, Roosevelt was one of the first politicians to discover the power of radio. Sitting in his wheelchair in front of a microphone, he could reach out to the American people through his famous "fireside chats" with no sign of his disability. When that strong voice boomed, "We have nothing to fear but fear itself," we were all too frightened to contradict him.

As President, Roosevelt was either loved or hated. A joke he told on himself in World War II sums it up.

During the fighting on Guadalcanal in the Pacific, an American marine was disappointed because he hadn't had a chance to shoot at the enemy. He hadn't even seen one of them.

"Okay," his commanding officer said, "go up on top of the next hill and yell, 'To hell with Hirohito!' Believe me, that'll bring the Japs out of hiding fast."

So the marine went up on the hill and hollered, "To hell with Hirohito!"

A Jap came out of the jungle and shouted, "To hell with Roosevelt!"

"Just my luck," said the marine, "I can't shoot a fellow Republican."

You will note, during World War II we called the Japanese "Japs." Now we sometimes call them "Boss."

When FDR died on April 12, 1945, just a month before Germany surrendered, William Allen White, editor of the Emporia *Gazette*, another of the newspapers that had criticized him most fiercely, started his obituary with the words, "We who hate your gaudy guts salute you."

★ ★ ★

Onstage right behind Roosevelt came another giant of history, Winston Churchill. He became prime minister of Great Britain after Neville Chamberlain got sacked, because the feeling in England was that although Chamberlain carried an umbrella just like Mary Poppins, Mary was much tougher than Neville turned out to be; Mary would have spit in Hitler's eye.

Churchill was a big, powerful-looking man with an impish twinkle.

It took quite a sense of humor to face Hitler and dare him to cross the English Channel after France had surrendered and most of the British army had been driven into the water.

"We shall fight them on the landing fields, we shall fight them in the streets, we shall fight them in the hills. We shall never surrender."

Pretty brave words from a prime minister whose most important victory up to that time was when English actress Greer Garson won the Academy Award for *Mrs. Miniver*.

Winnie wore a bowler hat and continually smoked big cigars. During the war he dressed in a one-piece jumpsuit, which was a full-length coverall he could leap into right out of bed and look fully dressed in thirty seconds. What a boon that could have been to Gary Hart.

Among the Churchill jokes we did over the years were these: "Winston is one of the world's great men. He's the first cigar smoker in history to have a cigarette named after him. . . . Now that the war's over, England needs money. When they met, President Harry Truman said, 'You look like a million dollars.' And Churchill said, 'That'll do for a down payment. . . .' Churchill brought Truman a present all the way from England, and Harry wanted to give Winston something to take back, but Eisenhower wouldn't fit in his suitcase."

Winnie had just as good a radio voice as Roosevelt, even more impressive because we heard it through the static crashes on the shortwave from London. We thought they were bombs falling. He was one of the truly great orators. About the Royal Air Force, which saved England by shooting the German Luftwaffe out of the skies over London, Churchill coined the line "Never have so many owed so much to so few."

England did owe a great debt to those kids of the RAF in their little Spitfires. They danced through the midnight sky over London like nightingales, but what the Germans didn't know was that the British had just invented radar, and those nightingales could see in the dark.

It wasn't a movie. It really happened. The British, all of them, stood the Germans off and made me proud that I was born in London. Of course, I left long before the war and never went back to live there. My birthplace is now marked by a large statue of a chicken. It stands at the spot where my father got his first look at my nose and said, "There's been some mistake. They've taken the baby and left the stork."

I really appreciated one speech Churchill made early in his career, especially after I made a few trips overseas during the war to entertain our troops: "Nothing in life is so exhilarating as to be shot at without result."

Amen, Winnie.

Another major actor in the Big Show was a fellow named Adolf Schicklgruber. It was pretty amusing when we found out "Schicklgruber" was Hitler's real name. You could understand why he was always so mad. We pretended he was very funny at the beginning of the war, but soon the only thing funny about Schicklgruber was that little moustache, which made him look like Charlie Chaplin in *The Great Dictator*. Jack

Oakie played Benito Mussolini, the Italian meatball who forced castor oil down the throats of those who disagreed with him.

In real life, there wasn't anything really comic about either of them, but on the Pepsodent show, we tried:

"Free speech isn't dead in Germany and Italy, merely the speakers. . . . When Hitler talks to himself, it's a cabinet meeting."

Hitler, too, knew the power of radio. He had a voice that sounded like Louis Armstrong shouting German from the bottom of a gravel pit, and he never stopped shouting. He developed that "Heil Hitler" salute that looked like a guy reaching up to goose a giraffe. Nobody described it quite that way to him, though.

Only after the Russians had taken Berlin at the end of the war and Schicklgruber had taken his own life and that of his girlfriend Eva Braun, did I get a chance to prove he didn't scare me. I walked right into Hitler's underground bunker in Berlin, after our Army assured me he had checked out. Even with him gone, the bunker was scary. I was one of the first to visit it when the shooting was over. I had been entertaining American troops in Germany, and somehow I had promoted a pass from the Russians. They were very friendly toward me because at that time nobody in Russia had ever heard my show. They drove me in a big car past all the rubble that used to be Berlin. It looked like the South Bronx after a rock concert. There were all these Russian sentries guarding a big concrete dome sticking up out of the ground, covered by grass and mud, surrounded by huge bomb craters. I went down inside the bunker with some American Air Force men who had just flown President Truman to the Potsdam Conference.

The place was a shambles, furniture scattered all around, as if the last tenant had just gotten a divorce and his ex-wife had tried to take the rugs with her.

Feeling very daring, we started picking up souvenirs. None of the Russian guards seemed interested in stopping us. I guess they figured they'd already gotten anything that had any resale value. I got some stationery with Hitler's initials — A.H. — and figured I could use it if I changed my first name. I also got the handle off his toilet. I guess it has sentimental value.

There was a huge swastika flag covering one wall. One of the fliers saw me looking at it and said, "Bob, would you like to have that?"

I was a little doubtful; I knew my neighbors wouldn't be too thrilled if I hung it out in front of my house on Flag Day. Besides, I didn't see how we could take it out of there. But those fliers just rolled it up off the wall, gave the Russian guard a couple of packs of American cigarettes, he gave them an Iron Cross he'd found, and the first postwar Russian-American trade pact was history. The guys had that tremendous swastika delivered to my home in Toluca Lake, where it's going to be part of the Bob Hope Museum, if I ever have time to get around to that project.

Adolf Schicklgruber. Among my souvenirs.

I like him better that way.

But to get out of this time warp and back to 1939; I spent that summer in England. I had promoted a trip from the Pepsodent Company so I could take Dolores back to meet my family. I guess my sponsor gave me the trip as a present to make sure I didn't switch over to Colgate. It must have worked, because I stayed with them so long, I went from Pepsodent to Polident.

It was the first time I'd seen my family since a short time after I was born. They came out of the rocks and trees to surround me at the local pub. I got up to tell some jokes, because I thought it might help them to understand why their checks were late, but my ninety-six-year-old grandfather told me to sit down while *he* told the jokes and did a buck-and-wing that brought down the house. Ninety-six years of solid talent. I was so lucky to be related to him. He prepared me for George Burns.

Three years later, when my grandfather was ninety-nine, I came back to England to do a show for the U.S. Air Force, and Grandpa insisted on coming along. I helped him up on the stage and he wished the boys good luck on their missions over Germany and bowed off to a tremendous hand. He died a week later in Birmingham, one week short of his hundredth birthday.

If he'd known, he'd have taken an extra bow.

When we finished our vacation on Pepsodent in 1939, Dolores and I sailed back for America aboard the *Queen Mary*. The first day out, Dolores got up and went to Mass. When she came back, she said to me, "We're at war." That woke me up. It was better than a cold shower.

I went up to the salon. It was jammed. The ship was overloaded with passengers, many of whom slept on the deck. They had paid any price to get aboard what they felt might be the last boat to freedom. Everyone was crying. It was one of the saddest moments I can remember.

The captain announced that the *Queen*

Mary would run without lights at night. There were German submarines in these waters.

I did a show for the passengers that evening to cheer them up and prove we weren't frightened, but it was tough dancing wearing that life preserver.

The date was September 1. Hitler had sent the German army to invade Poland. It was over so fast, not even Henny Youngman had time to think of any Polish jokes. Britain and France had a treaty with Poland, promising to come to her aid. To Hitler's surprise, they honored it.

When we got back to Hollywood without being sunk, I immediately called all my writers together and we worked through the nights and several gallons of vanilla ice cream on our opening show.

I have just been down in my vault to look up those scripts. I honestly do have a vault where I keep all my old jokes, something like the place Jack Benny used to keep his money, only deeper. It's a lie that I have to keep those jokes refrigerated.

The vault is in a separate building near my house, protected by security guards and several large, hungry dogs, who sometimes won't even let *me* in to take those jokes out.

At any rate, my secretary has a combination

to the safe, which is so large you can walk inside it. Over the years, various writers have gotten locked in there, and occasionally I run across bleached bones, still laughing. At their own jokes, of course.

The files for that opening show are a little smudged and faded, but unfortunately I can still read them: "How do you do, ladies and gentlemen. This is the Pepsodent kid, Bob Hope, starting to eat again with your teeth. . . . It was really hot the day I got back here to Hollywood. All my old scripts started popping."

As Abraham Lincoln remarked on another memorable occasion, the world will little note, nor long remember, what we said there.

But, as I recall, we really were aware of what was happening in Europe. What we were afraid of was that no one in America cared. Even if we could think of something funny to say about the fighting, nobody would laugh. This was Europe's war. We'd wait until they finished it, and then we'd go see the movie.

It wasn't until December 17, 1939, that a monologue mentioned the fighting. But it wasn't broadcast. In return for my vacation that past summer, I had to appear at the Pepsodent factory in Chicago, and do a show for the employees. The company promised

I wouldn't have to screw the caps on the tubes . . . until afterward.

"How do you do, ladies and gentlemen and fellow workers. Irium again!"

That was pretty funny if you knew that the secret ingredient in Pepsodent was something called Irium, pronounced "Eer-I-um." Nobody ever found out what it was.

"I'm really grateful to the Pepsodent people. They gave me a trip to Europe. Of course, they didn't know the war was going to start . . . I think. . . . The first night I was there, I went to see one of my pictures, and the whole audience was wearing gas masks."

The funny war. We didn't take it seriously. The enemy armies were stalled at the French frontier, daring each other like kids with a chip on their shoulder.

1940 dawned. It was a year in which Hitler's planes and tanks overran France and pushed the British army into the English Channel. That's when Mrs. Miniver saved them from going under. Still, we weren't too concerned over here.

You have to understand that, at a time when the German Wehrmacht and Luftwaffe were pounding France into flaming crepes suzettes with a couple of million soldiers and maybe ten thousand planes, the American army totaled all of 132,000 officers and men.

But they had been ordered to look tough.

In America, only the Boy Scouts were prepared.

In my life, the events in Europe were overshadowed by more important things, like beating out Jack Benny and Fred Allen in the ratings. We used to preview the Pepsodent show on Sunday nights, throwing in every joke we thought might have a chance. The laughs from the studio audience told us which were funny. In those days, we had no laugh machine to create hilarity on cue. If the show needed a lift, either we would throw in a brilliant joke, or I would drop my pants. I almost caught pneumonia, but it was worth it.

All the writers would sit up in a glass-enclosed compartment called the sponsor's booth and check off the laughs according to their volume. If a joke merely got a titter, it was a "one." A "two" or a "three" meant "fair." A large check $\checkmark$ meant a boff, and a really big check with a line through it meant it was a *super-boff* $\cancel{\checkmark}$. A truly earth-shaking laugh was a *super* super-boff $\cancel{\checkmark}$. Amazing how many of his own jokes a writer would give a $\cancel{\checkmark}$ to. You must remember, there was no tape recording in those days, almost no on-the-spot recording of any kind, so we had to rely on those checks and the memory — and honor — of the writers.

The Sunday previews sometimes lasted for two solid hours and were always a riot of ad-libbing and horsing around. Right afterward I would meet with the writers, and after a little lying about whose joke had been a √ or a ҉, we would put all the largest laughs together for the half hour on-the-air show the following Tuesday night.

Our show was performed first at 7 o'clock in the evening in California, and sent over telephone lines so it hit the NBC network on the East Coast at 10 P.M., Eastern Time. Since there was no recording, we had to redo the entire show, live, three hours later for the West Coast. So it shouldn't be a total loss, I would have the writers write new jokes between 7 and 10 P.M. to replace the ones that hadn't played.

Wouldn't it be great if life always gave you a second chance?

In 1939 and 1940, we created two infamous characters on the show, and lost a famous one. We called the infamous pair Brenda and Cobina, the two ugliest girls in the world, named after two aristocratic socialites of the period, Brenda Frazier and Cobina Wright, Jr. The "girls" were played by Elvia Allman and Blanche Stewart in a style that might be called Early Don Rickles. Since this was radio, we didn't need makeup to paint the ugly on them; the audience's imagination filled in the horrible details.

Here is the opening of their very first appearance — at least, on *this* planet — from the show of October 24, 1939:

> ELVIA: Say, Brenda —
>
> BLANCHE: Yes, Cobina?
>
> ELVIA: I can't wait for Robert Hope and Skinnay Ennis to get here. I'm shaking all over like I got PARSLEY! Do you think they'll go for my lovely long eyebrows?
>
> BLANCHE: Of course, but I think you'd look prettier if you combed them back over your head to hide your bald spot.
>
> ELVIA: Good idea. Now, if we could only get rid of those big bunches of grapes on the wallpaper.
>
> BLANCHE: Why?
>
> ELVIA: They take the edge off my tattooing.

The real Cobina Wright sued the program — you can't really blame her — and it was settled out of court when I agreed to bring her on the show as a guest. There's a little ham in all of us, no matter how blue the blood.

At the other end of the spectrum was Judy Garland. Judy was fifteen years old when she became our regular singer, and she was the sweetest, most unspoiled little girl who ever topped me in a comedy sketch. Judy was supposed to have a crush on me and I was always nervous about being so much older than she was. I asked her once, "Do your young friends think I'm in the groove?" And her diplomatic answer was "Well, they think you've got one foot in it."

She became very jealous when I would mention my feelings for Madeleine Carroll, the blonde British beauty of Hitchcock's *The 39 Steps*, and when Madeleine came on the show and I introduced her, Judy just stared at her silently and then said, "Hmmm . . . Peroxide."

Judy first appeared as a regular on the Pepsodent show on September 29, 1939. She came on singing a song called "Franklin D. Roosevelt Jones" so beautifully that even the Republicans in our studio audience applauded.

> HOPE: That was great, Judy. But tell me, last time you were here you were just a guest — now that you're a permanent member of our cast, how do you feel about it?
>
> JUDY: Oh, I'm really happy to be here,

Mr. Hope. You know, my school-teacher's happy I'm on your program, too. She says I ought to be happy to take anything to get started.

HOPE: But Judy, are you sure you'll feel at home on this program?

JUDY: Oh, yes, Mr. Hope. You should have seen the strange creatures I worked with in *The Wizard of Oz.*

HOPE: Judy, I want us to get along on this show. I want you to treat me as a father. When you get a little older, you can treat me as a brother . . . and when you get a little older than that, it's every man for himself.

We ended our little spot with Judy singing "Over the Rainbow." Solo. I was wise enough not to try to make it a duet.

The naïve child with the beautiful singing voice was taken off our show in 1940. We were innocent enough to think that what we called "Mexican cigarettes" were a good subject for laughs. When I would predict that I was a shoo-in to win that year's Academy Award, somebody would always say, "Give me a drag on that before you throw it away." It became a running line until we gave it to Judy. Mrs. Frances Gumm, Judy's mother, would often sit in the theater during rehearsals, watching her little girl grow up; maybe she thought Judy was growing up too fast. Whatever the reason, we lost her, and, much later, so did the world. "Mexican cigarettes" were only the beginning in her troubled career. But every year on CBS, Judy remains forever young, just the way I first knew her, still singing her way "Over the Rainbow."

What happened to Judy Garland reminds me that, some years later, we had Jackie Coogan, the former child star who was by then forty years old, balding, and overweight, on the program, and we had what we thought was a wonderful joke for him.

I said, "Jackie, I haven't seen you around Hollywood for years. What happened to you?"

And Jackie said, "I made a terrible mistake. I grew up."

Nobody laughed.

But there were a lot of laughs for me over at Paramount in those days. It was to be the start of a beautiful friendship, and I don't mean like in *Casablanca*.

I opened the Pepsodent show of February 27, 1940, with a plug for my new movie:

"Last week was a big week for me. I went to the preview of Paramount's new picture, *Road to Singapore*, starring Bing Crosby, Dorothy Lamour, and Bob Hope. It's a swell picture. I'd have enjoyed it even without Bob Hope."

Bing was an easy target for jokes in those days — he was rich: "Instead of paying income tax, Bing just calls Washington and asks them how much they need."

The early "Road" pictures helped keep America's mind off the frightening events overseas, as Schicklgruber's armies kept advancing. Bing was always throwing me to cannibals or selling me to Arabs, and otherwise endearing himself to the American public.

Many have tried to imitate the "Road" pictures in recent films. But something always seems to be lacking.

Bing.

It's hard to explain what that jug-eared groaner had that made us close friends through seven movies and innumerable radio and television shows. I know that some recent accounts of his family troubles portray Bing in a less-than-favorable light, but as far as I'm concerned, he could do no wrong. He had that warm, relaxed personal style onstage that, for me, carried over offstage into the best friendship I ever had. How could I fail to have a warm spot in my heart for a fellow who sold me into slavery to Dorothy Lamour?

The liner of one of Bing's albums sums it up best: "The voice of Bing Crosby has been heard by more people than the voice of any other human being who ever lived."

I miss that voice.

We started to insult each other from the moment we met. I called him "the sports shirt that walks like a man . . . the large, economy-size Sinatra . . . the only pot that ever got the rainbow." And he called me "The man with a nose like a bicycle seat."

It was love at first sight.

When we started working together on *Singapore*, Bing once stopped by my dressing room and I showed him some of the jokes my writers had written to punch up the script. Bing started laughing as soon as he read them, and when I told him the producer had thrown them out, Bing insisted we ad-lib them on the set. In those days, even though visitors weren't allowed, we would both invite lots of friends over to watch us shoot, so we always had a friendly audience. Finally there were so many of them around, the cameraman once spent half an hour lighting our visitors. He thought they were part of a mob scene.

Bing and I were having so much fun ad-libbing that word got out and when Don

Hartman, who had written the screenplay with Frank Butler, came on the stage to check it out, I hollered, "If you hear one of your own lines, yell, 'Bingo!' "

Don, who with Frank had created the whole concept of the "Road" series, hollered back, "Stick to the script or we'll put you both back in the trunk!" But when *Road to Singapore* opened and became a big hit, Don and Frank were happy to take bows for all those ad-libs.

Those two gifted screenwriters had a flat deal with Paramount that paid them a healthy yearly salary, but if they came up with an original story idea, they would get paid extra.

Needing money desperately, a chronic state with writers, they once stayed up all night and concocted a plot for a film to be called *Road to Moscow*. Buddy De Sylva, the songwriter who had sung his way to being head of the studio, received them in his office to hear their great new plot. Don and Frank didn't have a word on paper, but that never stopped a good writer. Or a bad one, either.

Don was the storyteller of the two, so he got up and ad-libbed the entire movie. Buddy started laughing, and that encouraged Don to greater flights of fancy, making up most of the story line as he went along. De Sylva kept roaring right to the very end, and then held out his hand and told the two geniuses they had a deal, now get to work and write the screenplay. *Road to Moscow* would be the next "Road" picture.

Hartman and Butler stayed up all night again just to celebrate their good fortune. The next morning, bright and early and badly hung over, they got together in their office and tried to write. But the well of inspiration had run dry. The story didn't work. Don couldn't remember what he had said in De Sylva's office, and Frank hadn't bothered to take notes. Finally, Frank asked, "What the hell was Buddy laughing so loud at?" And Don said, "I don't know. I was selling so hard, I wasn't listening to what I was saying."

They looked at each other for a moment. Finally, Frank said, "We'll have to bite the bullet. We'll have to go to Buddy and ask him to tell us what we sold him."

So the two went to De Sylva's office and Don said, "Buddy, when I tell a story I get so inspired, I sometimes ad-lib and then forget the best parts of it. I know it was great, you enjoyed it so much, but could you please tell us what parts of the story you were laughing so hard at?"

And De Sylva told them, "I was laughing so hard because you guys had come up with such a lousy story, you were going to have to break your asses to get a screenplay out of it."

They never did. *Road to Moscow* was never made. Neither was *Road to the Fountain of Youth,* which Bing and I were getting ready to shoot when Bing got that casting call from Upstairs. He left us on a golf course in the middle of a swing, which was, I suppose, the way he would have preferred. Just a drive and a chip shot to Heaven.

On June 3, 1940, 300,000 British and French soldiers surrounded by Schicklgruber's armies at Dunkirk were rescued from the beaches under heavy fire by everything in the British Isles that could float, from ocean liners to sailboats and a few Channel swimmers. Benito Mussolini promptly declared war on England and the French government decided to resign in a body, while they still had one. Adolf owned all of Europe.

On the Pepsodent show, we tried to continue as if it didn't matter. It can't happen here, America told itself. Other things were of much more importance to us on the show, like how we were climbing in the ratings. I was meeting with the writers and a fellow named Tom McAvity, the representative of Young & Rubicam, Pepsodent's advertising agency. Tom was a handsome, blond Scotsman who was assigned to our show to see we didn't forget to do the commercials. Sometimes, though, McAvity felt he had to help us creatively with the rest of the show, which didn't make him very popular with the writers.

Word came from New York during the meeting that the new ratings showed "The Bob Hope Pepsodent Show" had become Number One in the nation, passing both Jack Benny and Fred Allen. There was loud cheering and mutual back-slapping, and Tom, happily, put on his coat and announced, "Number One! I'm going home!"

And Milt Josefsberg, one of the crew of talented writers, said, "That's how we got it."

McAvity turned and accused him of canine ancestry on his mother's side. In a friendly way.

On June 18, I was on the road in Cleveland, Ohio, broadcasting my final show before giving the public a rest for the summer.

"Well, here I am back in my hometown, Cleveland. Hometown. That's French for 'I knew him when they called him Stinky.' "

We put on a review of the best bits we had done during the season, which saved the writers a lot of work, and bowed off to "Thanks for the Memory."

The radio season of 1939-1940 was over.

Nothing important had happened, outside of our show becoming Number One.

Except that while I was arriving in Cleveland, the German army was arriving in Paris.

CHAPTER TWO

1940-1941

"The Bob Hope Pepsodent Show
will not he heard tonight."
— NBC announcement,
December 9, 1941

During the summer of 1940, when the radio
show was off the air, I had a ball traveling
around the country with Dolores and the
cast, playing vaudeville dates. Our first stop
was at Joliet, Illinois, and at first I couldn't
understand what that howling mob was doing
on the platform when our train rolled in.
When I was told they were there for *me*, I
looked carefully for the rope. It was my
first experience with the power of radio; I
had no idea that the millions of numbers
that made up the ratings every week were
actually *people*.

We played one day at the Joliet movie
theater to break in the act — and the audience
— and then went on to the Chicago Theater
in Chicago. When we arrived, the line waiting

to get in ran around a whole city block. Since we were in the theater on a percentage basis, I said to the theater manager, "Let's yank a reel out of the movie so we can squeeze in an extra stage show today."

"You crazy?" the manager howled, "the audience will scream!"

"Let 'em scream on the way out, while they make room for more paying customers," I told him, unselfishly.

He finally agreed to cut out a reel. The audiences never noticed; they hadn't come to see the movie, anyway. I got the manager to cut out another reel, and another. Pretty soon there wasn't much left of the film but the opening credits and the end title, and still there were people waiting out on Lake Street to get in. I caught some of the kids in the audience staying on for two or three shows, and I went onstage and tried to shame them into leaving. They tried to shame *me* into putting the reels back so they could see the whole movie.

It was a tie. Neither of us had any shame.

This kind of success was brand-new to me, but I felt I could get used to it. I must have been pretty difficult to live with, because when somebody in the mob of autograph hounds outside the stage door asked Dolores if she was connected with Bob Hope, she replied, "No, I'm his wife."

After Chicago, we visited New York, Atlanta, Des Moines, and Cleveland, and I never came off the ceiling.

Adolf Hitler was also becoming a headliner that summer. He played France, Greece, Yugoslavia, and Eva Braun. None of them could resist him. *The New Yorker* magazine carried a famous cartoon, showing Adolf onstage addressing an audience. Five hundred storm troopers stood behind him, holding rifles with drawn bayonets. The caption: "I think I may say, without fear of contradiction. . . ."

Newspapers in America said Hitler's conquests were unequaled since the days of Napoleon, although Eva was no Josephine. But apparently Adolf liked her *Hasenpfeffer.*

In the midst of these momentous events, on September 24, 1940, the Pepsodent radio show went back on the air from Hollywood. In some ways, it seemed that the war had nothing to do with America. But there were signs that things were changing. Congress passed a law requiring all foreigners to report to the authorities, and that became the basis for one of Jerry Colonna's running lines. When I would say something to him like "Professor, you are a mass of obfuscation," Colonna would stare at me with those bulging eyes and ask, "Where does an alien go to register?" That was pretty funny to everyone in our audience except the aliens. I forgot I used to be one myself.

On September 16, Congress instituted selective service, and that was pretty amusing for a while, too.

"How do you do, ladies and gentlemen. This is Bob 'Military' Hope, telling you to use Pepsodent and your teeth will never be out in a draft."

From small beginnings.

"You should see all the young couples in love out driving in their cars, the fellow with his arm around the girl, and the man from the draft board with his arm around the fellow . . . Of course, I registered for the draft right away. They asked me in such a way I couldn't refuse. They were gonna draft my brother, but there was a little confusion. His body was one-A, but his brain was four-F."

In 1940, no one seriously believed we were going to be involved in a war. The Army wanted to draft you so you could go to their summer camp. It was all so amusing, Paramount had me make a film with Dorothy Lamour and Eddie Bracken called *Caught in the Draft*, which was a big success.

It's hard to realize today how funny the draft seemed. In those innocent days before

Pearl Harbor, lots of things seemed funny that later lost their humor. Take ethnic jokes. No one minded them as long as they were genuinely humorous.

In the fall of 1940 I was lucky enough to snag Chico Marx for a show. Chico was Jewish (his real name was Leonard Marx), but he played both an Italian and the piano at the same time. The public loved Chico's phony Italian accent, as it loved the phony silent act of his brother Harpo (real name, Adolph; no wonder he changed it). Harpo spent his whole onstage life silently chasing blondes with a cane and a honking auto horn. From anyone else, that might have been offensive; but Harpo chased blondes so lovably even the blondes loved him for it. When he didn't catch them, he took out his frustrations on a harp. When he did catch them, it must have been offstage.

When Chico appeared on the Pepsodent show, for some reason he was very nervous. Perhaps because he didn't trust any comic who wasn't his brother. At any rate, he lost his place in the script and couldn't utter a word.

I finally said to him, "Who do you think you are, Harpo?"

Everyone accused me of having Chico fake it so I could get off that ad-lib. It didn't matter. The Marx family got even the following week. I had his brother Julius on the show and I might as well have been silent.

Seldom is the word "genius" used to describe a comedian, especially by another comedian, but to me, Julius (Groucho) Marx was just that. The grease moustache, the huge cigar, the loping walk, the utter disregard for female sensitivities, and the puncturing of all the phonies in the entire world set Groucho and his style apart from every other ordinary mortal. He was outrageous, brilliant, savage, insulting, and hilarious at the same time.

The only problem with playing opposite him was getting a laugh if you didn't have an accent or an auto horn. Groucho's style made it almost impossible to top him, so very wisely I didn't try.

Our spot on the Pepsodent show went something like this:

HOPE: Well, Groucho Marx!
(*Applause*)
GROUCHO: You call that an introduction? The doctor got more applause when he took out my appendix. As I recall it, that's all he got. And furthermore, what do you mean by snatching my

brother Chico away and sticking him in front of a microphone? It's like stealing a man's wife. Suppose I stole *your* wife? How would you like that? More important, how would your wife like it? Never mind, I'll call her myself and find out.

HOPE: Why are you so upset? I want you to feel at home. I want you to feel as if you belong here.

GROUCHO: As if I belong here? Hope, I know when I've been insulted. My fawn-colored gloves! I'm leaving here immediately!

HOPE: Just a minute, Groucho — we've been friends a long time. I don't want you to leave hating me.

GROUCHO: Why not? That's the way I came in.

You may have noticed, all my dialogue in that exchange could have been read by Harpo. I wasn't just a straight man, I was a department store dummy. But since it was Groucho, I let him have all the jokes, out of respect for his great wit and timing, and the money I was paying him.

Even though much of America was still closing its eyes to Schicklgruber's march through Europe, we all began to pay more attention to the news. In 1940 FDR ran for an unprecedented third term against a successful businessman from Indiana named Wendell Willkie, who was young and handsome, and had dark, tousled hair that sometimes came down over his eyes. Willkie was so popular that he once addressed a political rally in Elwood, Illinois, and 200,000 people showed up. Until then, nobody knew there were that many people who could even spell Elwood, Illinois.

For the first time, both candidates had plenty of money to spend on radio advertising. It became a battle of the microphones. I opened one show by saying, "I want to thank both political candidates for giving up their time so this program can be heard."

There was a breath of fresh air in this political campaign, and her name was Gracie Allen. Gracie ran for President of the United States that year with the slogan, "Down with common sense, vote for Gracie!" She made a surprise appearance on our show and told me she had a real chance of winning, because half of all the married people in the country were women. Comics have been running for President ever since, but Gracie was the best; her rare combination of nonsense and sense made her sound at least as plausible as most of the real politicians.

Gracie Allen and George Burns were then reaching the peak of their, meaning *her,* radio career, although you mustn't take George at face value when he says, "For forty years my act consisted of one joke. And then she died." George was very much an equal partner in the act; his art of submerging himself to Gracie's comic talent was just that, an art.

Neither George nor anyone else would have believed that without his beloved Gracie he would achieve even greater success at an age when most men spend all their time looking around for a place to lie down more or less permanently.

When George was honored by Ronald Reagan in 1988 at the Kennedy Center, I got up to say a few words.

"When I was little I was brought up to respect God and the President of the United States. I never thought I'd see them sitting together in the same box. Look at them . . . two old actors looking for work. . . ."

We all really believe George could be God. He has the right attitude, the right combination of love, modesty, hope, cynicism, and old cigars. When he says, "When I created the world, I made only one mistake. Avocados. I made the pits too large," we believe him. We know God must be truly great to admit to such a foolish error. And if God is truly great, He could easily be George.

George Burns is of the earth, earthy, so I don't think he'll mind if I quote a line he once told me in private, even though we both know it's just a joke.

He asked me, "Bob, how old are you, really?"

I said, "George, I'm eighty-five."

George took a reminiscent puff at his cigar. "Eighty-five," he sighed. "Eighty-five . . . when I was eighty-five, I had a social disease."

Then he raised his right hand and with a wink he said, "So help me Me."

In the early days of the Pepsodent show, George was not yet God, but Gracie had us all believing she could be President.

In the middle of the campaign, Gracie did a walk-on on our show.

GRACIE: It's nice to see you, Mr. Hope.

HOPE: Just call me Bob. It's more friendly.

GRACIE: Oh, I don't want to be friendly. I just want to be President.

HOPE: President! How many supporters have you got now?

GRACIE: Two. One for each stocking.

Too bad the cold, printed word can't convey

the warmth and timing of great performers like Gracie Allen.

But if it could, writers wouldn't need *us*.

On election night, Tuesday, November 5, the Pepsodent show went on the air. It was 10 P.M. on the East Coast, where the polls had already closed, and 7 P.M. in California. There were no network computers to predict the results. We had to wait. As we were later to learn in the Truman-Dewey cliff-hanger, the opera isn't over until the fat lady sings, and Kate Smith didn't open her mouth that night.

Roosevelt or Willkie? We didn't have the foggiest.

"I hope nobody minds our breaking into the election returns like this. At last we're going to find out what it takes to get into the White House . . . a smile . . . or bangs."

FDR won the election — you weren't really worried, were you? — and our next broadcast covered it.

"The election was fun, wasn't it? I certainly do miss the campaign. It's such a queer feeling to turn on your radio and hear what's supposed to be on. . . . The Democrats really put on a demonstration last Tuesday night, but you can't blame them. It's not every day that Roosevelt is elected President. It just seems like it."

FDR lost no time in testing his power.

He decided to move Thanksgiving up a week; nobody was quite certain why. It was like trying to move your wife's birthday without telling her. Some of the states refused to go along. It caused quite a bit of confusion, especially among the turkeys.

"Well, that was a swell Thanksgiving . . . won't it be, Republicans? . . . This double Thanksgiving is quite a thing. Twenty-three states said it was last week, twenty-three say it's this week, and Maine and Vermont are still waiting to hear from Alf Landon. . . . Of course, I don't see why people get peeved at the Democrats for moving up the big meal a week. I remember when the Republicans moved it up six years."

That last reference to the Depression years seemed like ancient history, because events were moving so fast. Henry Stimson, the secretary of war, stuck his hand into a fishbowl in Washington and pulled out the number 158; if that was the number on your draft card, you got called up first. Sixteen million American men under thirty-five eventually registered for the draft. Brenda and Cobina almost went ape, which might have been an improvement. The "girls" announced on the program that they had seen a sign saying THE ARMY BUILDS MEN, and they spent four hours trying to find a lieutenant who could read blueprints.

Tens of thousands of draftees were now going through basic training, crawling on their bellies in the mud of a hundred army camps. Basic training for what? Nobody was sure, but it kept the laundries happy.

In 1940, we were still certain on this side of the oceans that we could never be attacked.

We were soon to learn better. In 1941, America lost her virginity.

Broadway was in a good mood that year. Three big musicals had opened, *Panama Hattie* with Ethel Merman, *Pal Joey* with a young dancer named Gene Kelly, and *Louisiana Purchase* with the team of Billy Gaxton and Victor Moore, which I liked so much I asked Paramount to buy it for me. I had made five more movies for Paramount by then, including *The Ghost Breakers*, with Paulette Goddard. I remember that one very well because at that time Paulette was Charlie Chaplin's girlfriend. One day I ran into him at the racetrack and he took me aside.

"Because of Paulette, I've seen all the rushes on your picture," he said, "and I must tell you how much I enjoy your work."

Chaplin enjoyed *my* work! Charlie didn't know it, but he was the one who had really started me in show business: I had done a

Charlie Chaplin imitation in a contest in Cleveland when I was twelve years old, and had won first prize — and that compliment set me up for the rest of the day, and maybe the rest of my life.

Shortly after that, I made *Road to Zanzibar*, the second "Road" picture with Der Bingle. Why Crosby had a German nickname I never figured out. Might as well call Adolf Hitler "Laughing Boy."

In those carefree times, almost every star made four pictures a year. The studios owned all the theaters, so your films were booked even before you started to shoot. Stars, directors, and writers were under yearly contract. You made the film the studio told you to make, or you didn't work.

The coming of war, the government's breaking up the theater chains, and the arrival of the one-eyed monster, television, changed all that. These were the last of Hollywood's golden days.

If anyone had told me then that one day I would look back on the era of Adolph Zukor, Sam Goldwyn, Louis B. Mayer, Jack Warner, and Harry Cohn as the good old days, I would have considered calling for the men with the butterfly nets. These powerful men didn't mind making an actor walk the plank occasionally. Once, when Cohn fired some star who refused to do a picture, Harry was heard to shout, "I'll never use that s.o.b. again until I need him!" Jack Warner was of the same stripe. When the draft started and stars like Clark Gable and Jimmy Stewart and Henry Fonda went into the armed forces, leading men were at a premium and could demand almost anything. Jack Warner — he was Colonel Jack Warner during the war and always wore his uniform to the studio and, for all anyone knew, to bed — once said, "Won't it be wonderful when the war is over and all the actors are starving again?"

Sam Goldwyn, on the other hand, considered himself a great patriot. He contributed greatly to Franklin Roosevelt's political campaigns, though later he asked to be rewarded for his generosity. FDR sent him off to England, supposedly to inspect the film industry, and promptly forgot about him. On Goldwyn's return, Roosevelt didn't bother to invite him to the White House to tell about his inspection. Sam promptly announced that he had decided to deliver his report, in person, to the United States Congress.

Even after thirty years in America, Sam still had a pronounced accent. He sounded a little like Weber without Fields. We all waited breathlessly for him to make that speech to Congress, and for Abraham Lincoln to turn over in his grave, but the congressional invitation never arrived. When I needled Sam about it, he said he had now decided to make his report directly to the American people.

I laughed because I knew he never would.

But Sam had the last laugh. The immigrant from Poland made a movie called *The Best Years of Our Lives*, with Fredric March playing a returned World War II veteran, which is still the most moving tribute to the American spirit that ever came out of Hollywood. In it Sam Goldwyn had made his report to the people of his adopted country, and nobody noticed his accent.

As for me, the Civil War seemed more real than the one going on in Europe, particularly since, in 1939, when David Selznick's *Gone with the Wind* was the big winner, the Academy had asked me to emcee my first Oscars show. I kept it up, off and on, for over thirty years. In that time, I must have been onstage with over a thousand golden Oscars, not one of which was ever awarded to Robert Hope for his acting. No wonder I began one of the shows with "Welcome to the Academy Awards, or, as it is known at my house, Passover." Still, I suppose I shouldn't complain, because over the years the Academy has awarded me two honorary Oscars, a gold medal, and a plaque. But I would gladly melt them down for the one I really want.

I opened the 1939 show with "Good evening, ladies and gentlemen. What a wonderful thing, this benefit for David Selznick."

Y. Frank Freeman, the warm Southern gentleman who was then president of Paramount, presented Selznick with the "best picture" Oscar with the words "David, that was a wonderful movie, but it was not historically accurate. If the Confederate Army had ever had as many men as you showed in that scene in the Atlanta railway station, you damn Yankees would still be runnin'."

It was the first time anyone had ever called Selznick a Yankee, so he didn't mind.

All through most of the next year and a half we were all still living in never-never land, despite the uniforms that were beginning to blossom on Hollywood Boulevard. The Pepsodent show was becoming a part of the national landscape, Professor Colonna and Brenda and Cobina were mobbed wherever they went. Colonna was always being asked if his flowing moustache was real. He had a stock answer; he would pull a moustache out of his pocket and say, "No, *this* is the real one." But the biggest laughs came when he introduced a running line whose popularity I've never been able to figure out: "Who's Yehudi?"

Let me try to explain that one. When Bill Goodwin's wife had a baby boy, Pepsodent ran a contest to pick a name for it. Yehudi Menuhin, the famed violinist, was in the news then, and we had Colonna suggest "Yehudi" as the baby's name. The audience howled for thirty seconds, and since we couldn't understand why, "Yehudi" became a mysterious personality, the little man who wasn't there, a figment of Professor Colonna's fevered imagination.

The question "Who's Yehudi?" produced a number of incredible answers, the absolute worst coming out of a haunted-house sketch we did on the air.

When actress Elvia Allman, playing a witch, was asked what Yehudi did for a living, she said, "Oh, Yehudi and his brother Mortimer are riggers for ghost ships." Not a bit surprised, I asked her, "Is Yehudi good at it?" And her answer, which I've been trying to forget for fifty years, was "Oh, yes, but he's not the rigger Mort is."

How could a little thing like a European war compete with that? Even though things *were* heating up.

The German general Erwin Rommel and

his Afrika Korps had entered Egypt. Hitler had given secret orders to invade Russia. His honeymoon with Stalin was over, and poor Uncle Joe would soon discover, after all those months in bed with darling Adolf, the marriage license was a phony.

The Pacific fighting had shut off much of our rubber imports, and other raw materials were also in short supply. On the show, we tried to pass it off with laughter.

"Well, gas rationing went into effect all over the country today. But here I am on the air, anyway. . . . The gas stations have a system with the ration cards. They use a large hose for people with the unlimited 'X' cards. Then they have a thin hose for people with 'B' cards. And if you drive in with an 'A' card, they bring out a hose with a nipple on it."

History was catching up with us. After one show, Al Capstaff, one of the sponsor's men, came up to me and said that Pepsodent wanted me to take the program out of its Hollywood studio for one show and visit March Field, one of our air bases.

I said, "What for? There's no war going on. Why should we drag the whole show down there? We're doing all right without going out of the studio."

I was resisting an idea that was to change

my whole life. Of course, I didn't know that Capstaff had a brother in the service who needed a little recreation.

The next Tuesday, I found myself on a bus with Jerry Colonna, Bill Goodwin, and the rest of the crowd, on our way to Riverside, California, and March Field. Also on the bus was Frances Langford, who had replaced Judy Garland as our leading singer. I had always thought her fragile and vulnerable, but we were soon to learn Frances was the bravest of us all. She was actually enthusiastic about March Field.

In those simple radio days, there were no cameras, no lights, no huge group of technicians; there were just me, the cast, the writers, the band, and two guys with a microphone. We didn't even need idiot cards. On radio, we all read from scripts.

May 6, 1941. Our first show for the U.S. Army. We had no idea we were going to discover an audience so ready for laughter, it would make what we did for a living seem like stealing money.

I'll never forget the moment when that bus pulled through the gates at March Field and we were mobbed by a bunch of homesick kids in badly fitting fatigues, screaming greetings. I got out my pen to sign a few hundred autographs, and they knocked me aside and went for Frances Langford. Frances, of course, was a real beauty, but it didn't really matter to those guys. After thirteen weeks in basic training, even Brenda and Cobina looked good.

Tom Harmon, then one of the biggest football names in the country, was in uniform at the base and helped us control the enthusiasm. Tom was later to marry movie star Elyse Knox, but at this moment he, too, was starving. He told us it was our duty to avoid the draft as long as we could, because what we were doing for the United States Army was the biggest thing that had happened to the military since Gettysburg; we had gotten live girls past the sentries at the gate.

It took me a long time to realize that all the rules of comedy were going to be changed. We represented everything those new recruits didn't have: home cooking, mother, and soft roommates. Their real enemies, even after war broke out, were never just the Germans or the Japanese. The enemies were boredom, mud, officers, and abstinence. Any joke that touched those nerves was a sure thing.

I've often wondered how many of those lonely kids we met at March Field on May 6, 1941, survived the war that was soon to follow. They were among the very first, and the odds were against them. I know in my heart that if it weren't for them, and a couple million like them, I wouldn't have had the springboard that has kept me eating regularly for more than half a century.

I hope a lot of those kids did beat the odds.

That night, we were in comedy heaven and didn't know it.

"Good evening, ladies and gentlemen. This is Bob 'March Field' Hope telling all aviators, while we can't advise you on how to protect your 'chutes, there's nothing like Pepsodent to protect your toots."

The laughter was so loud I looked down to see if my pants had fallen. I mean, there must have been something funnier going on than that joke. There wasn't.

"I want to tell you that I'm thrilled to be here. But I'm really here on business. I came up to look at some of the sweaters I knitted."

A howl. What was going on? I plowed ahead.

"One of the aviators here took me for a plane ride this afternoon. I wasn't frightened, but at two thousand feet one of my goose pimples bailed out."

I got goose pimples myself from the roar that followed that one. Then I started to understand. What I said coincided with what these guys were feeling, and laughter was the only way they could communicate how they felt to the rest of the country. I was their messenger boy. A ski-nosed Western Union.

The next week we were back in the studio in Hollywood. The civilian audience was tough and unreasonable. They had no gratitude for getting in free. They wouldn't laugh at the jokes unless they were funny. The memory of the generous laughter at March Field haunted me throughout the show. I had to get back to the military before my option came up.

The following Tuesday, we all climbed on the bus and went down to one of the largest pools of lonesome men in the United States — the San Diego naval base.

Most of the sailors didn't know who we were after we were passed through the gate. When the band got off, an officer took one look at their unkempt clothes and long hair and decided they must be another load of recruits. Before the musicians realized what was happening, they were in barber chairs, having their heads shaved. Since musicians never refuse anything free, they didn't protest. They thought everyone admitted to the base had to have his hair shaved off.

That should have forewarned us. The Navy is a world of its own, with its own customs and its own language. The sailors put their own interpretation on every joke we told them.

The climax came in a sketch with Barbara Jo Allen. Barbara played Vera Vague, an old maid more man-crazy than Brenda and Cobina, a tough acting assignment if there ever was one. Vera (Barbara) was supposed to respond to some insult from me by saying, "If you get fresh with me, I'm going to go to the head of the Navy, he's a dear friend of mine."

Barbara only got halfway through her line when the roof fell in. A frightening roar of laughter went up that could have beached a battleship and we almost had to call in the Shore Police to quiet the sailors down. We stood around dumbly on the stage, trying to figure out what they were laughing about.

It was only after the show that the Navy corrected our ignorance.

The laugh occurred when Barbara said, "If you get fresh with me, I'm going to go to the head —" and the rest of her line was never heard. "The head," as everyone in that theater but us was well aware, is a popular piece of naval plumbing.

We knew then that we had better learn

military language. Also, it might be a good idea to find out the names of some of the officers and poke a little fun at them, as long as they didn't carry live ammunition. The names of the hangouts for the local ladies whom, courtesy of the NBC censors, we always referred to as "B-girls," also were sure laugh getters.

I really think we helped create the term "G.I.," which officially stands for "government issue," by referring to one marine as having a "G.I. haircut." The whole nation soon became familiar with the new language, and so did the censors at the network. Once Frances Langford was forced to cut a hit song she was going to sing at another naval base.

The title of the song? "You Go to My Head."

By this time, Pepsodent had taken a good look at the sudden rise in our ratings and told me, "We'll pay for anywhere you want to go." That was the beginning of almost five solid years of hitting the road to service camps.

Our greatest surprise came after we were in the war a few months and the Women's Army Corps — the Wacs — was created. On our half-hour show, we always figured we would do twenty-three minutes of jokes and music, three minutes of commercials, and allow a little over three minutes for the laughter, usually more than enough. But once we started playing Army camps, we had to allow *six* minutes for the laughs. O, happy day!

And then we broadcast from Fort Des Moines, a base for the Wacs. The laughs spread more than twelve minutes and I had to cut while we were on the air.

The noise started when Wendell Niles, who was our announcer that year, stepped out onstage to do our warm-up. There was such a shriek from the assembled girls he immediately turned around, red-faced and embarrassed, and checked to see if his fly was open. It wasn't. Only then did it dawn on him that the girls were so hungry to see a man, even announcers qualified.

At Fort Des Moines, those girls were so hungry for anything that reminded them of men, Colonna made two dates just for his moustache.

When I stepped out in front of them, I got the same treatment as Wendell Niles. I started the show and the laughs were so big, I had to look down to see if *my* fly was open.

"How do you do, ladies and gentlemen. *(Big laugh)* This is Bob 'Broadcasting from

Fort Des Moines, Iowa' Hope *(a howl)* telling you Wacs that you're the bravest of the brave, and if you brush your teeth with Pepsodent, you'll have more whitecaps than the Waves. *(Cheers.* They were cheering the commercials. . . .) Well, here I am on Wac island. There are eight thousand beautiful Wacs here. *(Wolf whistles.* For want of something better, they were whistling at themselves.) One of the officers showed me all around camp, but she stopped at one place and put a blindfold around my eyes. I said, 'What are we going past now, a secret weapon?' And she said, 'No, the clothesline.' " *(Roof falls in)*

As time passed, we realized the reason for our overwhelming welcome from troops all over the world was that we spelled, more than anything else, "home." They knew us by our voices. When they heard us speak, they were back in the living room, Tuesday night at ten, in front of the Atwater Kent radio, with Mom and Dad and their pesky little brother or sister, although at that moment they might really be in North Africa or Sicily or Guadalcanal. That's why, many times when they were laughing the hardest, I could see some of them trying to hide their tears.

The girls were twice as generous with their laughter as the men we played to. Women were so new in the U.S. armed forces, they were all secretly worried about how they would measure up. Through their laughter they were telling the folks at home not to worry — they hadn't lost their sense of humor. Or their interest in the opposite sex.

I guess, when you get right down to it, there's very little difference between a man in uniform and a woman in uniform.

Need I add, *vive la différence?*

The fall radio season that began in September of 1941 followed a spring and summer of surprises in Europe. As I mentioned, Hitler had broken up his love affair with Uncle Joe Stalin by tearing up their friendship treaty and trying to get him to eat it. German troops did an about-face and invaded Russia.

Stalin was outraged. He had planned on doing it to Adolf first. You can't trust house painters.

In the middle of August, Roosevelt announced he was going fishing. Since he'd never gone fishing before, the fish weren't worried. All he caught was Winston Churchill, in a secret meeting on a British warship off Newfoundland, where they signed something that became known as the Atlantic Charter, pledging the United States to do all it could to help Britain defeat Adolf. It also pledged the United States to stop Japan in China, where they were making chop suey out of the Chinese army. When Winnie wanted to know how Franklin was going to manage the Japanese, FDR winked and said, "I think I can baby them along for a while."

Franklin didn't know it, but the baby was already climbing out of its crib.

When the radio season began that fall, we were blissfully unaware of how close danger was. After all, we were in Hollywood, the capital of bliss.

I opened one show with "I had a date with a pretty girl last night, and let me tell you, there's a lot of defense work going on around here."

But not enough. At 3 A.M., December 7, 1941, Lieutenant Commander Kanjiro Ono was listening to Bing Crosby singing "Sweet Leilani" on the all-night musical program from KGMB in Honolulu. He wasn't really a fan of Der Bingle. What he was waiting for was the weather report, which was obligingly provided at regular intervals. "Partly cloudy, ceiling thirty-five hundred feet, visibility good."

"Domo arigato," said Kanjiro. Thank you very much.

Commander Ono was in the radio room of the aircraft carrier *Okagi*, at the head of a task force including 6 carriers, 353 planes, and 34 submarines. Nobody had spotted them, except perhaps some tuna, who wound up as sushi. The Japanese were some 250 miles northwest of the Royal Hawaiian Hotel, which they have since bought for $100 million, but at that time they hoped to get it for nothing.

What happened after that would have made a good routine for Abbott and Costello, if the results hadn't been so tragic. It probably provided some good material for a lot of Japanese stand-up comics. For instance:

When the first wave of Japanese planes hit the fleet at Pearl Harbor, the band on the U.S.S. *Nevada* had lined up on deck to play "The Star-Spangled Banner." Right next to them, the battleship *Arizona* was sunk by bombs and torpedoes. The band kept right on playing. The leader said later, "It never occurred to me I could stop the national anthem once it was started."

A coast artillery bugler realized he didn't know how to blow the call to arms. It had never come up before. So he blew pay call. It worked even better. The entire unit came out in twenty seconds.

Mrs. Hall Mayfield, wife of an intelligence officer, saw her husband standing in pajamas on the back lawn, watching the blazing harbor through binoculars.

"Hall!" she shouted, "you go right back inside and put in your teeth!"

Gunners from the cruiser *Argonne* shot down the 14th Naval District radio tower.

Forty U.S. shells hit downtown Honolulu.

It was amateur night. America was going to have to turn pro very soon. Those kids at March Field were going to become very popular very fast. So were the marines at San Diego.

In a way, the sneak attack awoke the John Wayne in all of us. It united a peaceful country in a way a mere declaration of war never could have. Up until that time, we hadn't taken the Japanese seriously. As one wounded U.S. sailor put it, after being dragged out of the smoke and flame of Pearl Harbor, "I didn't even know they were mad at us."

That Sunday morning, I had just finished going over the monologue with some of my writers when Dolores rushed in and said, "The Japanese have attacked Pearl Harbor!" I laughed.

This sounded like a Colonna line, like the one when Jerry hurried in during a war sketch and shouted, "Hope, I've just delivered our ultimatum to the enemy!"

"Are you sure they got it, professor?"

"How could they miss it? I put it in an ultimatum can!"

Dolores insisted I turn on the radio. She had gotten it right. On CBS, Artur Rodzinsky was conducting the New York Philharmonic. But this Sunday, as the performance was about to end, the orchestra began to play "The Star-Spangled Banner." And the audience in Carnegie Hall stood and sang the words.

Patriotism was back in style.

It still didn't seem real. That afternoon, I went to a football game at Gilmore Field, the Hollywood Stars' stadium. There was a big crowd until half-time, when orders came over the public address system for all men in uniform to report to their units immediately. They didn't mean football uniforms. Half the men in the stands got up and left.

That night, we held our preview as usual. We were all too shocked to react normally by canceling it. The audience laughed in little spurts, on the edge of their seats in case they had to make a hasty exit. There was no real fear. No tears. No one knew quite how to handle it. So we told jokes.

"I did my shopping early this year. I wanted to make sure they have the stitches out by Christmas." And into a Christmas shopping routine. No mention of what had just happened, because we didn't really know. The size of the debacle at Pearl Harbor was kept secret until months later. But already things were changing. There had always been a good sprinkling of uniforms at our shows; that night, there were none. They had other things to do. Some in the audience noticed, and were as nervous as we were. Any minute we expected to hear the announcement that the Japanese were invading Santa Monica.

To my surprise, a few of the laughs seemed bigger than the previous year, a reaction to danger I later found wherever we went during the war. The closer we got to enemy fire, the louder the laughter. If it started getting hysterical, I knew it was time to dive for a foxhole.

Tuesday, December 9, NBC made the announcement " 'The Bob Hope Pepsodent Show' will not be heard tonight."

The President of the United States took our place.

"My fellow Americans: I must report to you tonight that many American soldiers and sailors have been killed by enemy action. American ships have been sunk. American planes have been destroyed.

"The Congress and the people of the United States have accepted that challenge.

"We are going to win the war and we are going to win the peace that follows, so help me God."

CHAPTER THREE

1942-1943

"We're off on the Road to Morocco.
This camel is tough on the spine. . . ."
Road to Morocco,
Paramount, 1942

We were in it. No one believed the Japanese fleet had turned around after Pearl Harbor and gone home. Being in show business, we all expected them to put in a guest appearance on the West Coast and take bows.

The show of December 16, 1941, began in a subdued mood: "Good evening, ladies and gentlemen. This is Bob Hope, and I just want to take a moment to say that last Tuesday night at this time, I was sitting out there with you listening to our President as he asked all Americans to stand together in this emergency. We feel that in times like these, more than ever before, we need a moment of relaxation. . . . All of us in this studio feel that if we can bring into your homes a little laughter each Tuesday night, we are helping to do our part."

I don't know if that argument would convince any draft board, but it made us feel better about what we were doing.

Patriotism even extended to the commercials:

"Every hour of work that is lost through illness pushes victory just a little further away. . . . Avoid wet feet, drafts [!] and watch your throat, because that's where illness often starts. Gargle with Pepsodent antiseptic regularly."

Pretty sneaky.

The jokes were still the show. Whole new vistas had opened up:

"Well, Los Angeles had its first blackout the other day. Every electric light in the city went out. I saw one guy standing in the street and laughing like anything. I said, 'What are you so happy about?' And he said, 'At last I'm not alone. Look — this month, *nobody* paid their bills. . . .' There's nothing to worry about, though. California alone could beat Japan. After all, how long could the Rising Sun hold out against the Drifting Fog?"

In Beverly Hills, the movie colony pressed some of its most prestigious members into service as air-raid wardens. Among them were director Otto Preminger, an Austrian, and producer Henry Blanke, a German. One midnight during the blackout there was a false alarm when a barrage balloon broke loose from its moorings and was thought to be a Japanese plane. The antiaircraft guns in the Hollywood Hills started firing furious salvos at it, and Otto and Henry ran up and down Rexford Drive shouting, "Close de vindows! Close de vindows!" One frightened movie star leaped out of his front door, hollering, "Run for your lives! The Germans are here!"

War had come to us uninvited and we were still trying to figure out how to handle it. You would have thought our experiences with grateful military audiences in the spring would have had us on a bus to an army camp while FDR was still addressing Congress. But, no. Seven weeks went by before it dawned on us that some of those sailors who howled at Vera Vague in May might have been on the U.S.S. *Arizona* in December. We went back to the military and never left until the war was over. It was no great hardship. I wasn't very old then, but somehow, in my mind, they all became "my kids." It's hard to remember, but in those days lots of them must have been older than I was. Today, as George Burns once said, I've got ties older than they are. They're my kids now, all right.

But before we went back, we kept playing for those civilians in Hollywood who were going through all those terrible ordeals on the home front:

"I've been digging a bomb shelter under my cellar and I can't quit now. The tunnel almost reaches Hedy Lamarr's house. . . . And the shortage of everything is worrying me. This morning when the bank sent back my check, it was marked 'Insufficient Rubber.' . . . The women are worried about their figures, now that they're not going to make any more girdles or garters. It's a case of loosen your hip and knees so we can strangle the Nipponese. . . ."

And how about this intriguing line at the end of one Pepsodent commercial:

"We urge you not to throw away your old toothpaste or shaving-cream tubes. Save them. And listen for a future radio announcement that will tell you what to do with them."

By this time, Germany and Italy had declared war on the U.S. The British had surrendered Hong Kong to the Japanese. And the Japanese had landed at Manila and it had been declared an open city, while U.S. and Filipino forces held out inside the fortress of Corregidor.

Not many jokes in the headlines then.

Finally we took the show back to the guys who would be fighting the war for us. On January 27, 1942, we returned to the sailors of the San Diego naval base, and to show how ignorant we were, our guest star was Robert Young.

He was great, but do I have to tell you he was nothing like a dame?

We tried to make up for it by keeping the jokes on Topic A:

"I really don't think there are enough girls around this base. Today I saw twenty-six sailors standing in line to buy tickets to see a hula dancer tattooed on a guy's chest. . . . I made expenses. . . ."

Two weeks later, we were doing similar jokes for the Army at Camp Hahn, and when the show was over, I drove my own car back home, with two of the writers as ballast. They swear I hit a hundred miles per hour going over the Ridge Route and then had to jam on the brakes when we hit a traffic jam at the top of the mountain.

We couldn't figure out why there were hundreds of cars stopped in the middle of nowhere, with dozens of police fanned out on the highway. Finally, one of the cops recognized me and came over. He pointed to the sky over Los Angeles, where we could see flashes of light, and told us to keep it secret, but a Japanese submarine was shelling the city.

I shouted, "A Japanese submarine!" and he almost blackjacked me. The writers were shocked out of punch lines. While they were whispering shakily to each other and wondering if the entire city would be destroyed, I announced there was absolutely nothing we could do about it and crawled into the backseat of the car and fell sound asleep. It was my vaudeville training. I had taught myself to catnap whenever I wasn't a direct target.

When the firing stopped, I woke up. We made our way down to Los Angeles, looking for signs of devastation. None. The coast artillery had been shooting at another lost barrage balloon.

But the writers never got over my catnap. It was, one of them later remarked, like watching someone sleeping through the battle of Armageddon and World War I at the same time.

And enjoying it.

In the midst of all the war hysteria, with the news from the Pacific getting worse and worse as the Japanese took Corregidor and organized the Bataan death march, life at home continued almost as usual.

But there was one bright spot that spring of 1942. Out of the blue, a formation of U.S. Air Force planes firebombed the center of Tokyo. It was the first American strike of the war. Nobody knew where they came from or where they landed. In the jubilation at home that followed, a smiling FDR announced they had come from Shangri-la, under the command of a colonel named Jimmy Doolittle.

Long after the war, I emceed a banquet for Doolittle's Raiders. I told them, "I don't know why we make such a fuss over you guys; nothing's changed with the Japanese. Instead of dropping bombs on Pearl Harbor, they're dropping Toyotas."

But at the time they were national heroes. Only years later did we learn they had flown in B-17 bombers that had been modified so they could take off from the deck of an aircraft carrier. They had only enough fuel to drop their bombs on Tokyo and crash-land somewhere in China. It was the kind of boyish daring that had an explosive effect on American morale. The raid didn't do much lasting damage to Tokyo, but it destroyed a lot of Oriental pride and dreams of empire. I think I knew, at that moment, that Mr. Moto was finished as a military threat. Babe Ruth had just hit a home run in Hirohito Stadium.

The whole adventure became a movie, *Thirty Seconds over Tokyo,* starring Spencer Tracy, and "Jimmy Doolittle" became a synonym for "good old American know-how." Years later, at another of the many testimonials to the guy who was now General James Doolittle and had commanded Air Force units from North Africa to Europe, I went into this routine:

"It's nice to see Jimmy Doolittle again. You all know General Doolittle. He has a better war record than Warner Brothers. . . . He's all Air Force. He wasn't born. He was built by Boeing. He's been decorated more times than Elizabeth Taylor's finger. He's the only man George C. Scott is required to salute. Once, when his tail gunner yelled, 'Zeroes at eleven o'clock!' he said, 'What are you worried about? It's only eight-thirty.' I first met him during the war in the South Pacific. He was always wonderful to me. He made sure they had my blood type around, even if he had to kill the chicken himself."

The euphoria created by the Doolittle raid was something the country needed badly. It was recognized early on that morale was as important to a nation's survival as armaments, although it's nice to have a little heavy artillery in your backyard, too. Another thing about war that has hurt its popularity in recent years is that it's expensive. Even Donald Trump couldn't afford to finance a really *big* war today. The U.S. needed cash then, Trump wasn't around, so the Treasury Department came up with the same great idea Judy Garland and Mickey Rooney used to arrive at in their MGM musicals — let's put on a show!

Of course, Treasury didn't have any trouble getting stars; who in Hollywood had the guts to tell the IRS he was going to be out of town? The Victory Caravan, it was called, a trainload of fifty Hollywood names making whistle-stops across the country to sell war bonds. Among those hoping to avoid an audit were Cary Grant, Joan Bennett, Groucho Marx, James Cagney (who had just won an Oscar for *Yankee Doodle Dandy*), Desi Arnaz, Pat O'Brien, Charlotte Greenwood (the British dancer and comedienne), Merle Oberon, Charles Boyer, Olivia de Havilland, Spencer Tracy, Irene Dunne, and Betty Grable. Crosby couldn't stand not being part of the mob scene, and he joined us in Chicago. This group of ordinary citizens sold a billion dollars' worth of bonds in the days when that was real money. When Howard Hughes heard about it, he shook his head and said, "A billion dollars! That's a small fortune."

It was a long train trip across the country

from Los Angeles to Washington, D.C., and sometimes the close quarters got on the nerves of all that patriotic talent. Desi Arnaz, who looked about nineteen at the time, insisted on playing "Babalu" on his bongo drums, over and over. Finally Pat O'Brien, who had hoisted a few Irish lemonades, grabbed Desi by the throat and said, "Listen, you Cuban so-and-so, we beat your brains out in '98 and we can do it again!"

But all was sweetness and light by the time the train rolled into Washington. When Groucho saw the screaming mob of citizens jamming the station, jumping up and down and hollering their lungs out at the sight of so many movie stars, he said, "If this is the American public, we ought to surrender right now."

Groucho could never understand that off the stage, without that grease moustache and cigar, he was not easily recognizable as the Great Groucho. He got off the train without his cigar, and nobody applauded. So he went around the back of the train, got on again, pulled out a cigar and went into that Groucho lope. When he got off the second time, he got the big hand he was expecting. Once when we were walking down a Washington street we passed a woman carrying an armload of bundles. Julius Marx gave her the usual

Groucho leer and said, "I see you're doing your Christmas shoplifting early." He didn't have the cigar and grease moustache. The lady obviously didn't know who the hell he was and immediately took one of her bundles and started hitting him over the head. Groucho turned to me while fending her off and said, "Let's get outta here. That's Milton Berle's mother."

The climax for the Victory Caravan came when we all visited the White House. For once, Franklin was away and Eleanor was at home, and greeted us all warmly. None of the stars like Cagney or Grant needed an introduction, but Charlotte Greenwood worried that Eleanor wouldn't know who she was. When Charlotte was presented, she did a vaudeville high kick over the First Lady's head. Groucho turned to Mrs. Roosevelt and said, "You could do that too, if you put your mind to it."

Cary Grant and I sort of shared the emcee duties. I was there to attract the women and Cary told the jokes. That's one of them. Cary was wonderful; I gave him all the old corny vaudeville bits, like two farmers meeting and milking thumbs, and Cary would perform them with such British dignity I almost forgot he had started in vaudeville himself as a stilt walker. Maybe that's why

I looked up to him.

I spent a lot of my time on the Victory Caravan with Grant, Jimmy Cagney, Charles Boyer, and Spencer Tracy. It was really a tough trip. You were lucky if you could mention your own pictures once every half hour.

After the Caravan was over, and our radio show was off the air for the summer, the War Department asked me to make a trip to Alaska and thaw out some of the troops from Juneau to the Aleutians who had been waiting for someone to explain to them what they were doing there. Since there was no shooting reported in that area, I bravely agreed, if I could take Frances Langford along, figuring they would never send a girl if it wasn't completely safe. What's more, she wouldn't go. That was before I realized that Frances was really Joan of Arc and happily went places a guy like me could get killed. Once she realized she had become a symbol to our soldiers of the girl back home, nothing could stop her from performing on the very edge of the battle zone. Even when those more faint of heart were ready to turn back, I could never persuade her to follow me.

Frances immediately agreed to make the trip to Alaska, and so did Jerry Colonna, and also Tony Romano, a tough little guitar player from San Francisco I introduced to the troops by saying, "He's taking the place of Skinnay Ennis, who's in the Army now. They're using Skinnay to clean rifles." Tony was even thinner and could have been used as an Italian pipe cleaner.

Skinnay and his band had gone into the Army and were based as a unit at the Santa Anita Race Track, which was now an Army base instead of a rest home for Crosby's horses. The guys in the band didn't know anything about "Army." A sergeant would come around and wake them up and say, "It's eight-thirty!" and they would tell him, "Forget it. We sleep till eleven." They could get away with it because they played for all the general's parties.

The soldiers in Alaska were the loneliest guys in the world. Also the coldest. They didn't even have enemy troops close by to pump up the adrenaline and keep them warm. Only in the farthest islands of the Aleutians had the Japanese made landings. On an island called Umnak we did a show for a bunch of fliers who had just come back from a bombing mission in dense fog. We never found out whom they had been bombing. I'm not sure *they* knew, either. They all crowded together in a Quonset hut (that's an upside-down foxhole) and laughed at jokes like "This is our first trip up North and the Army has really taken care of us. They gave us a plane that was flown by a four-star general . . . Pershing. . . . I knew it was an old plane when I saw the pilot sitting behind me wearing goggles and a scarf."

But what those fliers were really interested in was Frances. She was the first white woman ever to visit Umnak, and for all I know, the last. While she was singing, "Isn't It Romantic?" with Arctic wolves howling outside — and *inside,* too — I looked down at the audience, and one of the fliers had his arm around a buddy. The buddy was crying. Neither of them dared to look up, and I had to look away. It was a sight I was to get used to, the farther we got from home. It was seeing a pretty girl and hearing her voice that brought the war home, and home to the war, to men who might never make it back themselves.

Later, I did a little crying of a different sort, after I'd foolishly insisted we try to make a night flight from Cordova, Alaska, to Anchorage, in what turned out to be a record sleet storm. We got up in the air, and our radio went out. Our pilot, a guy named Marvin Setzer, from Pomona, California, believed we could fly out of it. So did Bob Gates, our copilot, who was from South Dakota. Both officers were about twenty years old at the time. Setzer, being from Southern California, thought it was like at home, where the chamber of commerce censors the weather reports and "sleet" is officially "frozen orange juice"; you don't try to fly through it, you drink it.

By the time we arrived over Anchorage, fog had closed in. Our radio was still out. The wings were icing up and so were my knuckles. We knew there were mountain peaks all around and we couldn't even see our propellers. Never did so many men think so seriously about getting down on their knees without even one pair of dice.

I looked over at Colonna, who was wearing one of those woollen caps pulled down over his head against the bitter cold, and he just shrugged.

Frances? She was hoping she'd have to jump.

Setzer called to the crew chief, whose name was Dubowsky — funny, but in movies all crew chiefs are named Dubowsky or Winsocki, never Smith or Jones; unfortunately, this was no movie — "Dubowsky!" Setzer hollered, and the crew chief came forward. They had a whispered conversation and then Dubowsky motioned to Frances and handed her a life preserver and a parachute.

"Put on the Mae West," he told her, "not that *you* need it. We're gonna have to bail out."

"What about the old rule?" I asked him, "women and comedians first?"

Just then we felt a *whoosh* as another plane lost in the fog tried to hold wings with us for comfort and we were caught in its prop-wash.

Colonna deiced his moustache and said, "Anybody see a station wagon?"

He was referring to the old gag about the nervous paratroop recruit who was assured by his top sergeant that all he had to do was jump and pull the ripcord, and the parachute would open, and a station wagon would meet him when he reached the ground and drive him back to the base. He jumped, pulled the ripcord, and his parachute failed to open. The private looked down at the ground whizzing up at him and grumbled, "I bet that station wagon won't be there, either."

It didn't seem so funny when Dubowsky was handing each of us those life jackets and parachutes and issuing instructions that I could barely hear above the noise the motors and my teeth were making. My whole life flashed before my eyes. I let it flash by twice. There still was no sign of a happy ending.

Suddenly, Setzer called out, "It's there!" and pointed down, where the ground was rumored to be. We could see a faint glow trying to break through the fog. It got brighter and brighter. We found out later the plane that had almost brushed us was a United Airlines plane. When it landed, the pilot reported our presence and General Simon Bolivar Buckner had the Army corral all the antiaircraft searchlights in the area and make a cone of light over the airfield. We rode that lovely cone down to the ground and made a perfect landing.

Later, when I got up off my knees and managed to make it to the PX, I gave Setzer and Bob Gates, our copilot, watches engraved with THANKS FOR MY LIFE.

By the time we returned to Hollywood, the War Department had created AFRS, the Armed Forces Radio Service, to broadcast entertainment to our troops. Several of my writers escaped there, where as privates they were paid the huge sum of twenty dollars a month; but at least, they reminded me, Uncle Sam didn't make them jump for their checks.

Every star in Hollywood contributed his or her services. Armed Forces Radio Service produced such shows as "Command Performance," "Mail Call," and "Jubilee." "Jubilee" was the first — and only — all-black Army radio show. These programs were broadcast by shortwave, and also were recorded on phonograph records, which the Air Force flew to fronts all over the world.

AFRS headquarters on Western Avenue at Sunset Boulevard in Hollywood was a military madhouse. Trying to impose army discipline on comedy writers was a sure way to chaos. The stories that came out of that unit would have given a tremendous amount of aid and comfort to the enemy if they ever heard them.

Some of the stories might even have been true. Here's one you'll have to make up your own mind about:

For a while, an actor named Captain Ronald Reagan put in a short hitch at AFRS headquarters. Captain Reagan's only military experience up to that time had been saluting Colonel Jack Warner whenever Ronnie's option came up. On one careless occasion, someone decided to make Reagan Officer of the Day. One of my writers, now part of the unit, phoned him, disguising his voice.

"Captain Reagan? This is Lieutenant Colonel Whitney of the Fifty-fourth, on secret orders from General McNair. I have a company of one hundred men en route to Camp

Roberts and we're running late. Can you provide bivouac?"

There was a short pause while Ronnie quickly consulted his military dictionary.

"Yes, sir!" he replied, and immediately hung up and called Abbey Rents to deliver a hundred army cots. There was no arrangement for sleeping at AFRS. All the sleeping was done at typewriters.

Almost immediately, the telephone rang again.

"Lieutenant Colonel Whitney here. Very sorry, I miscounted, captain. Our unit on this maneuver actually consists of one hundred and *fifty* men. Does that present any logistical problem?"

"The impossible we do immediately," Reagan said, believing he had just coined a phrase. He hung up and frantically phoned Abbey Rents for fifty more cots.

Then came the final phone call.

"Captain Reagan? You know, of course, the Fifty-fourth is a cavalry unit. Be sure you have enough hay."

And the "colonel" hung up.

Ronnie phoned the prop department at Warner Brothers.

They tell me there was straw blowing around in the wind at Sunset and Western for weeks after that.

★ ★ ★

Another of the fighting men at AFRS headquarters was a private named Peter Witt, a refugee from Hitler's Germany who had become an American citizen and had immediately been drafted. Peter is now a well-known theatrical agent, but at the time his only claim to fame was the U.S. Army uniform he wore proudly down Hollywood Boulevard. There he saw a woman who was registering voters for the upcoming presidential election, seated at a table on the sidewalk.

Anxious to exercise his new citizenship, Peter stopped to register. After getting his name and address, the lady asked Private Witt, "What is your political affiliation?"

"What does that mean?" Peter wanted to know, bewildered.

"Are you a Republican or a Democrat?"

"I don't know."

"Listen, Private," the lady said, understandably annoyed, "just tell me, who did you vote for in the last presidential election?"

"Von Hindenburg," Peter answered, truthfully.

One final incident in what came to be known as the War on Western Avenue:

A regular Army officer had been mistakenly assigned to the post and assumed he was dealing with soldiers. He got annoyed at the way the writers were forgetting to salute and neglecting to shine their shoes, so he ordered all of them out to police the parking lot and pick up the trash with pointed sticks. Happy to be away from their typewriters, the writers stormed into the parking lot and cheerily began the job. A Hollywood agent who was still a civilian sidled up outside the fence and hissed softly to Private George "Rosie" Rosenberg, himself a well-known agent before getting number 158 on his draft card. Both of them knew that all the big radio shows were in trouble because so many writers were in the service. Rosie, seeing the regular Army officer watching him, pretended to be spearing chewing-gum wrappers as he moved closer to the fence.

" 'The Ann Sothern Show' has a problem this week," whispered the first agent. Of course, both of them knew it was illegal for civilian shows to employ soldiers to write under the table.

"How much?" whispered Rosie.

"Five hundred bucks. One show."

Rosie nodded and edged toward a short, badly uniformed private named Al Lewis, who was diligently spearing a Kleenex.

"Ann Sothern," whispered Rosie.

"How much?"

"Five hundred bucks."

Al carefully lifted a cigarette butt with his pointed stick.

"What?" he said, "and give up *this?*"

Discipline may have been lacking, but talent was not. The world's worst soldiers sat at their typewriters in their ill-fitting uniforms and provided all the material for the AFRS shows that circled the globe, with the cream of Hollywood reading their lines. The shows were hilarious and sometimes touching, as stars read letters from troops scattered from the foxholes of the South Pacific to the trenches of southern Italy, never knowing if any of them were still around to hear their requests for entertainers and songs answered. Most of these great radio programs were never heard by the American public. These were only for service men and women, their very own shows, and they were meant to be special.

Only once, on Christmas Eve, 1942, did "Command Performance" go public, on all four American radio networks and all independent stations simultaneously.

The program opened with a bugle call and the words, "Command Performance U.S.A., the greatest entertainers in America, as requested by you, the fighting men and women of the United States armed forces throughout the world, presented this week and every week till it's over 'Over There.' "

Then the orchestra played George M. Cohan's famous song.

"And here is your commanding officer and master of ceremonies — Bob Hope!"

I know I've sometimes been criticized for "having been knitted by Betsy Ross," but there was something overwhelming about knowing that all around the world, the men and women fighting and dying for a cause you and they believed in were waiting to laugh at the jokes. It had me shaking a little.

Until I heard that first laugh. After that, I was solid ham again.

"How do you do, ladies and gentlemen. This is Bob 'Command Performance' Hope, telling all you soldiers, sailors, and marines that although Johnny Doughboy found a rose in Ireland, what he really wants is that stink-weed in Berlin. . . ."

It got more than a laugh. Every G.I. in town with a night to kill had been given a pass to the show. They all had heard the stories about the first American troops train-ing in Ireland and they howled. I knew I was home.

"Last week my aunt gave her girdle to the scrap drive, now she's dreaming of a wide Christmas. . . . These days wives are no longer backseat drivers. They sit up on the hood with a straw and siphon the gas of the cars in front of them."

Fortunately, there was a lot more to the show after that, including the Andrews Sisters, Red Skelton, Spike Jones and the City Slickers annihilating "Jingle Bells," Ginny Simms, Kay Kyser, and, oh, yes, the Groaner.

"Say, Bing, do you realize we're being heard by a billion people in over thirty countries?"

"When you lay an egg tonight, Ski Nose, it's an international omelette, isn't it?"

In addition to "Command Performance" that Christmas, I was asked by the War Department to send a yuletide message to those RAF kids I mentioned earlier. I didn't know if they'd ever heard of me, but I'd certainly heard of *them*.

"Dear fellows of the RAF, this is Bob Hope talking to you from the United States. You remember the United States, don't you? It's the place Mrs. Roosevelt starts from. You know, I was born in England, no matter how much Parliament tries to deny it. Right now, every smart person is coming to England. Even Rudolf Hess knew enough to come in out of the rain six months before it began pouring. . . . While Schicklgruber is in Russia having nightmares of a White Christmas. . . ."

By now the winds of war were shifting. Rudolf Hess was one of Adolf's closest associates. He had stolen a Messerschmitt and parachuted into Scotland to suggest the British join Adolf in attacking Uncle Joe Stalin. The British listened politely and locked him up for forty-five years. U.S. marines had conquered the island of Guadalcanal in the Pacific. The Navy had won the battle of Midway against the Japanese fleet. The German army had been stopped at Stalingrad by the Russian army and the subzero weather.

That last reminds me of an old story about the farmer whose land was on the Russian border. After the war, he was told the boundaries had been redrawn and his farm was now in Poland.

"Thank God," he said, "I couldn't stand another Russian winter."

Neither could Adolf, so he turned his attention to an easier target. By the end of the year he went into the business of building gas chambers, where there was less competition.

As 1943 rolled around, the U.S. was more and more deeply involved in the war. American G.I.'s had invaded French North Africa, under Ike Eisenhower's command, and alongside the British and Free French had taken Casablanca, Oran, and Algiers.

Life at home went on. On February 2, the Pepsodent show played the Army Gunnery School in Las Vegas. Imagine, a gunnery school in Las Vegas! What great training for sore losers.

I opened the monologue that Tuesday night saying: "There are a lot of historical places here in Nevada, but there's one place in the middle of the desert that's very famous. It's the only place in the world where Roosevelt and Churchill haven't met. . . . Imagine Roosevelt and Churchill having a meeting way out in Casablanca. Just shows you how crowded those Washington hotels must be. . . ."

At Casablanca, FDR and Winnie were planning the course of the war. They didn't know Humphrey Bogart was soon to follow them and let his girl Ingrid Bergman fly away with Paul Henreid, while Bogie walked off with his arm around Claude Rains.

The fighting in North Africa was becoming tougher and tougher. Ike Eisenhower had commanded his first major battle with raw American troops at a little place called Kasserine Pass, and Erwin Rommel and his Afrika Korps had stamped all over them. Casualty reports started appearing every day in American newspapers. I didn't feel quite right about only playing Army camps safely in the U.S. As for "Command Performance," it had its heart in the right place, but I knew *I* wasn't. There was something wrong with packaged entertainment sent out to the troops in the front lines, while the entertainers were safe at home. You had to go to *them* to be truly appreciated.

I was determined to be appreciated if it killed me.

In the summer of 1943, I signed up to play the European Theater of Operations for a new organization called the United Service Organizations (U.S.O.), which had the same idea. The European Theater was a little like vaudeville with foxholes. In both places you could spend most of your time diving for cover.

My deal was arranged by Abe Lastfogel, the head of the Williams Morris Agency, who was doubling in brass as president of U.S.O. Camp Shows. I was to get no salary, hire my own cast, and pay my own expenses. With that kind of deal, it didn't matter if I ever came back.

Colonna wasn't available so I decided to recruit an old friend named Jack Pepper. I found him slinging hash in the officers' mess at Loew Field in Texas. When he saw me he hollered, "Get me outta here!" I knew

Jack from vaudeville, when he was in an act called "Salt and Pepper," which will give you some idea of why he was no longer in vaudeville. He was not only very funny, he was large enough to hide behind if the shooting got serious. He joined Frances Langford and Tony Romano on the first overseas trip of the Hope Gypsies.

Our little troupe was booked to open for American troops in England, and after that, North Africa. Fortunately for us, by that time Ike and the Americans, British, and Free French had picked themselves up off the desert floor and booted Rommel and his Afrika Korps out of Bizerte and Tunis and into the Mediterranean. But we were still going to be flying around in a war zone, and even though I figured the Luftwaffe didn't make a habit of targeting comedians, it was possible that Adolf had heard some of the "Schicklgruber" jokes and wanted to have the last laugh.

We spent six anxious days and nights in New York, waiting for word that we could leave. The Army doctors filled our time by inoculating us against every disease known to man and a few known only to horses, judging by the size of the needles.

At one A.M. on a clear, moonlit summer night, our Pan American Clipper was finally ready to take off from the waters of New York harbor, leaving from the Marine Terminal at La Guardia Field. It didn't do me much good to remember that a few short months before, another Clipper with a U.S.O. troupe had been shot down in flames near Lisbon, seriously injuring Jane Froman, a lovely singer, and killing Tamara, the beautiful star who had been in *Roberta* with me on Broadway. Ironically, Tamara's big number in the show had been "Smoke Gets in Your Eyes."

Maybe Dolores was thinking about that when she said good-bye to me at the gate to the Clipper.

"Be careful," she told me.

I knew there was no point in my being careful if the pilot wasn't, but I didn't want Dolores to worry, too.

"Okay," I said, "I'll be careful."

We kissed each other, and that was all. One deathless, mundane moment. But we both knew what we meant. Little did I know then there were going to be lots of moments like this in my future. And hers.

There was only one other woman on the flight besides Frances, and she was a secretary to our ambassador to Britain, and she *had* to go. I was there because it was too late to back out. Frances was there because she *wanted* to be. I was glad she was. I kept asking her to help me with the oxygen mask until she reminded me we hadn't taken off yet.

The Clipper finally got off the water and headed out over the Statue of Liberty. At least, that's what I was told. The plane was blacked out and we couldn't see out of the windows, which was all right with me. I pretended we were in Glendale.

We stopped in Newfoundland to refuel, and naturally we did a show for the Royal Canadian Air Force stationed there. After we took off again, we did a show for the other twelve passengers on the plane. The Clipper was only in the air an hour when we ran into headwinds and had to return to Newfoundland. Six more shows and a day or so later, we took off yet again and headed for Ireland, which they told us was a neutral country, although we couldn't understand how an Irishman could be neutral about anything. We came in hugging the clouds. Our captain explained it was in case any German planes were around, we could duck into the mist and hide.

I came in hugging the captain. He was my kind of war hero.

After we landed, we had to take a plane to Bristol, England, and a train from there to London.

I had been in London only two years before, but it looked like a different city. Whole blocks of buildings were gone. Piles of rubble had been carefully pushed together. The damage went on mile after mile, but some buildings, like Claridge's Hotel, where we were staying, were almost completely untouched. Claridge's, of course, wouldn't have stood for being bombed. That sort of thing was beneath them.

The doorman said the bombings actually might have been a good thing. They kept everyone's mind off the war.

The first thing I wanted — and needed — when I got to my room was a bath, so I phoned down to Room Service and told them there was no soap in my bathroom.

"Sorry, sir," said Room Service, "there is no soap in the King's bathroom, either."

I felt honored. The King was as dirty as I was. This was war, all right.

Our little group was taken in tow by Bill Dover, head of the U.S.O. in England, and soon we were given shots all over again, fingerprinted — I understand I wasn't the first of my family in England to be honored that way — and almost press-conferenced to death before we finally were allowed to go into our act. In the next eleven days we covered 1,306 miles, and played something like four dozen American bases.

At that time, any thought of invading Adolf's playroom from England was a long way off. Most of the U.S. forces were bomber groups, engaged in what was called the "softening-up" process over Europe. They may have been softening up targets in Germany, but the operation was hardening up our bomber crews, those that were lucky enough to make the roundtrip. And they didn't get any frequent flier bonus, either.

One of the bases we played was headed by General Frank Armstrong. They told us about the speech he made to his men when he took over the command:

"Fifty percent of you fellows might get killed. Forty percent will never get home again. But you'll have a better chance if you follow me in close formation. I'm going to lead you. I want you to listen to me. We're going to get through. From now on, this is a military camp. We're going to live and die in a military manner. If any of you are afraid, you can walk out now."

One or two guys did walk out. And that took courage, too.

It certainly took a little courage for me to go on in front of those guys and try to make them laugh. It was the first time an audience I faced was in more danger than I was.

I needn't have worried. They were so happy to see friends from home they laughed at almost anything. I had shakily scribbled some jokes on a sheet of V-mail I had found in the plane on the way over. Later, the U.S.O. supplied me with a great comedy writer named Hal Block, and the jokes got a lot less shaky.

Hal was stationed in London for just such emergencies. He quickly learned to write funny in bomb shelters, jeeps, and on the backs of camels. He later said he wished they'd start a war in Hollywood so we could go home.

That first routine in Britain started something like this: "Well, here I am in good old Jolly. You know, England — that's the place Churchill visits when he leaves America. . . . Here in England, everything is strange. Everybody drives on the wrong side of the street. Just like California . . ."

After I did some jokes with Jack Pepper, Tony Romano plucked out a few jazz tunes on his guitar, and finally Frances got up and sang. The fellows hollered and cheered and wolf-whistled just the way they do at home.

At home. That's what it was all about.

As we left, we learned these guys were just about to leave on a mission over Germany. In broad daylight.

We went off to play a military hospital. A fellow who wrote a lot better than I can was accompanying us. His name was John Steinbeck, and this is how he described it for his column for the *New York Herald* syndicate:

LONDON, July 23 — Probably the most difficult, the most tearing thing of all, is to be funny in a hospital. . . . The time hangs very long. Letters, even if they came every day, would seem weeks apart. Everything that can be done is done, but medicine cannot get at the lonesomeness and the weakness of men who have been strong.

And Bob Hope and his company must come into this quiet, inward, lonesome place, and gently pull the minds outward and catch the interest, and finally bring laughter up out of the black water.

There is a job. It hurts many of the men to laugh, hurts knitting bones, strains at sutured incisions, and yet the laughter is a great medicine. . . .

Finally, it came time for Frances Langford to sing. The men asked for "As Time Goes By." She stood up beside the little G.I. piano and started to sing. She got through eight bars when a boy with a head wound began to cry. She stopped, and then went on, but her voice wouldn't work anymore, and she finished the song whispering and then she walked out, so no one could see her, and broke down. The ward was quiet and no one applauded. . . .

That afternoon, we were driving back to our hotel at Sharpington when we heard a tremendous roar and spotted a bomber formation right above us. When I got out from under the car and realized they were U.S. B-17's overhead, it occurred to me they might be coming back to General Armstrong's base and were being flown by those kids we'd played for that morning. So we raced back to the base and a young lieutenant offered to take us to the place where the flight crews were debriefed.

We climbed into a jeep and got there just as the bombers were coming in, one after the other, kicking up clouds of dust and shaking the whole countryside. They didn't seem to be shot up too badly. Of course, that was only a civilian's opinion. No one had been shooting at *me*.

Pretty soon trucks and jeeps full of fliers began rolling in. When they saw us they began to cry and laugh and holler. They grabbed Frances and hugged and kissed her, and she patriotically kissed back.

"You brought us luck!" they kept screaming.

"How was it?" we asked.

"A milk run!" One kid grinned. "Eighteen went out and eighteen came back!"

This made all of us feel pretty great, too, as if we were part of it, which of course we weren't.

Later, a colonel told me of one mission where twenty-one bombers from one base went out and only one came limping back.

The feeling in England was entirely different from what I experienced later in Vietnam. Yes, a lot of innocent civilians were being killed by American bombs over Germany and the Continent, as well as a lot of German soldiers who felt they were fighting for *their* country. But this, as has been said, was the last *good* war. The madmen running Germany honestly believed they could dominate the world and "liquidate" those who didn't like them. It was already happening in all the countries they had occupied and would certainly have happened in America if Adolf had developed the Bomb first. We didn't know about that at the time, but it was Hitler's boast that he was building a "secret weapon" that would win the war. It might have, if his timing hadn't been off.

The U.S. fliers we met felt they were truly protecting their families and their homes. They didn't organize any protest marches in England. They fought and they bled and they laughed at the jokes and sometimes, they died.

Perhaps the world has grown up enough now so I won't have to play any more American Army camps in the future.

Or Army hospitals.

One more insight into what was going on over there came when we played the Flying Fortress base at Polebrook, in northern England. When we drove up, the guard told us excitedly that Major Clark Gable was stationed at the base and was just returning from a mission. We raced over to the runway just in time to greet Clark leaving his bomber after a run over Germany. When he climbed out of the plane, I saw his hands were shaking. Catching my eye, he said, "This is a lot of crap."

The bombs and the ack-ack were real now.

Clark had been on many combat missions over Europe, and he no longer considered himself a movie star, although the British girls who were driving our troupe did everything they could to get me to introduce them.

I started my routine by saying, "I hear you have another handsome leading man permanently stationed here. But it isn't true he's been forbidden to ride in B-17's because his ears destroy the lift. They've fitted their leading edges with deicers."

After the show, Clark and I talked about what it really was like in one of those bomber units. All of our Hollywood ideas about war were just fairy tales, he said. We'd gotten them from movies like *Gone With the Wind*, where an orchestra was always playing "Dixie" behind all the dying.

In real war, heroes don't act like heroes. Take it from Rhett Butler.

Clark told me about youngsters back from their first mission over enemy territory who would jump out of the battered bombers and hit the ground with their fists and cry, "I'll never go again!"

Some of them became truly hysterical and the flight surgeon would quietly slip his arm around them and suggest a little R & R. And perhaps some psychiatry. After all, at that time the whole crazy world could have used a little psychiatric help.

I met Gable after that when he could get leave, in London, at the Embassy Club, with John McClain, a newspaperman from Cleveland. The war Clark was fighting was a contrast to the jokes I was telling at the time. The G.I.'s didn't have to be reminded of what it was really like. They preferred lines like "I arrived at this base around six o'clock in the morning. Just in time to sneak into the bugler's tent and fill his bugle with ketchup. Five minutes after he blew reveille, Walter Winchell announced the Red Army had advanced as far as Liverpool. . . . By the way, you know what the gunner on the rear end of a plane is. That's the guy who's supposed to get the lead out of his tail. . . . They took me up and let me work the guns for a while. I wouldn't say my aim was bad, but it's the first time in aviation history anyone ever shot his own plane down."

I guess the jokes didn't seem that funny to Clark. But he fought his way through the war and came back to Hollywood to play a general in *Command Decision*. Make-believe must have been a relief.

The Hope Gypsies were about to leave England for North Africa when I finally got to meet Winston Churchill. I'd like to say he called me for advice on what to do next, but I guess he didn't have time. What actually happened was that "Happy" Chandler, then a senator and later the governor of Kentucky, who finally got a real job as commissioner of baseball, was in London with a senate committee. He gave a big party. Eisenhower and a lot of the big wheels were there, and I told Chandler I had heard Churchill had seen some of my movies, and I wanted to explain the plots to him.

Happy didn't think that was possible — he'd seen the movies, too — but he said, "Would you like to go with me to the Houses of Parliament tomorrow?" I said, "Sure," and was supposed to meet him at the Savoy Hotel at noon. I was ten minutes late and he was already gone, but his military aide, Captain Bock, said to me, "Come on. We're going to Ten Downing Street."

When we got past all the guards and entered the prime minister's house, down at the end of the hall I saw Churchill shaking hands with a line of VIP's. Happy hadn't bothered to tell anyone I was coming, which was just as well, because most of them had led sheltered lives and wouldn't have known who I was, anyway.

I joined the line where John Winant, our ambassador to Britain, was introducing everyone. Winant glared at me, like you glare at a fly in your soup. Although Winant knew who I was, he must have been wondering how the hell I'd gotten in, but before he could say anything, I held out my hand to Churchill. He took it, looked a bit doubtful, and started away. Then he turned back and did a fast British double take.

Two things must have gone through his mind: One, I've seen that face someplace before; two, this fellow must be harmless — no self-respecting spy would ever wear a nose that obvious.

Winnie started into his office and all the VIP's, who included several U.S. senators, followed him in, so naturally I tagged along. I hadn't been elected to anything, but then, I'd never been defeated, either. Until this moment. Because Churchill picked up a hat and said, "Let's go into the rose garden and talk," and I figured they were going to discuss which country to blow up next, and that was a little out of my territory. They all went out, and left me alone with Captain Bock.

So there we were in Winston Churchill's study with all those confidential papers and war secrets around. And no one was watching. If I'd been a spy, I could have earned the Iron Cross in no time. But I didn't want to be kissed on both cheeks by Adolf Hitler, so we decided to leave. We went into the anteroom, and I saw one of Churchill's hats and tried it on. It didn't fit. So that the afternoon wouldn't be a total loss, I stole some of Winston's stationery and shoved it into my pocket.

On the way out, one of the guards indicated for me to sign the visitor's book. I noted that I was signing right after General Henri Giraud, the French war hero who had been rescued from a German P.O.W. camp to help the Allies in the North African invasion. That made me feel very important, until I remembered Giraud was out in the garden, smelling the roses and talking to the prime minister, while I had been treated like the gate-crasher I really was.

I was so mad I made up my mind to write a letter to Churchill and explain everything.

But I decided not to.

I didn't want to waste his stationery.

It was shortly afterward that the Hope Gypsies were off on the Road to Morocco, but Dorothy Lamour was nowhere to be seen when we landed in Marrakech. Not long before, Allied troops commanded by Ike Eisenhower had sailed from near this area to invade Sicily. The Italian fleet that was supposed to stop them never showed up. It was rumored they had tied up at a pizza parlor in Naples. Right now, General Patton and his 4th Army and General Montgomery of the British 8th were battling their way around both sides of the Sicilian island in a race to see who would be the first general to reach the capital, Messina, just off the toe of the Italian boot, which by now was pointing at Mussolini.

We were among the first entertainers to be invited into North Africa after Rommel and his Italian pals had made their hasty exit. We didn't really consider it an honor. But as we got off the plane, I saw a line of cars and a group of officers waiting. I figured they were there to congratulate us for having flown safely over the submarine-infested waters from Prestwick, Scotland.

I told the gang, "Look at that brass! We're finally getting the kind of reception we deserve!" And I guess we did, because when we walked by them, they didn't make a move. They were there to greet some African king who probably couldn't even tell jokes.

The only welcoming committee we could find were two lonely camels and a cobra who had dropped by looking for a quick lunch.

After our nonreception at the airport, we went off to kill time at the bazaar in Marrakech, which looked just like the back lot where we shot the "Road" pictures at Paramount. Apparently, neither the Arabs nor Paramount had enough in the budget for paint and street cleaners. Someone finally found us fighting off the flies and the rug merchants and told us the Army had given up on us when our plane was two days late, but that General Doolittle — Jimmy had been promoted since leaving Shangri-la — had insisted on keeping a B-17 waiting to fly us to Algiers.

We were happy to be on our way until we came in over the Algiers harbor and saw the devastated boats. The Luftwaffe had recently paid a courtesy call. One ammo ship was still on fire.

I tried to persuade the pilot I was ready to use the rest of my roundtrip ticket, but he wasn't listening.

By the time we got into the city, we were so bushed we didn't care what happened to us. We hadn't had any sleep since we left Prestwick, so we all fell into bed at what was left of the Aletti Hotel. Unfortunately, it was only two blocks from the most inviting target in town: the harbor. I was happily dreaming about being in a Moroccan harem, with Madeleine Carroll and Hedy Lamarr painting my toenails, when I was jolted out of bed around 4 A.M. by the sound of air-raid sirens and a voice hollering, "Run for your life!"

It turned out to be my voice.

I raced across the hall and pounded on Frances Langford's door and screamed, "Frances, get up! This is it!"

By the time she opened the door the "all clear" had sounded and I was standing there in a bedsheet only Rudolph Valentino would have looked good in.

I apologized and told Frances it must have been a false alarm, like we'd had in Hollywood. The Army wouldn't have let us visit anyplace where there were *real* air raids.

At that time, I also believed in Santa Claus.

The next day, we arrived in Tunis to start playing the air bases. The Tunis harbor and waterfront had been bombed out more thoroughly than in Algiers, but at least nothing was smoking except Tony Romano, who had found some of those black Italian cigars.

The Army told us Tunis was full of spies. As a matter of fact, the bellhops in our hotel, the Transatlantique, were German P.O.W.'s. It was the first time I ever had my bags carried to my room by a guy who looked like Erich von Stroheim. I didn't know whether to give him a tip or hand him my wallet.

We played all the bases and hospitals around Tunis. One afternoon we played in the middle of the desert for seven thousand men of the tank corps.

"Boy, is it hot here. This is the first time I ever laid fried eggs. . . . But I must say we're staying at a wonderful hotel. I have a room with an adjoining Arab. It's the only way I could get a sheet. . . . The rates are thirteen francs a day and a bounty on anything you catch in your room. I broke even. . . . The only problem is that every time the sand shifts, I'm on a different floor."

Hal Block, my writer who'd preceded us overseas, rejoined the troupe at Bizerte with the good news that if we lived through the next week, we were scheduled to broadcast a complete show by shortwave from Algiers to the United States, and Hal hadn't had time to write a line for it.

But he had thoughtfully brought a pencil.

He didn't have much chance to use it. We were on the go all the time. We did one show in the desert at Ferryville, outside of Bizerte, for 7,500 soldiers, sailors, and Wacs, who were spread over the desert sand on jerry cans, boxes, and anthills, whistling and cheering as we climbed up onto a little stage. The announcer said over the PA, "Ladies and gentlemen . . . Bob Hope!" and you could have heard the screaming all the way to the Pyramids. The guys had caught sight of Frances behind me and were yelling for me to get out of the way.

Just as I ignored them and told my opening gag — "What a time we had in London before we came here. The fog was so thick one night, the antiaircraft shot down three submarines" — I saw a tank burst through the crowd and come toward the stage. I didn't think the joke was that bad, but I'd never met a critic with a Sherman tank before, so I got ready to jump off the platform, when suddenly it stopped right in front of me. The turret popped open and a guy crawled out wearing a tanker's crash helmet. He dragged a folding chair up after him and sat down on it and crossed his legs.

"Make me laugh," he said.

Of course, it was a setup, and I got a good chuckle out of it as soon as I crawled back on the stage.

From Ferryville we were ferried back across Lake Bizerte to the Bizerte naval base, waving to the boys in the L.C.T.'s (Landing Craft Tanks) and the L.C.I. (Landing Craft Infantry) in the harbor, none of us realizing we were all to be Targets for Tonight. The harbor was jammed with every type of equipment to help an Allied invasion of Italy, if Sicily was taken. We had dinner at the base, where Lieutenant Bob Peoples, former football star from U.S.C., was the mess officer. He could pass the mashed potatoes from fifty yards away.

After dinner, we did a show for ten thousand more guys. It was a little tough getting laughs. There was a report on the radio that the Germans were planning to blast Bizerte off the map. Shortly.

I cut two minutes out of the monologue. This is what I delivered. Hurriedly.

"It's wonderful being here in Africa. Ah, Africa. That's Texas with Arabs. . . . Of course, you can get *out* of Texas. . . . You know, you can't date one of these Moroccan girls unless you take her mother along as a chaperone. You know what a Moroccan mother is. That's an M.P. with bloomers."

We spent the night at our hotel in Bizerte, which had been pretty well plastered in previous air raids. It was nice, though. All the rooms were fully ventilated. There was a sign in the lobby: KEEP THE DOORS LOCKED AT ALL TIMES. IT HELPS HOLD THE WALLS UP.

And then came the sirens, and the smudge pots started sending a fog over the city to hide it from the German planes. The ack-ack started crisscrossing the sky. A whole forest of antiaircraft searchlights blazed on. It was the first time I had ever seen so many klieg lights without feeling the slightest urge to take a bow.

We were all out in the street by that time and an M.P. shouted for me to crawl into a sewer. Did you ever see the inside of a

North African sewer? It'll never be on the Universal Tour. I hit the opening at the same time as Jack Pepper, and we didn't get much farther. Jack's waistline took up most of the acreage. Tony Romano had thrown himself over his guitar. If there was a direct hit, Tony wanted to go out in the key of G. "Mother" Langford was running up and down calling, "Are you fellows all right? Speak to me! Speak to me!"

It was all over fast, apparently just a reconnaissance raid, and we all went back to bed, which was a mistake. The North African mosquitoes had located some tender tourist meat and sent out an all-points bulletin. They spent the rest of the night playing kamikaze.

By that time, I decided we needed to find lodging a little farther out of town. Passaic, New Jersey, for instance. That's when Colonel Blesse, who ran the 56th Evacuation Hospital up in the hills, invited us to stay there. It was three miles out of town, so I agreed. I felt a little strange about sleeping in a hospital when I was perfectly healthy, and then I remembered a story that Al Schwartz had told me. Al had relocated from the Pepsodent show to Jackie Gleason and the Honeymooners. Gleason liked to live at Doctors Hospital in New York, because it was quiet, no one knew he was there, and he could hold uninterrupted meetings with the staff of the show. One day, Al and the other writers arrived at Doctors Hospital clutching their hilarious material and found the door to Gleason's hospital room locked. Surprised, they asked a nurse on the floor where Jackie was.

"Oh," the nurse told them, "Mr. Gleason didn't feel well, so he went home."

The next day we went out to do a show at a B-25 bomber base, which was a relief, the B-25's being smaller than the mosquitoes. In fact, B-25's were sometimes called "The Flying Prostitutes — no visible means of support."

The colonel in command told us most of the men were already assembled for the show, but he would appreciate it if we could wait. Some of the boys were due back from a mission in fifteen minutes. Twenty-four planes had gone out. The men who came back would be counting on him to hold their seats.

We waited in the colonel's tent while he explained that we'd be able to tell how the mission went by the way the planes came in.

"If they come in high," he told us, "and circle the field, it means they have wounded. If they buzz us, things went pretty well."

About five minutes later we heard the

sound of approaching bombers. The sound grew louder and louder until we realized they were buzzing the base. The colonel gave a shout and ran outside and started to count.

He stood there in the field, the wind blowing his hair, screaming the numbers exultantly as the planes skimmed in for a landing.

". . . twenty-two . . . twenty-three . . . *twenty-four!*"

We must have brought luck with us again.

We had a happy audience for that show. I opened with a description of our stay in Bizerte:

"We just moved out of our hotel. I had a lovely little closet overlooking a moth. . . . The room was so small that every time I turned the doorknob I rearranged the furniture. . . . The ceiling was so low, the mice were born round-shouldered. . . . The mosquitoes were so big they had to use landing strips. . . . I prefer the runway you fellows have out here, where the B-25's take off for the Big Show. What a job you're doing. I'd like to have the aspirin concession in Rome right now. . . . And whatever happened to the Italian fleet? Eisenhower ordered out ten planes, four submarines, and a chopper to look for it, but it was no use. He finally sent a note to Mussolini saying, 'I give up, where is it?

We don't want to fight it, we just don't want to run over it.' "

The adrenaline ran out after that show. We were all bushed from playing so many camps, and from lack of sleep. A major asked if we would play a few of the wards in the base hospital, about twenty miles from Bizerte, and for the first time on the entire trip, we hesitated.

We held a meeting and took a vote. We decided to stay a little longer and visit the hospital. That vote may have saved our lives.

We walked into one of the wards and there were seven operating tables, all in a long row, almost as far as you could see, where teams of medical corps surgeons were stitching guys up. Those surgeons all looked twelve feet tall to me.

We walked into another ward, and went into our regular routine. I started kidding with one of the boys, who was wearing a one-piece plaster cast that went up above his ears.

"How do you get a razor in there?" I asked.

He said, "I've *had* my close shave, Bob."

I would have crawled into the woodwork if the termites hadn't beaten me to it.

Playing those wards took an extra forty minutes. How lucky could we get? Twelve miles out on the way back to Bizerte, we suddenly saw all hell break loose in the sky over the city. It was all the Fourth of Julys you ever saw rolled into one. We could see the planes up there in the searchlight beams twisting and turning and spitting fire. Every so often one would blow up with a flash of flame and we'd wonder, was it ours or was it theirs?

We had stopped and gotten out of our car. We all had helmets on, but I was worried about the rest of me. The Luftwaffe had started running in on Bizerte right over our heads, spitting fire like Carmen Miranda dancing the flamenco. The sergeant with us hollered for us to hit the ditch, and I did a fast Nijinsky toward it and felt a terrible pain. I had either been killed or sprained my ankle. No matter. I still managed to beat Frances Langford to that ditch.

When it was over, she helped me crawl out and get to the car. I don't think she carried me, but knowing Frances, she probably tried.

We got back to Bizerte and drove around and looked at what was left of the real estate. Smoke all over the place, and rubble. A body lying stiffly on a caved-in floor of a room with only two walls. A shoe sticking up from a pile of timber and plumbing and stucco. If we had returned on schedule, we might have been a statistic.

We arrived at the 56th Evacuation Hospital, our Hilton for the night, and Colonel Blesse insisted I have my ankle and knee looked at. The G.I. who bandaged me looked a little nervous, and I asked him, "How did you get into the medical corps?"

"Drafted."

"Were you an intern?"

"Nope."

"Medical student?"

"Nope."

"How did they put you in the medical corps?"

"Screening test. They asked me to write down who I worked for last. I put down, 'Dr. Pepper.' "

Somehow, we both survived.

The next day we got the good news. Patton and Montgomery had just captured Messina. The Army wanted to celebrate. It would be nice if the Hope Gypsies played Loew's Sicily before the smoke cleared. We should consider it an honor. We would be the first entertainers ever invited into a war zone only three days after it had been captured from the enemy.

There was nothing to worry about. Most of the snipers had been knocked off. *Most* of them?

We didn't feel flattered. But we went.

Our little group flew into Sicily in a B-17 with gunners manning all the turrets and a guy from New York Life tearing up my insurance policy and swallowing the pieces.

We landed outside Palermo and as we drove into town, it looked just like Southern California. Mountains, ocean, sunshine, everything but real estate offices. The road was jammed solid with American Army troops who had just helped capture Messina. As we rolled by, we'd lean out and wave and holler to them, and a couple of seconds later five thousand men would be doing a double take and shouting our names.

Within twenty-four hours, every person on the island of Sicily knew we were there. They probably knew all the jokes I was going to tell, too, but they came to our shows and laughed, anyway.

The largest audience of the whole war was the one we played to outside Palermo, the 1st Division under General Eddy. It was late one Sunday morning and there were nineteen thousand boys sitting there in a gully, terraced up the hillside in that bright Sicilian sun, half of them stripped to the waist, all of them with their helmets full of grapes, and rifles at the ready. Did you ever try to tell jokes looking down the muzzles of nineteen thousand rifles? As Colonna would have put it, non-habit-forming, isn't it?

I started the monologue and my voice was almost wiped out by the sound of airplanes flying over us. I started to complain, but they told me they expected German bombers in the area and the P-38's above were flying cover.

I stopped complaining and just talked louder.

"We just flew over from North Africa. What a place! I won't say it's dusty there, but it's the only place I know where they spit cement. . . . And those troops over there. What hardships they go through! Night after night they went without sleep, always alert, always keeping their eye on the objective. Finally Frances Langford pulled down her shade. . . . But they're all great guys except for one kid I met who was doing K.P. This fella had been breaking all the rules, shooting dice, going A.W.O.L., running around with women. So I said to him, 'What's the big idea, son?' And he said, 'Mr. Hope, did you give a pint of blood to the Red Cross last year?' And I said, 'Yes,' and he said, 'Well, shake hands with the guy who got it.' "

We did a few more shows and went back to Palermo, where that night I had a great thrill. We went to a showing for the Air Force of *My Favorite Blonde*. The thrill came after the movie, when the Germans arrived in a hundred JU-88 heavy bombers and plastered the town, the harbor, and our hotel, knocking us out of bed and smashing the place to bits. I've taken a lot of criticism in my time, but this was ridiculous. I didn't even know they'd seen the picture.

I've tried to make all of this sound like a comedy routine, but it really wasn't. A comedian is supposed to be funniest when he's frightened. If that's true, I must have been hilarious all the time we were in Sicily.

My good friend Ernie Pyle, the great spokesman of the enlisted man and the finest columnist of World War II until he got too close to it later on a little island in the Pacific, wrote this in his column of September 17, 1943:

The Hope troupe, which included lovely Frances Langford as the fourth member, really found out about war when they were over here. . . . I was in two different cities with them during air raids and I will testify that they were horrifying raids. It isn't often that a bomb falls close enough that you can hear it whistle. But when you can hear a whole stick of them whistling at once, then it's time to get weak all over and start sweating. The Hope troupe can now describe that ghastly sound. . . .

If this column appears in Hollywood let it be taken as legal testimony in verification that no matter what narrow escape story Bob tells when he gets back, it's true.

We were always being kidded about not being in uniform, and I had a few standard answers. I said Jack Pepper was classified two-F-two-F, meaning "too fat to fight," Tony Romano was double-S-double-F, meaning "single man with children," and I was in class four-Z, meaning "coward." The truth was that both Bing and I had been offered commissions as lieutenant commanders in the Navy, but FDR had said, "No way. I want these people to play for *all* the services." I guess he didn't want us in the armed forces. After all, he had sworn to protect and defend the United States.

We flew back to Algeria after our last show, actually a little sad about leaving those guys who would soon be crossing the Strait of Messina to storm the beaches at Anzio and Nettuno, while we were back in the peace and quiet of Algiers.

We were up to our ears trying to prepare our broadcast to the United States, when we got word that Ike wanted to see us. I tried to figure out what we had done wrong. After all, he was preparing for the invasion of Italy and certainly had more important things on his mind than a ski-nosed comic and his vaudeville troupe.

What Eisenhower wanted was just to thank us. He knew everywhere we'd been and every show we'd done. I grabbed the opportunity to tell him I'd like a picture with him — meaning I wanted to pose beside him. He opened a drawer and took out four or five glossies of himself and asked me which one I liked best?

He pointed to one and said, "That's my favorite."

I'm no fool. I took them all.

Ike told us he wanted to be sure we'd keep doing shows for the RAF in addition to those for Americans, because it was important not to neglect our Allies. We were all going to need each other terribly in the near future. The Germans and the Japanese were far from defeated.

That was the bad news. The good news came when he said, "I understand you people have had some excitement on your trip. Well, you're perfectly safe here in Algiers this time. We're well protected by guns and planes and warships. We haven't had a bombing in six months. We're too strong for 'em here now. They can't get in. You'll get a lot of rest tonight."

We all heaved a sigh of relief. We were to do our broadcast at midnight. That meant we could go back to our hotel afterward and get a good night's sleep; we had it on the highest authority.

I had a sneaking suspicion a little praying wouldn't hurt. After all, even Hebrew National frankfurters insist there is a *higher* authority.

As midnight rolled around, we were falling all over each other getting ready for the broadcast from the Red Cross building in Algiers.

Andre Baruch in his Army uniform was our announcer and also doubled as stagehand. He and Jack Pepper moved the microphones around, and Tony Romano led the Army band that was to accompany us. A lot of the script Hal and I had written was in pencil; a lot of it wasn't even there. We hadn't had time.

In those days, international broadcasting was an event; broadcasting of entertainment from a battle area was almost unheard of.

Midnight in a war zone. Sounds like a song title.

Baruch handed me a set of earphones so

I could hear the cue from New York over the rush of static.

Then he put a finger in his ear so he could listen to his own voice and announced, "From somewhere in North Africa, through the cooperation of the United States Army and U.S.O. Camp Shows, we bring you Bob Hope with Frances Langford, Tony Romano, and Jack Pepper. And now, here he is in person, Bob Hope!"

I was there in person, all right; I couldn't find a stand-in for a job like that.

"Good evening, ladies and gentlemen and fellow tourists. This is Bob 'Just Got Back From Sicily' Hope, who went to Sicily to get some spaghetti for this ham, but wound up with meatballs made of Spam. . . . Believe me, you really have to take it in Sicily. The hot sun, the dust, the Atabrine. You know they give Atabrine to our troops to get rid of malaria. Then the troops gave it to the Italians and they got rid of Mussolini . . ."

After that, I did a few jokes with Frances:

"What do you mean, you've been looking all over Algiers for Charles Boyer? What do you like about him?"

"Oh, Bob, when he looks at me and flutters those eyelashes . . . oh, my . . . !"

"What do you want, love or air conditioning? After all, what has Boyer got that

I haven't got?"

"Nothing, but his doesn't look like it's government issue."

A few songs from Frances, Tony Romano and his guitar, some more insults from Jack Pepper, and the show was over.

It doesn't sound like much, but pulling it all together in a war zone in those days, with no staff and no equipment, wasn't exactly a piece of cake. We all felt we'd done a good day's work. The power shortage had grounded all elevators in Algiers, so we happily climbed five steep flights of stairs just to listen to ourselves again on the recording of the broadcast and pat each other on the back.

One of the reasons we were so happy was that we were booked to fly back home the next day. We got to our hotel around 3 A.M. and we all hit the sack and slept soundly for all of forty-five minutes. Then all hell broke loose. The sirens, the ack-ack, the bombs whistling, the explosions. Jack Pepper pounded on my door and hollered, "Air raid! Go to the shelter!" As if I needed any encouragement.

I raced down with the others, hollering, "Tell those Germans what Eisenhower said! He's gonna be mad at them!" But it didn't sound very funny, even to me.

We huddled together in the air-raid shelter under the hotel. It used to be the wine cellar, but a quick investigation proved the Army had gotten there first.

The warships in the harbor were putting up a screen of flak and the noise of the fighter planes and the bombs dropping made it all seem like a B movie with the sound turned up too loud. When you're actually in it and you know it isn't the projectionist's fault, your throat chokes up and you can see the ceiling above you shaking from the concussion and every explosion reminds you of all the wrong things you've done in your life, including coming to North Africa in the first place.

The bombing went on and on and on. I felt someone clutch my arm, and it was Frances. Alaska, Bizerte, Palermo, those dangers had never made her lose her beautiful calm, but here, cooped up in a cellar in Algiers, she started to tremble and cry.

I tried to break the tension by telling a true story I'd heard about an officer in this same bomb shelter who had comforted a hysterical woman by saying, "Don't worry, lady. Don't be frightened. I'm a fighter pilot." She pulled herself together and glared at him and said, "What the hell are you doing down *here?*"

Finally, it was over. I got off Frances's lap and we all went upstairs and got a little shut-eye.

The next morning I sent Ike a telegram: "Thanks for the rest."

The streets were littered with flak and debris as we made our way to Algiers airport to catch a military flight for England. They took a look at our tickets and told us we only had a "4" priority and might have to lay over four or five weeks.

After screaming for several fast minutes, I grabbed a cab and raced back to Algiers to ask for help from the Army. If we had to stay, I threatened to do a lot more shows using the same jokes.

We got switched to top priority.

As we took off and flew out over the peaceful blue ocean, I heaved a deep sigh of relief. I felt we could head for home knowing we had done our job.

But what about all the guys who didn't have any priority at all? I remembered over-hearing two commandos chatting.

One said, "Ain't I met you before?"

And the other said, "I dunno. What part of hell you from?"

I wondered, in spite of what FDR had said, if I shouldn't have been emulating Gable, instead of making jokes like "There's a notation at my draft board that says, 'Unconditional surrender is preferable to calling this man up.' "

When I got back to Hollywood I found a letter waiting for me.

Dear Mr. Hope,

I thought you might like to see this note from my son, Lt. John D. Saint, Jr., who was in Sicily when you were.

This is the note:

Dear Mom and Dad,

It was not officially announced that I know of, but the word spread like wildfire, "Bob Hope is in town!" When I arrived where I was told he was coming, there was a tremendous crush. Fifteen thousand is a conservative estimate. All of a sudden Hope came in riding in a command car followed by two more. He came up on the grandstand dressed in baggy trousers, an ordinary coat, and an open-neck collar. His nose was really sunburned and caught the brunt of a lot of his own jokes. He brought out Jack Pepper and Tony Romano, and they were great. And then all of a sudden Bob said, "Here's Frances Langford!" There was a din you would not believe. She sang and she sang from the very bottom of her heart. "You Made

Me Love You." "Embraceable You." Every one of those thousands of men went home to their wives and sweethearts. There was not a sound and there was not a movement. . . . She will never know what it did to us. It was almost more than a man could stand. . . ."

I felt better when I read that. Maybe four-Z wasn't such a bad classification, if it meant I could bring the men Frances and the rest of the Gypsies.

CHAPTER FOUR

1943-1945

"God bless those kids across
the English Channel."
— *Pepsodent show,*
June 6, 1944

Getting back to California was something of
a letdown. Hollywood was tinsel and make-
believe and happy endings. Where we had
been was mud and reality and horror. None
of us in the Hope Gypsies would ever be
the same after what we had seen. Whoever
said "There are no atheists in foxholes" had
it right.

We missed all of them already, the guys
and the girls who couldn't leave and fly
home. We knew we were going to have to
go back to them.

It was great to see Dolores again, to be
back in the comfortable house in Toluca Lake,
where the milk and the eggs weren't pow-
dered and there were no bomb craters in
the front lawn. It was good to get back to

work with the writers and start another season touring Army camps; the trouble was, these camps were in the United States. I think I was suffering from adrenaline withdrawal; I had gotten hooked on fear, the real thing, not the sort you felt when a joke didn't play or a movie got panned. Danger, real danger, hyped up both the performers and the audiences. The bombs weren't just in the monologues. In Palermo and Algiers, the audiences and the performers all knew they might never hear laughter again. So we all laughed.

I suppose there's something wrong with me. Even at my present age, somewhat past puberty, my doctors tell me I don't react like a normal, grown-up person. My nervous system won't let me slow down. I seem to recharge as I discharge energy. If I was still a kid, they'd say it was hyperactivity, and what I needed was a good spanking. Whatever the reason, I don't seem to get tired the way most people around me do. Time is my friend, not my enemy.

My writers like to tell a story about me, which I don't believe. They say that when the Pepsodent show was in Atlanta I woke some of them up in the middle of the night because I'd thought of a new topic for the monologue. I told them to get busy writing jokes, and then I remembered we had just hired a new writer, a kid named Norman Sullivan (the kid was to stay with me for more than thirty-five years), and I asked them to get Norman working on it, too.

One of the writers protested, "But Bob — Norman just got here today, and it's three o'clock in the morning!"

The writers claim I answered, "He doesn't know anybody in Atlanta. What else does he have to do?"

Maybe I didn't want Norman to feel lonesome. Sleep has never been important enough to me to interfere with work. In vaudeville, I learned how to grab ten-minute catnaps between shows. It kept me alert on stage in case the audience started up after me.

The home front followed the war news more closely than the soldiers, who were too busy fighting to read the newspapers. I didn't know until I got home what had happened in Italy when we were right next door. I don't think the Italians did, either. Schicklgruber didn't trust his own allies, so on September 9, he ordered German troops to kick the Italian army out of Rome and take over control of the Eternal City. This revised an old Hungarian proverb to read, "When you have Adolf for a friend, you don't need an enemy." At about the same time, somebody located the Italian fleet and they were so embarrassed they immediately surrendered.

After arresting Mussolini, the Italians locked him up in a deluxe hotel on top of a mountain in central Italy and took away his American Express card. German commandos led by Colonel Otto Skorzeny staged a daring glider raid and got Benito out without paying his bill. He seemed reluctant to go until they brought along his mistress, Clara Petacci. What happened to Mrs. Mussolini, nobody seemed to know. Maybe there wasn't room in the gliders for excess baggage. Benito didn't even mail her his allotment check afterward.

Shortly after the Hope Gypsies left the area, Italy surrendered to the Allies. It may have been part of a secret deal with Eisenhower to get me out of Sicily, but I could never prove it.

To complete the ring-around-a-rosy, the Italians decided to switch sides and declare war on Germany. For a while, you couldn't tell the players without a program.

To add to the confusion, I had come back to the United States to discover that the way people looked at me had changed, too. In my own mind, I was nobody's hero; I was just a comic willing to take chances to find an audience that would laugh at anything. I felt I was nothing special. After all, the soldiers and sailors I was entertaining were taking life-and-death chances every day, and nobody put them on the cover of *Time* magazine.

But that's what happened to Robert Hope. The cover of *Time* and the line "First in the hearts of the servicemen." People started to look at me as if I were Mount Rushmore. Now that I *look* like Mount Rushmore, of course, they've stopped.

I really couldn't figure it out. I was no different than a couple of dozen other entertainers that year. In the Middle East were Jack Benny, Larry Adler and his harmonica, and Al Jolson; Ray Bolger was in the South Pacific, Judith Anderson in Hawaii. Martha Raye visited the foxholes of Tunisia, and in New Guinea there were others within earshot — and gunshot — of the Japanese army. Fred Astaire and the Groaner were to invade Europe together after I left.

These last two, I reluctantly admit, could sing and dance almost as well as I could.

And what about the rest of the Gypsies? There should have been a statue to Frances Langford, wearing a parachute. And one complete with moustache for Jerry Colonna. And awards to Tony Romano, Jack Pepper, Patti Thomas, and all the other troupers. They took the same chances and worked just as hard as the boss, knowing that when they got home, only the so-called "star" would get the headlines.

So I was a little embarrassed when I saw my face on that *Time* cover. It's not true I later had it tattooed on my chest. But I can still quote every line of the story. It was so well written.

Besides, it's engraved on my bathroom mirror:

"From the ranks of show business have sprung heroes and even martyrs, but so far only one legend.

"That legend is Bob Hope. . . ."

The trouble with being a living legend is that you have to keep working at it. We did our first Pepsodent show almost as soon as we got back from Europe, playing the Pasadena Civic Auditorium to decompress before we hit the camp circuit, and it was like old times. Our guest was the old Groaner himself. Bing and I were both back on familiar territory:

"Welcome home, Ski Snoot. My, my, look at you. No more pot tummy. How'd you manage?"

"I didn't. During an air raid, it went round back to hide."

The other jokes were old friends, too:

"I've just returned from a tour of Army camps. The U.S.O. sent me to Europe to boost the morale of the soldiers . . . in the United States. . . . Yes, sir, I heard they were going to open up a second front. So here I am. The first back."

But I had changed. At the end of the show, I took a moment off from being funny and made a stab at being serious. I was no Ed Murrow or Elmer Davis. And, of course, I was certainly no Walter Cronkite. In a later time, nothing was news until Walter said it was. It was rumored that on his honeymoon, Walter said to his bride, "And that's the way it is," and rolled over and went to sleep.

I just did the best I could, and hoped someone would listen. After all, they listened to the commercials.

"Well, folks, during the summer we popped in on your son overseas. We ate army chow and jumped into ditches with him when the Junkers came over. We saw the shadow of pain and tragedy on his face, and we've seen a belly laugh chase the shadows away. We came home, and found that all some people are talking about is the high cost of living. Maybe they ought to figure the high cost of dying on that beachhead at Salerno. . . ."

On the home front, Hollywood was doing its best. The Hollywood Canteen opened on a side street off Hollywood Boulevard. Movie stars all pitched in and entertained, waited on tables, washed the dishes, and danced with the soldiers and sailors passing through. I once washed dishes with Vice President Henry Wallace, who wanted to show what a clean politician he was.

No officers were allowed. In fact, it was like a crap game after taps has blown. It got so crowded that if a soldier wanted to tune the radio, he had to squeeze past Lana Turner, Hedy Lamarr, Dinah Shore, and Betty Grable just to change the station. In five minutes one night I must have heard 148 different programs. Bette Davis was practically the den mother; she showed up almost every night. Even Marlene Dietrich made it, singing "Lili Marlene," the German war song that was so popular it was adopted by troops of both sides. Dorothy Lamour came down, but she almost had a disaster. She was standing in the kitchen in her sarong when a nearsighted soldier reached for a dish-towel.

Some of the guys took advantage of the situation. One of them would walk up to a beautiful star, smile bravely, and say, "Will you please dance with me? I'm going over soon. It worked great until they found out he was going over to the Pantages to see a movie.

After that we hit the G.I. trail again — Terminal Island Naval Base, Minterfield air cadets, Camp Luis Obispo, and Las Vegas Gunnery School. As Christmas approached, we were at Camp Callan. The war in Europe seemed to have reached a winter stalemate, and things didn't look too bright in the Pacific, either. I took time out from laughter to say, "It is Christmastime. Over there, American soldiers move through the streets stepping over the dead and wounded; and the Christmas smells are not of sage and pine needles, but powder and smoke and blood."

I've waited too long to give credit for lines like those to the one writer who was responsible for seeing that I didn't get laughs. His name was Glenn Whedon, and his difficult job was to make a former vaudeville comic sound like Henry Kissinger without an accent. In my new role as Mount Rushmore, I needed someone like Glenn to help me say what I wanted to say, better than I could say it myself. I'm glad he was there.

That Christmas Eve, America got a present it would never forget. FDR and Winnie announced that General Dwight Eisenhower had been selected Supreme Commander of the

Allied Expeditionary Force for the inevitable invasion of Europe.

We all hoped Schicklgruber found that news story in his Christmas stocking. Everything the Allied armed forces had to offer was soon to climb down Adolf's chimney under the command of one man, the best soldier America had, Ike Eisenhower, whose family had come from Germany itself. We were a nation of immigrants and children of immigrants, a melting pot, and we were going to prove that Schicklgruber's "racial purity" theories were a crock of sauerkraut.

For the Japanese, if they read the papers, there was a presentiment of future defeat hidden in a small announcement on an inside page. A tiny Tennessee town called Oak Ridge had suddenly become home to fifty thousand scientists. Nobody knew why a small town in the Tennessee hills needed fifty thousand scientists — unless the Li'l Abner Skunk Works was looking for a new recipe for home brew — except for a few people like FDR, Albert Einstein, and a guy named Robert Oppenheimer.

On a lighter note, we had a real gift for the Waves at the U.S. Naval Hospital at San Diego when we played there right after Christmas.

"Here he is, girls — the star of *Destination*

Tokyo — MR. CARY GRANT!"

The shrieking and cheering just wouldn't stop. I finally had to shout "Please, please! *We* have to talk too, you know!"

Cary had just returned from entertaining the troops in the South Pacific and was at the height of his popularity.

The green-eyed monster showed up in our dialogue:

"I've seen you on the screen, Cary. How did you learn to kiss like that?"

"Practice, Bob. Constant practice."

"Yeah? What do you do with your old targets?"

Cary once took me aside and talked to me about my Passover problem with the Oscar. In all the years of his great career, he never won an Academy Award. In fact, he was only nominated once.

"You see," he explained, "people have to *know* you're acting. You have to scream or holler or bleed to death in front of them. Now, when I act, I usually have my hands in my pockets and speak quietly. The audience believes I'm just being myself, and can't understand why I get paid for it. But when I made *None But the Lonely Heart* I played a coalminer. I wore old clothes and the director let me take my hands out of my pockets and scratch my ass. Immediately, the audience could see I was acting, and I got a nomination."

Cary did get an honorary Oscar once, but he never got the big one, the Academy Award for acting. I'm a member of a large club.

Another talent even less recognized was a little pink-cheeked, bald-headed ex-vaud-villian named Barney Dean. Barney was the sweetest, kindest, wittiest, most loyal friend a fellow ever had. We had met in 1928, when we were both on the bill at the Stratford Theater in Chicago. Barney and his brother Sid were part of an act that Barney described as "the slowest whirlwind dancers in show business." The funny part of it was that Barney and Sid were not really brothers; they just thought it looked better on the program. Barney used to fake all his tapping. Sid got a little suspicious one time and stopped dancing to listen to him; when Sid didn't hear any tapping, he slapped his "brother" right in the face. The audience roared. Sid wanted to keep it in the act, but Barney refused. He felt it was beneath them. After all, *something* should be.

I was the emcee at the Stratford in those days and was barely getting by, but Barney was a good friend of the booker — Barney was a good friend of everybody who ever met him — and gave me such a buildup that my one-week stand stretched into six months and a career. I never plucked a chicken in my brother's meat market again.

Barney never asked for gratitude. He just got embarrassed and disappeared when I tried to thank him.

I didn't see him again until years later when he walked on the set at Paramount where Bing and I were shooting *Road to Singapore*. I was so happy to see him I almost kissed him, but Dorothy Lamour was watching and I didn't want to give her any mistaken ideas.

"Where've you been?" I asked him, "What have you been doing?"

"Same old thing," Barney said, "selling handcuffs."

Actually, he was selling Christmas cards, but he didn't want his Jewish mother to find out. He said he was afraid she'd make him turn back his circumcision.

Bing knew Barney and loved him, too, and together we got Paramount to put him on the payroll as a writer. Not that Barney ever wrote anything. But he was fun to have around and would sometimes come up with wild lines that were funnier than anything in the script. And most important of all, he wasn't afraid to tell us when a scene or a joke wasn't playing. Of course, we would usually glare at him, and Barney would pretend to tremble and call out, "Where are my dancing shoes?" But quite often, he was right.

Barney once got stopped for jaywalking in Beverly Hills and apologized: "I'm sorry, officer. How fast was I going?"

Perhaps his most famous remark was engraved on the back of a gold watch he gave to Buddy De Sylva, when Buddy was president of Paramount.

"This is a lot of crap," the inscription read, "but when you got no talent, you got to do these things."

Bing once took him along when he went to visit Nelson Rockefeller at his plush mansion in Westchester. Barney stopped short in front of a huge oil painting of a polo match and said to Bing, "Why don't we do that anymore?"

And once Barney heard Crosby mention that he was going to New York. Barney asked if Bing would do him a favor.

"Sure," Bing said, "what can I do for you?"

"Go up to 1225 167th Street and climb up to the fifth floor, the elevator isn't working. Knock on the door of the first apartment and a nice old Jewish lady will open it. She's my mother. Say hello and give her five thousand dollars."

Barney was with me until the day he died, but that's a story for later. There was a lot of wonderful fun and laughter in between.

My picture career had taken off as a result of the success of the radio show. I was very lucky. One medium helped the other, and I was climbing in both at the same time. Paramount even allowed me to get the girl, unless it was a "Road" picture. In *Road to Morocco,* what I got was the camel. This uncouth dromedary had spat in my face during one take, which I assumed would be cut out of the picture. But David Butler, the director, thought the camel was funnier than I was, and kept the beast's ad-lib in the final print.

The camel stole all the notices and almost got an Oscar nomination.

David was large enough to be an Irish Santa Claus. When the Rams football team first came to Los Angeles, Butler got a season ticket on the fifty-yard line at the Coliseum. When the Rams scored their first touchdown in the opening game, David raised his huge bulk out of his seat and cheered at the top of his considerable lungs. When the guy seated in back of him started yelling for him to sit down, David turned to glare at him and said, with great dignity, "I got a right to cheer. I *went* to Ram!"

Butler directed several of the "Road" pictures, including one in which Bing and I were almost run down by a stampede of horses, and *Road to Utopia*, where we were almost chewed up by a live bear. David got big laughs out of both situations. He was a believer in animal rights.

Butler also directed *They Got Me Covered*, a flick I made with Dorothy Lamour while doing the radio show at the same time. It wasn't as difficult as it sounds. In those golden radio days, all I had to do was show up at the NBC studio for the preview Sunday and the show on Tuesday night, and read the jokes from the script I held in my hand. It wasn't until television came in and loused up a good thing that actors had to take the time to memorize their lines. Some of them never did bother. Necessity became the mother of the idiot card.

They Got Me Covered, my first movie for Sam Goldwyn, came about when Paramount refused to give me a raise — the studio had the foolish notion that actors should honor their contracts, no matter how much money their films earned. Doc Shurr figured that if he could get Paramount to lend me to Goldwyn, we might be able to hustle Sam into raising my ante. Paramount agreed — too easily, for my taste — and there was a long struggle with Goldwyn until Doc finally assured me we had a deal.

But when it came time to sign the contract, there was no figure in it for my salary. When I mentioned this slight oversight to Goldwyn, all he would say was, "Trust me."

Sam had just made *The Westerner*, starring Gary Cooper, and asked me to go to Dallas with him and help promote it. On the cuff.

After I'd played my fourth free show, I brought Sam out on stage in front of the audience. Without realizing what I had in mind, he told them how I was the greatest comic he had seen since Eddie Cantor, and how proud he was to be making a picture with me.

"Pride is fine," I told him, "But what about money?"

"Trust me," he said.

So I lay down on the stage with the microphone and said, "Let's talk about it now. Lie down."

The audience roared. Goldwyn always prided himself on the dignity and quality of his movies, but the truth is, there was always something of the pixie about him. In the days when Danny Kaye was making films for him, Danny could always throw Sam into convulsions by making funny faces. Once Danny was in New York and he phoned

Sam in Hollywood and said, "Sam, I'm making the fish face," and Goldwyn fell off his chair, laughing.

He couldn't resist the theatrical moment in Dallas, so he lay down on the stage beside me and we started to negotiate my salary in front of a theater full of Texans. They howled. A *Life* photographer was with us and shot the whole crazy thing. I figured that gave me all the evidence I needed and stood up and announced Sam and I had a deal. It was the best money I'd ever gotten in films. The audience applauded, with Doc Shurr clapping louder than anybody. After all, he was getting 10 percent.

That night at a party, Billy Wilkerson, who published the *Hollywood Reporter,* told Sam he ought to be ashamed of himself for taking part in such a silly stunt. It was beneath his dignity.

Sam thought it over and killed the photographs. But he stuck by the deal. He had told me to trust him and he wouldn't go back on his word.

That was Samuel Goldwyn's real dignity.

Some of the stories that grew up about Sam in Hollywood were hilarious, and probably as false as the ones my writers tell about me, but knowing Sam, they all *could* have happened.

Garson Kanin, then at the beginning of a great career, was hired by Sam as a production assistant and promptly told Goldwyn the script for one of his musicals was terrible. He urged Sam not to make the picture, and Goldwyn promptly fired him. The movie was made and released and lost millions. Some years later, after Gar had gone to Broadway and written *Born Yesterday*, a tremendous hit, someone suggested to Sam that he hire him to do a picture.

"Kanin?" Goldwyn snorted. "He was connected with one of my worst failures!"

Sam had a real sense of humor. One day, when I was resting in my dressing room, he brought all the Goldwyn girls in to meet me. He had a big fan in his hand and fanned me to cool me off.

There was also the tale of the time Goldwyn was making an expensive Technicolor musical with Eddie Cantor and had everybody worried sick about going over budget. There was one sequence in the film where Cantor was supposed to be caught in a waterfall made of ice cream. To their horror, the camera crew discovered that nothing would photograph in Technicolor like ice cream except real ice cream. They waited until they knew Goldwyn was out of town and then ordered five thousand gallons needed for the shot, without telling him.

While they were shooting the scene with a ton of real ice cream cascading over a fake mountain and into a tank on the sound stage, Goldwyn walked in unexpectedly. Everyone held his breath. Sam just stood there and watched. When the shot was over, Goldwyn walked up to the huge ice cream waterfall, stuck his finger in it, put it in his mouth, and said, *"Mmmm.* Strawberry."

The Goldwyn story I like best concerns Billy Wilder. Billy came to Goldwyn one day when Sam was in his office with his wife, Frances. Wilder reminded Sam that when he sold him the story for a movie called *Ball of Fire,* Goldwyn had promised him an extra $10,000 if it ever got to the screen. The film had just been released, with Gary Cooper and Barbara Stanwyck in the leads, and was making a pot of money. Billy wanted his $10,000 bonus.

Sam's face turned red.

"You Hungarian thief!" he thundered (Billy is Austrian, but never mind). "I never promised any such thing! Get out of my office!"

Billy left, upset, and Frances turned to her husband and said, "Sam, I was sitting right here when you promised Billy the extra ten thousand dollars."

"What are you talking about?" Sam

shouted. "You're out of your mind!"

Around midnight that night, Frances awoke in their bedroom to see Sam, in his pajamas, pacing the floor.

"What's the matter?" Frances asked.

"I can't sleep," Sam told her. "I just remembered, you're absolutely right. I did promise Billy the money."

"What are you going to do?"

"What *can* I do?" Sam asked. "I'm going to sit right down and write him out that check for five thousand dollars."

Although I enjoyed making films — especially for Sam — I always felt the radio show was closer to the real world. Every week, we were heard by more people than attended Radio City Music Hall in a year.

Meanwhile, the troops in our Army camp audiences were headed for more drama than you could find in a dozen Bette Davis movies.

That spring of 1944, the world was waiting to see what was going to happen in Europe. Everyone knew that Eisenhower was building up tremendous forces in England and that the Allies were going to attack across the English Channel. Everybody's spies were breaking everyone else's secret codes: the Germans knew exactly what the signal for the invasion was going to be; the British had broken Schicklgruber's top military cipher and knew where all his submarines and tanks were and what he did after lunch with Eva Braun. The butler to the British ambassador in Turkey was a Nazi spy, code-named Cicero, and he had pilfered the combination to the ambassador's safe and given the supposed secret date of the invasion to the Germans.

The fact was that all these attempts at deception canceled one another out. It wasn't very good espionage, but each one of those incidents made a good movie.

At the time, our group didn't pay much attention to all this spy-and-counterspy stuff. Our minds were on the South Pacific. The Hope Gypsies were preparing to take off with Frances Langford, Jerry Colonna, Barney Dean, Patti Thomas, Tony Romano, and Jack Pepper for New Guinea, Tarawa, and similar remote real estate recently taken from the Japanese, and we were occupied with getting shots and going to confession.

We were due to head for the distant, steaming jungles of the Pacific as soon as we played our last Pepsodent show of the season.

We never did that show.

It was Tuesday night. June 6, 1944.

"Folks, this is Bob Hope speaking from a P-38 airfield near Van Nuys, California. We've looked forward to being with these men, and doing our regular show here, but of course nobody feels like getting up and being funny on a night like this. What's happened during these last few hours none of us will ever forget. How could you forget? You sat up all night by the radio and heard the bulletins from England, and you thought of the hundreds of thousands of kids crossing the English Channel. Then the sun came up and you sat there looking at that huge black headline, that one great black word with the exclamation point, 'INVASION!'

"God bless those kids across the English Channel."

Frances Langford sang "Ave Maria."

There wasn't much else on the show.

There didn't have to be.

Those planes and ships and tanks and kids who stormed onto the beaches of Normandy under a hail of bombs and bullets and shells made up the largest armada the world had ever seen. It was the start of the greatest invasion in history, retaking the continent of Europe from the Nazi hordes who had conquered, destroyed, occupied, and gassed millions upon millions of civilians: Jews, Poles, Russians, French — whomever Adolf was annoyed with. It would take almost a year of fierce air, tank, and infantry battles before it was all over and Schicklgruber took his own life, which by that time nobody else wanted.

But all that was still several months down the road. For the Hope Gypsies, our eyes were on the South Pacific, where that summer of 1944 Abe Lastfogel and the U.S.O. had scheduled us to play Loew's Malaria Circuit, in the steaming jungles of that other war, where booby traps, machine guns, and hand grenades hadn't yet been replaced by Mary Martin and Ezio Pinza singing "Some Enchanted Evening."

This was to be Barney Dean's first experience in a combat zone, outside of Nate 'n' Al's Delicatessen. He was not thrilled, but he wanted to go.

Barney, "Mother" Langford, Stash Colonna, Jack Pepper, Tony Romano, Patti Thomas, and I all boarded a plane at March Field that didn't exactly inspire confidence. It was a C-54 litter plane headed for Saipan to pick up some wounded. We wondered if they might include the previous U.S.O. unit.

Our first stop was to be Honolulu, which was Grand Central Station for the entire Pacific area. The basic strategy the Allied big brass had chosen was to drive the Japanese back island by island and then use the recaptured territory to build air bases needed for the big planes that would one day have to bomb the sashimi out of the Japanese mainland. Men and supplies flew into Honolulu from the States, and returning hospital planes never lacked for cargo.

We were told we were going to play the Pineapple Circuit: Eniwetok, Tarawa, Kwajalein, New Guinea, Saipan, Majuro, and a few less popular neighborhoods. The Japanese were still very much in control of the suburbs. If we laid a bomb, they quite likely might return the favor.

The Air Force kindly provided us with maps of the Pacific area. We were a little disturbed to note that some of the islands we were scheduled to play weren't even on them.

To give you an idea of how remote they were, when we got off the plane at one, a monkey ran up and grabbed my hand and said, "Help! I'm lost."

And I loved the facilities at the next base. When I asked for the washroom, they handed me a shovel.

One of our early stops was Eniwetok, which had been the scene of a very bloody battle. But our guys had won. The worst part about winning a rat-infested, malaria-ridden South Pacific atoll is that you have to stay there. With no women anywhere. Hal Kanter, who had written for me in the prewar days and was now stationed there with Armed Forces Radio, said guys would start howling at the sight of two coconuts close together. You can imagine what happened when the Hope Gypsies showed up with Frances Langford and Patti Thomas. The wolf whistles blew three planes off the runway.

I remember that when I saw the place, I told them, "So this is Eniwetok. What an island! It's so small, when the tide comes in, you guys should get submarine pay. . . . You're not defending this place, are you? Let them take it, it'll serve them right."

It felt good to bring girls and music and laughs to places where the only thing breaking the monotony before was finding a new fungus growing on you. Every time I'd start to puff up from all that applause, Barney would remind me it isn't so tough to be more popular than jungle rot.

That reminds me of the story of Marilyn Monroe, who made an overseas trip to do some shows during the Korean War. When she got back, she told her husband, Joe DiMaggio, "Oh, it was so exciting! When I would walk out on stage in front of those thousands of men, you've never heard so much shouting and cheering!"

And Joe said, "Oh, yes, I have."

He's still hearing those cheers.

Off Eniwetok, I ran into another living legend. I had been invited aboard a Navy ship to have dinner with Admiral Hoover, when I unexpectedly ran into Henry Fonda. We were so happy to meet somebody else from never-never land we almost kissed right there on the deck. Hank was in the Navy, but at the time he was quartered down about three decks where you could die of suffocation. So I said to him, "Come on and have dinner with me and the admiral," and he said, "Oh, no. No, no, no." I could see he wanted to, but he was doing his shy Jimmy Stewart impersonation. So I went to the admiral and said, "You know, Henry Fonda's aboard and he looks hungry. Why don't we invite him to dinner?" Well, it seems the admiral had wanted to, but he was reluctant to do it himself. *Both* of them were playing Jimmy Stewart. Hank might have starved if I hadn't persuaded them to play themselves. We had a great dinner together, and of course we didn't know that in 1955, Hank would make a sensation as a Navy lieutenant in *Mr. Roberts*, and Jack Lemmon would walk away with the supporting Oscar for the same picture. Fonda didn't even get a nomination. I just mention that for the record — mine.

Speaking of the admiral's dinner reminds me that food became one of the most important items to the Gypsies on that trip.

In *Annie Hall*, Woody Allen had a line about two old ladies in a Catskill mountain resort. One complained to the other, "The food at this hotel is terrible!" And the other agreed, "Yes, and such small portions!"

Our problem was that our portions weren't small enough. The Army and the Air Force were occupied with battling their way closer and closer to Japan for the final assault, and food was not the top priority. At most bases it was typical Army chow. Half the time we expected it to crawl off our plates.

And then we flew into the island of Majuro, which was a big naval base in the Marshall Islands. They hit us with steak, peas, mashed potatoes, ice cream — none of it on a shingle. I felt I'd died and gone to heaven and found a "21" Club up there. This was another kind of war, the Park Avenue war, that we hadn't known existed. We ate high on the hog for two days without stopping.

And on nearby islands, the Japanese army was eating raw fish. We felt sorry for them. We didn't know that in America after the war, you wouldn't be able to get into a sushi joint without a reservation. And we thought they lost.

After Majuro, we island-hopped all over the Pacific, the islands getting smaller and smaller, the Japanese getting closer and closer, the bases getting more and more primitive. I got big laughs with lines like "What a beautiful swamp you got here. This'd be a great spot to build a cesspool. . . . It's a top-secret base. Even the snakes can't find it. . . . If you wanna hide from your draft board, this is the place to do it."

We had just done a show in a place called Noemfoor, where they based the Black Widow Night Fighters, when a fellow came in with a communiqué and handed it to the general. It read, "They killed a Jap two hundred yards from the stage during the show."

And Colonna said, "Was he coming or going?"

I told you we did shows from places that weren't even on the map. One of them was a tiny island called Pavuvu. We were at an island base in the Pacific called Bonica when the commander told us that the men of the famous 1st Marine Division had been training at Pavuvu for almost six months. They were preparing to invade another unknown island called Peleliu, a tiny dot in the Carolines north of New Guinea and east of the Philippines. Peleliu was rumored to be one of the most dangerous of the Japanese-held positions on the way to Tokyo. In all those six months, the almost-forgotten marines on

Pavuvu had never had any entertainment. The island had no airstrip; we'd have to land on a road. Would we consider making an attempt?

We all climbed into Piper Cubs, two or three to a Cub, and flew out over the Pacific. When we finally located Pavuvu, we buzzed the baseball field and it was the most exciting moment of the tour when we saw fifteen thousand men waiting for us, looking up and cheering every little plane as it came in.

We gave them the best show of the tour.

When the marines finally made their assault on Peleliu they found the coral reefs steep and jagged, the temperature 115°, and the Japanese entrenched in caves they had turned into fortresses of reinforced concrete. Of the fifteen thousand kids who cheered that day, 40 percent never went home.

I was going through a hospital in Oakland some months later, doing the usual "Don't get up" comedy routine for a ward full of wounded marines, when a guy half-covered in bandages suddenly stuck his hand out of the bed and hollered at me, "Pavuvu!"

He didn't have to say anything else. I just went over and shook his hand.

I said, "You were there, huh?"

And he said, "All of us in this ward."

I kept shaking hands going down through

the beds, and finally came to an enclosed space at the back, where they were fanning a guy just coming out of an operation. I stood there watching. He opened his eyes and said, "Bob! When did you get here?"

I had to turn and walk away. As Adlai Stevenson said, I was too big to cry, and it hurt too much to laugh. When I got a little bit farther away from that kid, I wasn't too big anymore.

Compared to the guys who were digging Japs out of caves with machine guns and flame throwers, our little group was a Sunday school picnic in South Pasadena. I guess I felt the need of a little danger to even things up when we hit Australia, otherwise I don't know why I would have asked to handle the controls of the Navy Catalina flying boat taking us from Brisbane to Sydney. Up to that time, my flight training consisted of a trip on the Flying Dumbo ride at Disneyland.

I waited until everyone else in our group was asleep before begging our Navy pilot to let me do the driving. He was a little dubious about turning over the controls to a civilian, especially after I asked him which way was reverse, but he wanted an introduction to Frances and he figured, how much harm could a stupid civilian do in only a couple of minutes?

He put everything on automatic pilot and went back to talk to Frances. I have an idea the Catalina discovered who was flying it and the left engine fainted. The pilot came racing into the cockpit and ordered me out of the seat. He started checking the instruments and the motor kept complaining until finally he feathered the prop. We went into a dive and he yelled, "Jettison everything we don't need!"

I raced into the back and tripped over Barney, who was just getting out of his berth. I had kidded him so much about how the planes we were in were always going to crash, he didn't believe me when I told him we were in serious trouble.

"How can it be serious?" he asked. "Your option was already picked up."

I dragged him up to the cockpit and showed him the feathered prop.

"That's supposed to be going around," I told him.

Barney swallowed hard and said, "Spare me the technical crap. How long have we got to live?"

The plane kept losing altitude and by that time everybody was awake and throwing everything overboard including the Scotch. Barney got indignant when we started eyeing *him*. He told me to throw my wallet overboard, since it was the heaviest thing on the plane.

We were over a little Australian town named Laurieton, which naturally didn't have an airport. The pilot hollered from the cockpit for all of us to strap ourselves in. He had seen a small lake and on one complaining engine he brought that big boat down on a tiny spot of water. It skipped twice, hit a sandbar, and sighed deeply as we lurched to a stop.

We crawled out on a wing and shouted with relief when we saw a small boat start out from the shore as we started to sink.

An Aussie was rowing the boat, and when he saw us all clinging to the wing, he hollered, "I say there, do you chaps have any American cigarettes?"

We had traveled nine thousand miles for a Lucky Strike commercial.

We finally talked him into taking us ashore, where, naturally, someone asked us to do a show for "The Forces," the Australian U.S.O. They had a small stage and an audience of about five hundred, so I went out to knock 'em dead with a couple of surefire routines. Nothing. They just sat and stared. American Army jokes meant nothing to them. If one of them hadn't saved our lives, I would have canceled the engagement. But I was too stubborn to quit until I got a laugh.

So I said, "I was up in Brisbane the other day, and I met this woman who was wearing a big hat. It started to rain, and she took her dress and held it over her hat. I said, 'What are you doing that for? Your legs are getting all wet.' And she said, 'The hat's brand-new. My legs are fifty years old.'"

I got my laugh with that joke that was as old as her legs, and quickly said, "And here's Tony Romano!"

But the people in Laurieton got even; they never sent out word that we were safe, and for three days Dolores heard news reports that our plane was missing. We finally got to Sydney, and there was a crowd of ten thousand waiting to cheer us. Our hotel was so jammed we couldn't get through the lobby.

A few days later, we were aboard a big C-130 headed back to the jungles.

No one asked me to fly the plane.

One of our last stops was a place called Hollandia. We were expecting tulips and wooden shoes until we found out Hollandia was in New Guinea. The Japanese had invaded it first, and the Allies had figured we wouldn't be strong enough to attack it for at least another year. But General MacArthur was in a hurry to get back to the Philippines — I think he'd left his pipe tobacco in Manila — and had decided to take a long shot by attacking New Guinea ahead of schedule. It worked. Hollandia was now in our hands, and our troops were pushing forward all over New Guinea. But the Japanese were still there, pushing back.

We didn't know what we were going to meet when we hit the beach there. We were in for a big surprise. Twenty thousand troops and General Robert Eichelberger were waiting for us. It was one of the biggest audiences we had ever faced in a war zone, and I kept wondering who was watching the store. Among all the shouting and cheering when Frances, Patti, Colonna, and Pepper walked out on the stage, I thought I heard a few voices hollering "Banzai!"

I pulled myself together and told the troops, "I'm happy to be here. What part of Miami *is* this? I don't know how we're going to get back home when we leave here. Two mosquitoes ate our chopper."

Then I introduced Colonna and said, "Isn't that a beautiful moustache?" I stroked it and said, "What a jungle!"

Jerry backed off and hollered, "Careful! Snipers!"

Of course, the girls were what they really wanted to see, and France's voice and Patti's dancing had them leaping to their feet to cheer. Or maybe they just wanted to get a better look.

We did a second show that night for about five thousand Seabees, the guys from the Construction Battalions, in a natural amphitheater near the beach. It was a lovely, moonlit night, and when Frances stepped out and sang "I'm in the Mood for Love," some guy stood up in the middle of the crowd and hollered, "You've come to the right place, honey!"

Biggest laugh I ever heard.

I called out, "Are you the guys who build the roads the marines land on?"

And some guy answered, "No, we're the Seabees. We build the roads the Japs retreat on."

What they built was almost as important as what the fighting men captured, because it allowed supplies to be brought up through the jungle and airfields to be constructed in places so remote even Club Med hasn't yet found them. And MacArthur, who had left Corregidor wading through the ocean to a submarine — it's not true he left his footprints on the water — had promised the Philippines, "I shall return!" He was pressing the men to work harder and faster. He had established his headquarters on top of a steep hill three quarters of a mile almost straight up from

Hollandia, and the G.I.'s had to build a road to get up there. The soldiers hated it. Somebody had even written Congress about it. Every time we drove up the hill the kids would hiss us, thinking I must be MacArthur.

At least, that's what I thought. But Barney said it was because they thought I was going to do another show.

When we finally got back to the United States, we caught up on what had been going on that summer in that little war in Europe we had forgotten about while I was learning to pronounce "Kaopectate" in four native languages.

We learned that on July 20 there had been an attempt to assassinate Adolf Hitler by some of his own generals. Unfortunately, it didn't work, but the handwriting was on the wall. The Nazi supermen had all turned back into Clark Kent and were stuck in a telephone booth.

After liberating Paris, Allied troops crossed the German border. Victory seemed in the air as the first Pepsodent show of the season broadcast from the Marine Corps air station in the Mojave Desert. I gave my report on the more important events of the past summer.

"We played for a lot of marines on our U.S.O. tour to the South Pacific. I won't say I did a lot of flying, but ever since I came back, I sleep with my nose under my left arm. . . . On the way over, we skimmed about ten feet above the waves. I asked the pilot, 'What's the idea?' And he said, 'We can't go any higher. The tail gunner's doing our laundry.' On our way back, over Australia we developed motor trouble and the first thing they wanted to do was throw all the useless weight overboard. But I wouldn't let go of my seat. . . . I won't say I was excited, but I was in such a hurry to get into a parachute I could hardly wait for Frances to take it off."

A lot of things had been happening on the Hollywood front. Vincente Minelli had directed a film called *Meet Me in St. Louis*, starring the little girl who used to adore me on the Pepsodent show. Judy had asked me to wait for her until she grew up. While I waited, Vincente married her. I felt cheated. As Brenda once told Cobina, "You waited so long for your ship to come in, your pier collapsed."

My world collapsed even more when I went to see a flick starring God's gift to elderly horseflesh. The picture was *Going My Way*, and when I next emceed the Academy Awards, I had to present Harry Lillis Crosby with the Oscar for the best acting performance of the year, knowing in my heart that *I* should have gotten it for smiling while I handed it to him.

The presidential campaign heated up. FDR's opponent was the governor of New York and former racket buster, Tom Dewey. Dewey's chances of becoming President were sadly damaged when some commentator noted he looked exactly like the groom on a wedding cake, complete to the moustache. The image stuck and Dewey could never get off the icing.

I've been making jokes about Presidents for a long time. I don't know exactly who was President when I started, but he was wearing a coonskin hat. The first presidential joke I ever told was about George Washington: "George told his father, 'I cannot tell a lie.' I don't know how he ever made it in politics. . . ." And Thomas Jefferson called the presidency a splendid misery. " 'Splendid misery.' That's like watching your mother-in-law drive off a cliff in your new Chrysler." Since I was then sponsored by Chrysler Motors, that was a laugh and a commercial at the same time. About Abraham Lincoln: "Lincoln said, 'You can fool all of the people some of the time and some of the people all of the time, but you can't fool all of the people all of the time.' Abe made that statement right after he'd seen my act." And I find I can still get laughs with lines about Calvin Coolidge, who was known as Silent Cal: "Coolidge never said anything. In fact, a monk once broke a vow of silence to ask him to speak up."

Of the more recent Presidents, I've known most of them personally, played golf with them, and learned they all have a sense of humor, or they wouldn't be in politics. Or try to play golf.

They all seemed to get a kick out of the jokes; that's how I got away with lines like "Wasn't that a wonderful meeting at the White House between Eisenhower and Kennedy? Eisenhower said, 'Congratulations on your victory,' and Kennedy said, 'I had to win. It's so tough these days to find a place that'll take children.' "

To get back to the presidential election of 1944, Franklin Roosevelt and Harry Truman ran against the little guy on the wedding cake. I've forgotten who ran for vice president on the Republican ticket. Whoever it was probably prefers it that way.

I guess "charisma" is the most overworked word in the English language. I'm not exactly sure what it means, but I know it describes Roosevelt.

Maybe Churchill said it best: "Meeting Franklin is like opening a bottle of champagne."

I would have felt that way even if he hadn't laughed so loud at my jokes.

"I went to Quebec when Roosevelt and Churchill were holding that conference. Professor Colonna almost missed our train. He bumped into Dewey and it took the porter an hour to untangle their moustaches."

November 7, 1944, was a Tuesday, but the Pepsodent show did not go on the air; some foolish listeners preferred to hear the election results.

It was another FDR landslide. Even so, it had been a tough battle. Roosevelt was running for an unheard-of fourth term, and the strain was beginning to show.

Nineteen-forty-four was also memorable for one line in *Road to Utopia*, which was made that year. Bing and I are at the bar in a tough saloon in the Klondike during the gold rush. Crosby asks for a double slug of rotgut and when the bartender looks at me, I say, "I'll have a lemonade." When every mean-looking miner in the saloon turns to glare, I quickly add, "In a dirty glass!"

Material like that was really helping my movie career, but I wasn't making many pictures. Just one a year, compared to four before the war. Working on a Hollywood soundstage just didn't seem as important while guys were still fighting overseas for their lives. They hadn't heard all the jokes, either, which may have influenced my decision to keep going back.

Just before Christmas, 1944, it looked as if we were going to get to Berlin before the new year. Then the kids of the 106th Infantry, green American troops who had never been in battle, were attacked in the Ardennes Forest by the desperate German army. It was trying to drive across Belgium to the Channel and split the Allied forces in two, hoping to get a negotiated peace so they wouldn't have to surrender to the Red Army, which had shown a disturbing tendency to carry a grudge over what the Nazis had done to Russian civilians. In blinding snow that prevented Allied air support, the U.S. 101st Airborne, which had been dropped into the fight, was surrounded at Bastogne during what became known as the Battle of the Bulge. When the German general gave General McAuliffe of the 101st an ultimatum to surrender or be annihilated, McAuliffe's answer went down in history as World War II's best and shortest one-liner: "Nuts!"

I don't know how that translated into German, but the 101st held out until Patton and his men could break through and free them on Christmas Day. Santa Claus arrived in a Sherman tank.

A real Hollywood ending.

When 1945 dawned, history was moving so fast we hardly had time to write monologues about it. The war in Europe had become a race to get to Berlin before the Russians arrived and drank up all the beer.

Then came our broadcast of April 17.

"This is Bob Hope, ladies and gentlemen. It was only last Tuesday that we were laughing and whooping it up with an audience of a thousand marines. Only seven days ago tonight, but I want to tell you it feels like a thousand years. A few seconds ago we listened to the voice of Harry S. Truman, Thirty-third President of the United States of America. No man on earth, today or all the way back through history, has faced so great a responsibility as President Truman. One hundred and thirty million Americans are serving notice that they will stand beside him to the completion of the task to which Franklin Roosevelt gave his life."

The whole nation mourned the death of one of our greatest leaders.

We were also nervous at the thought of having Harry Truman as President of the

United States. Truman used to be a Missouri haberdasher. He was the first politician to have a legitimate reason for sticking his hands in your pockets. Later, when he told America to tighten its belt, it was a fashion tip. He put that famous sign on his desk in the Oval Office, THE BUCK STOPS HERE. Of course, in those days it was still worth a dollar.

I got to know him quite well and we became friends. I liked him because he always said exactly what he thought. When he was in the Senate, he became known as "Give-'em-Hell Harry," and when Truman became President, he was great copy. Unfortunately, most of it was unprintable. He once called a reviewer a son of a bitch for criticizing his daughter Margaret's singing. Margaret read the review and immediately became a novelist. But the most famous story about Harry was told by his wife, Bess. She said, "Harry made a speech to the Washington Garden Club and kept referring to 'the good manure' that must be used on flowers. Some society woman complained to me, 'Bess, couldn't you get the President to say "fertilizer?" ' And I said, 'Heavens, no. It took me twenty-five years to get him to say "manure." ' "

Everything started happening at once in the war, as if both sides were rushing to get off the air. The Italians captured Mussolini and hung his mistress upside down beside him. Knowing this might upset Benito, they shot him first.

The Russians captured the Reichstag in Berlin, and before Hitler turned the gun on himself, he shot *his* girl friend, Eva Braun.

Love, your magic spell was everywhere.

May 8, 1945, was VE Day. The war in Europe was over. The battle to see which American soldiers would get back home first was on. But the invasion of Japan still loomed. U.S. soldiers in occupied Germany didn't know if they were going to be shipped to the States, or the meat grinder in the Pacific. By the end of the war in Europe, they were a bunch of tough, war-weary, confused guys. The government decided they should have a little entertainment to pass the time.

Sure, nobody knew if they were in a mood to laugh at comedians or shoot at them. The Army decided to send in a clay pigeon. If anything happened to me, they could always blame it on the jokes.

I rounded up some real talent to hide behind, including Colonna, Gale Robbins (who had a beautiful voice and a figure that made hiding behind it a pleasure), and Ruth Denas, who sang and pumped an accordion. There was also Patti Thomas again, and Jack Pepper, and a new recruit, Roger Price, who wrote jokes, drew cartoons, and took out the laundry.

We left New York on the *Queen Mary*, a ship fast enough to outrun anything in the Atlantic except a frightened comedian. The captain tried to calm me by explaining that there was no danger, the German submarines had surrendered and all the Japanese submarines were in the Pacific, but I was never very good at geography. I kept seeing periscopes in front of us until I realized it was my nose.

We did our first show at the Albert Hall in London, on the Fourth of July, before ten thousand G.I.'s. After the first laugh, I stopped being nervous. More than ever now, our group represented home to them, the one place in the world they wanted to be. I guess a lot of the laughter was homesickness, but like I said, I'll take 'em any way I can get 'em.

War jokes had now become nostalgia; I could get laughs by telling guys how it used to be. "We flew quite a bit in those days and those English fliers had their own way of doing things. I was over enemy territory with an English flier and I said, 'Why don't you look through the bomb sight?' And he said, 'I can't. We're boiling tea in it. . . .' But I wasn't nervous until I noticed how small my parachute was. Then I looked at it again and it said, 'Lipton's Orange Pekoe. . . .' Of course, coming back here this time on the *Queen Mary* was quite different. What a reception we got! I was met at the dock by the Bob Hope Fan Club and its keeper. . . ."

Then the entertainment began. I felt that the wolf whistles for the girls didn't sound quite as sex-starved as they had in the South Pacific, and then I remembered the war here was over and these guys had had time to meet some English girls. It reminded me of a sketch Ken Murray did in his "Blackouts" show in Hollywood during the war. A G.I. in Sydney had an Australian girl on his lap as he telephoned his girl friend in America.

"Honey, our engagement is off," he told her, "I've found another girl."

"But, darling — what's she got that I haven't got?"

"Nothing. But it's *here!*"

From England we went to U.S.O. headquarters at Châtou, near Paris, where I felt as if we'd walked into a combination of Broadway and Forty-second Street and Hollywood and Vine. Talents like Alfred Lunt, Lynn Fontanne, Bea Lillie (who had just lost her son in the war), Reginald Gardiner, Connie Dowling, and Joy Hodges, among others, were over to entertain the servicemen. And we were told we just missed Jack Benny, Larry Adler, Ingrid Bergman, Jimmy Cagney, Al Jolson, Gary Cooper, and Ann Sheridan. Fred Astaire and Der Bingle had been there and moved on to Paris.

Bing told me how he'd met Ike the first time.

"We were staying at the Ritz Hotel just after Paris had been liberated. Nobody had a car. You'd see a colonel drive up in a jeep and chain it to a fire hydrant. When he came out of the hotel, the hydrant would be gone, too. We went to Eisenhower's headquarters at Versailles to do a show for him and his staff, and I grabbed the first opportunity to tell him our problem.

"He said, 'Take my car. And my driver.'

"I couldn't believe it. I asked him when he wanted it back, and Ike said, 'When you're finished with it.'

"Did you ever drive a car with five stars on the license plate? You could park it on the sidewalk and the M.P.'s would salute. I got saluted so many times, I almost caught cold from the draft. Believe me, those five stars were parked in front of some very questionable places in Paris. And nobody dared ask any questions.

"A week later, I regretfully gave it back

to Ike and asked if there was anything I could do for him.

" 'Sure,' he said, 'I love hominy grits and there's no way I can get them over here.' "

Bing said that when he landed in New York, he sent Ike a couple of pounds and mentioned it to the press. They printed the story. A month later, Crosby got a desperate cable from Ike: "Stop it! I'm up to my rear end in grits!"

Our last show in France was a big, all-star benefit in the ballpark in Nice, where the second U.S. invasion had taken place. I spotted a Frenchman sitting in the audience whom I had known when he had his dressing room near mine at Paramount. His straw hat and drooping lower lip had feminine hearts doing back flips all over the world. He had made millions of American housewives dream of him, and in those days of strict movie censorship, they could only *imagine* how Maurice would make love. Maybe he kept that straw hat on. It wouldn't have mattered. They all adored him. He was Maurice Chevalier, the soul of France. What was he doing in the bleachers, or whatever they call the cheap seats in a French ballpark?

I was just about to call him up on the stage when a major, whose name I've forgotten to protect the guilty, motioned me to one side and whispered, "Don't introduce Chevalier. He's suspected of being a Nazi collaborator."

I was shocked. "I'm not a judge and I'm not a jury," I said, "I'm just the emcee here and this guy is one hell of an entertainer."

And I called out, "Hey, Maurice, come on up!"

He held off a moment, and then he bounded up on the stage. I can remember he was completely unprepared to do a show; he was wearing a white turtleneck sweater and red pants. He stood next to me hesitantly, not knowing what the reaction of that audience would be, an audience including French and American fighting men who had been in battle against the Nazis only a few short weeks before.

They stood up and applauded. They, at least, were willing to give him the benefit of the doubt. He was still Maurice to them.

Chevalier was almost in tears. And then the old fire returned, the old *jambon*, which I've been told is French for "Bob Hope," and he launched into "Louise," and "Place Pigalle," and all the songs he had made famous, until the audience rose in another standing ovation and he had to beg off.

Later that night I met him at a party at someone's château, and he grabbed my hand

and said, "Bob, thank you for introducing me." And he kissed me — on both cheeks.

Chevalier told me his story, which I believe. After France surrendered, he was asked by the Nazis in Paris to entertain French prisoners of war who were being held in German prison camps. And he did it.

Maurice felt he had to. The French singer he was in love with, the girl he was living with, was Jewish.

One final French note. Many years later — I keep saying that, but there have been *so* many years later — after Maurice had charmed the world again in *Gigi*, with Leslie Caron and Louis Jourdan, a lovely film that won nine Academy Awards but not even a nomination for any of its stars (if I sound bitter, it's from long practice), I went to the Greek Theater, outdoors in Hollywood's Griffith Park, to see Chevalier's one-man show. He must have been seventy-five or better at the time. He went through the whole repertoire I had heard him sing in Nice — "Louise," "Place Pigalle," and the others — and then into the songs from *Gigi*, finishing with, "I'm Glad I'm Not Young Anymore." He bowed off to a standing ovation that brought back that afternoon at the ballpark in southern France.

I went backstage after the show to congratulate him. That last number had really knocked me out.

"What a song!" I said, " 'I'm Glad I'm Not Young Anymore!' "

And Maurice smiled a sad Chevalier smile.

"Don't believe a word of it," he said.

I knew exactly what he meant.

Back again in the summer of 1945, we finally got up the courage to leave the French Riviera and go into occupied Germany. Our first show was at the General Ike Stadium, a racetrack and athletic field on the edge of Bremen, where the audience was eight thousand guys from the 29th Division. Ninety percent wore the Purple Heart.

I didn't care too much for my introduction: "Well, here he is, fellows, the only man in Germany who wears his hat on his unoccupied zone — Bob Hope!"

But they were generous with their applause. They all had enough points to be rotated back home and wanted me to bow off so they could get back to their packing. I insisted on making them wait through lines like "I asked one guy here which had been the worse, D day or D day plus one, and he said, 'Pay day minus two. . . .' " Everything in Germany now is sold for cigarettes. The Fräuleins don't say yes or no. They say if's or butts. . . .

In the U.S., "Two Cigarettes in the Dark" means a song. In Berlin, it can mean anything. . . . But I have to be careful what I say here. A comic in the Russian zone told a joke about Stalin last week, and before they knew it the audience had laughed themselves all the way to Siberia."

That week, the Hope Gypsies were scheduled to go to Nuremberg to do our show during the G.I. Olympics. That was a big outdoor affair the Army had scheduled to keep the soldiers occupied with strenuous sports that didn't involve Fräuleins.

Then Secretary of War Stimson, who was in Berlin with Truman for the Potsdam Conference, received a cable from Washington that read, "Operated on this morning. Diagnosis not yet complete but results seem satisfactory and already exceed expectations."

English translation: The first atom bomb had just blown a hole in the Nevada desert.

The nuclear age had been born, while I was rehearsing lines like "I'm pretty sure we're in Germany. Just before we landed here, we flew over a field of liverwurst."

Using the atomic bomb on Japan was one of the toughest decisions Truman or any President of the United States ever made. Afterward, right or wrong, Harry was willing to take the full blame; it was his decision and no one else's. He gave the Japanese the chance to surrender, and when they refused, he gave 'em hell. Literally.

I was in the Nuremberg Stadium watching the G.I. Olympics in a rainstorm, when they announced over the loudspeaker system that Japan had offered to surrender. It was a moment I'll never forget. That whole stadium full of guys seemed to rise twenty-five feet in the air. Nothing in my life had prepared me for that experience. The cheering, the shouting, even the crying. Thousands of men who knew at that one moment they were going to live. There were no questions, no doubts. A G.I. next to me hollered, "Now I can go back to God's country — Flatbush!"

It changed history. It eventually made the Cold War a joke. It had a lot to do with what happened in Europe in December of 1989. Science had triumphed over politics. For the moment.

The future? I don't have a crystal ball, but as usual I do have a story.

A couple of years ago, a group of Hollywood VIP's were flown in a C-130 transport to a Strategic Air Command base in Nebraska to be briefed on America's nuclear capabilities, possibly for the next Batman picture. They were taken fifty feet below ground and shown the tremendous banks of huge supercomputers that control all our military nuclear operations, and regulate the fail-safe mechanisms that prevent errors and accidental firings.

Then they were all given Bachelor of SACology diplomas to honor their recent education; except for one visitor, Jay Kanter, a well-known Hollywood executive.

It was announced that since this was Mr. Kanter's second visit to the base, he would be given a *Doctorate* of SACology. He was handed an ornate diploma with a gold ribbon, and driven in an Army limousine to the plane that was to take all of them back to California, while the others were loaded into an ordinary bus to the airport.

On the plane back to Hollywood, one of the other VIP's said, "Jay, I didn't know you'd been through this whole thing before."

And Jay said, "I never was in Nebraska before in my life."

"Then how come they gave you that doctorate diploma?"

Jay shrugged. "Their computer screwed up," he said.

I tell the story only to remind all of us that machines have no conscience. They must be carefully watched by men who have.

But those who weren't even born when Hiroshima shuddered under that mushroom cloud may not fully understand. Some outlaw, mad-dog nation may build the Bomb in an attic and ignite it with a marijuana cigarette.

We can only hope our kids were paying attention on August 6, 1945.

And have told *their* kids why it mustn't happen again.

CHAPTER FIVE

1946-1953

"There are no psychiatrists in Korea.
They know you're nuts or you wouldn't
be here."
— *Seoul, Korea, November 7, 1950*

All of us heaved a sigh of relief that the
war was now over and the Bomb had made
it impossible for it ever to happen again.
Strawberries and cream forever. Everyone
down to the seashore and out to the ballpark.

But we had underestimated the ingenuity
of men. Somehow they'd figure out a way
to keep shooting at each other.

Nineteen-forty-six started out as a pretty
good year. Irving Berlin wrote "There's No
Business Like Show Business," and Hermann
Göring committed suicide at the Nuremberg
Trials.

Noël Coward and David Lean made a won-
derful British movie about love called *Brief
Encounter*. It was so wonderful that later,
Norman Panama and Melvin Frank borrowed

the plot for a flick I made with Lucille Ball, *The Facts of Life,* which was considered very daring because Lucy and I played husband and wife. Somebody else's.

It had seemed simple in *Brief Encounter.* But somehow, adultery is very difficult if you're not British. If you *are* British, it's okay, if you're in the cabinet. If you're an American presidential candidate named Gary Hart, you can get your picture in the paper if you're careless enough to do it on a yacht named *Monkey Business.* To this day, if you sneak out the backdoor of your girlfriend's house, it's called a Hart Bypass.

As you can see, in today's world politicians have made it very difficult for comedians to be funnier about sex than *they* are. But back in 1946, adultery was still considered bad manners in this country. Lucy and I weren't playing presidential candidates, we were playing ordinary people, and the rules were different. It could easily have been considered bad taste, but Lucy was a consummate actress evoking such innocent worldliness that people really believed she could fall in love with the schnook I played, who couldn't even find the motel room where the two of us were shacked up.

The Facts of Life turned out to be one of my better movies, and for that I have to thank Lucy Ball and Norm Panama and Mel Frank. It took all of them to make me credible as a great lover.

Other things that happened in 1946 went almost unnoticed. The U.S. announced it was going to keep troops in Korea until the Russians pulled out. That reminded me of the ball player who swore he wasn't going to shave until his team won a game, and wound up playing for the House of David. (You have to be as old as I am to understand that one, so I'm not going to explain it. Ask the other two guys who remember.)

We began the new radio season in the fall of 1946 with something that made another kind of history. Lucy Ball had come to me and asked me if I had heard a mariachi band led by a little-known enchilada named Desi Arnaz. She thought maybe I could use a little chili pepper music on the show. It happened that Stan Kenton, who was our bandleader at the time, was taking his group to England to play some dates, and I could see Lucy's interest in Desi was more than musical, so I agreed. In checking back in the vault, I find we introduced Desi as being from "somewhere in South America." Nobody had heard of Cuba in those days. It was before Barbara Walters discovered Fidel Castro.

We tried giving Desi some lines, but his accent was so thick he could barely get them out of his mouth. Nobody could understand a word he said. He turned out to be a Cuban stage wait. So instead of giving him too many lines, we did jokes about him, like, "Desi Arnaz and his rhumba band were at the party with us. What a bunch. You ask them to pass the food and they beat you to death with maracas. . . . And the way they ate. The butler didn't say, 'Dinner is served.' He just stood in the kitchen and hollered, 'South America, take it away!' "

Desi lasted just a season with us, and I felt sorry about having to let him go. I think he was married to Lucy by that time, and I worried about how they were going to eat.

Just two years later, "I Love Lucy" was the biggest thing in a new electronic medium. I remember I met Desi in Palm Springs and said, "*You're* getting laughs?" And he cracked up. He knew what I meant. He'd learned how to turn a bad Cuban accent into a hundred million dollars and immortality. He and Lucy helped turn the struggling infant called television into the King Kong of the entertainment world, and changed the love life of a nation. "I Love Lucy" helped sell the millions of TV sets that kept the old folks at home and drove the kids out of the house to have sex. Then the kids got married and came back to sit in front of the television set again. And now the old folks have to go out to have sex.

We didn't know much about TV in 1946 and 1947. After all, it had been put in mothballs for the duration of the war, and there didn't seem to be any pressing reason to let it out. I'm not sure there is one now.

And then, the dam broke. The Federal Communications Commission announced it would license commercial television broadcasting, and along came Milton Berle. While most of us thought television would be too much work — you couldn't read from a script in your hand, any more than you could in movies — Miltie memorized an entire one-hour television show every week and loused it up for all the rest of us. His "Texaco Star Theater" became number one on the new tube, and Uncle Miltie became "Mr. Television."

Jack Warner signed Berle to make a movie called *Always Leave Them Laughing*, with Jerry Wald as the producer. I knew Wald almost too well, because he used to be the theater critic for the old New York *Graphic* when I had just arrived on Broadway. I was co-headlining with Bea Lillie at the Palace Theater. A flag outside the theater read BOB

HOPE — THE MIDWEST SENSATION! Wald opened his review with " 'The Midwest Sensation' — why did he come East?"

When Miltie's picture previewed, it got such glowing notices in the trade papers that J. L. Warner called Jerry into his office and accused him of paying off the critics. But when it opened around the country, it never really became the tremendous hit it deserved to be. Warner had forgotten that, while Milton Berle was Mr. Television, there were only about twelve television sets in the U.S. that worked, and they cost so much that the guys who owned them couldn't afford to go to the movies.

Jack Warner got so upset, he immediately decreed that you couldn't mention TV or show a television set in a Warner Brothers movie. When Warners filmed a living room after that, the whole family would just gather around a fireplace.

Warner almost threw two unsuspecting songwriters, Sammy Fain and Paul Francis Webster, out of the studio. They hadn't heard about the new edict, and they came up with a new song for a Warner Brothers musical, "I'm in Love with the Girl on Channel Nine."

Berle went back to TV and nightclubs after that. I talked to him once when he was having some trouble getting laughs in the clubs. I told him I once had the same trouble when I was playing in Kuala Lumpur (Miltie thought that must have been the club next door to the Copacabana, until I explained it was a city in Malaysia) and they had seated the prime minister all alone at a table right in front of the stage. The rest of the customers were seated out in the boondocks behind the dance floor, out of deference to his position. I told them to move everybody up to the stage, and I started getting yocks again, even from the prime minister.

Miltie thought that might be the answer, and checked the club on his next date. He saw the tables were all back of the dance floor and raised a tremendous howl with the owner. Then he phoned his agent and said, "I told that so-and-so to move the tables up to the stage or I'm taking a walk!"

And his agent said, "Miltie — you don't open until *tomorrow* night."

In those early days, I got a lot of offers to do television regularly. They weren't exactly offers. They were dares. I was ready for it, though, until Niles Trammel, who was head of NBC, said to me, "Bob, television is just a baby. We'll call you when it needs changing."

But eventually, I made the plunge into network television because of a sensational technological advance. They offered money.

I went on "The Ed Sullivan Show" on CBS in 1949 (Ed was on TV two years before it started). All I did was go out onstage and tell a few jokes, and I got poison pen letters from movie exhibitors. They feared and hated television and said it was ruining their business. They threatened to stop booking my pictures and end my career, because people were staying home to watch Ed Sullivan. Ed was perfect for the new medium. He couldn't tell a joke, he couldn't sing, he couldn't dance, and he couldn't move. Boy Scouts had been rumored to create fire by rubbing Ed with Charlie McCarthy. The TV crew only had to light one spot on the stage for Ed, and the camera could be nailed down. But Sullivan succeeded in making his show one of the most popular in television. He was a smart, although muscle-bound, showman.

Then the movie studios discovered they could make a bundle by selling their pictures to television, and suddenly it became their pal. Today, they sell the films even before they're made. And Ted Turner came out of Atlanta and bought *Gone With the Wind* and the entire MGM backlog for two billion dollars that he didn't have. And he's getting it back.

Today, it certainly pays to be in love with the girl on Channel 9.

On April 9, 1950, I finally went on NBC with my own TV show for Frigidaire. They were very generous with me. They told me I could have my salary any way I wanted it, big or little cubes. The show was called "The Star-Spangled Review" and included such stars as Doug Fairbanks, Jr., Bea Lillie, Dinah Shore, Les Brown and his Band of Renown (who were to spend the next few decades playing "Thanks for the Memory"), and Jack Cole and seventy-five dancers. On a ten-inch screen, they could have gotten by with seventy-four dancers, but this was a *big* show. The producer was Max Liebman, who later helped make TV history with Sid Caesar and Imogene Coca and "Your Show of Shows." They did one timeless gag I'll never forget. Sid, playing a kookie leader of a rock band, was pointing out the musicians — "This is the guitar player, this guy plays the drums, and this is the radar operator." Imogene said, "What does the radar operator do?" And Sid answered, "He warns us if we're approaching the melody."

My opening line for Frigidaire showed how nervous we all were about the frightening new medium of television. We felt that every joke had to be visual.

"How do you do, ladies and gentlemen. What a fine-looking audience. (Looks audience over and counts with his fingers) Oh, I thought I was still at the Paramount Theatre, working on percentage. . . . I decided I'd better get into television before Milton Berle used up my material."

Looking back, I realize I've been under contract to NBC in TV or radio since 1938. I find that hard to believe. Who would have ever thought they'd last that long?

For a while, I kept doing both my regular radio show and television specials. I mentioned on the air, "I'm on radio for a cigarette sponsor and on television for Frigidaire. Chesterfields satisfy, Frigidaire makes life easier, and they're both trying to figure out what I do. I'm afraid to tell 'em."

But it proved too difficult to do shows both on radio and on television, and I had to make a choice. My double-dipping days were over, and it was with a lot of regret that I gave up the radio shows that had been my bread and butter and K-ration for so long. I miss those early days, the excitement of going on the air live every week, the ability to take the Hope Gypsies anywhere in the world at almost a moment's notice, to broadcast live from a war zone as we did from Algiers in 1943. Sure, we still do the same things; most recently we've been moving targets in places like Beirut and the Persian Gulf, but that's with cameras, film, tape, weeks of careful editing afterward, sweetening the laughs and picking the best shots. A month later, the television show finally hits the air. The audience already knows we're back home safely, nobody shot me or blew up the stage, and part of their reason for watching the show is gone.

No suspense. Only wishful thinking.

I miss the immediacy of feeling you're a part of history, even though you're not. Yes, I miss the wars, probably because I had the best of the excitement and the least of the danger. You always had to pretend you were brave, even though your insides had turned to raspberry Jell-O. And the feeling we got from the G.I.'s in World War II, who were fighting what has been called "the last good war" and made the world's greatest audiences, is something we'll never forget. We all felt we were doing something worthwhile, not just making a buck.

And looking back, I guess the best part of it for all of us was that we were so young.

The very best part of it.

That's why I enjoy going back now to the year 1948. I was forty-one years young then. That's "very young" only to someone my age today, when I have to hire somebody to stir my prune juice.

There was an election that year. The Man on the Wedding Cake was running against Truman. In the primary campaign, so was almost everybody else. Senator Robert Taft of Ohio ran against Dewey for the Republican nomination. Henry Wallace bolted the Democratic party and ran on his own ticket. Everybody thought that Eisenhower might run, but nobody knew if Ike was a Republican or a Democrat. He probably could have been elected on both tickets if he had cross-filed. But Ike couldn't decide what he was.

I opened one show with "This is Bob Hope telling all you presidential candidates to use Pepsodent and you'll never have to pout, 'cause your teeth won't be like Eisenhower and decide to drop out. . . . General Eisenhower is going to become president of Columbia University instead. He figures it's easier to flunk 'em than veto 'em. . . . Yes, sir, here I am in Washington. That's a small group of buildings surrounded by presidential candidates. Last night I spoke at the radio press correspondents' dinner. Truman was there. We have a lot in common. We're both trying to get our options renewed."

For a while, there was some talk that General MacArthur, who was by then military governor of Japan, might run for vice president on the Republican ticket, with Senator Taft. I put it this way: "Everyone's happy that Congress is back in session. General MacArthur sent a telegram to Taft that said, 'Good luck. . . . Signed, Anxious.' "

Tom Dewey won the Republican nomination and started a slashing campaign. Nobody thought Give-'em-Hell Harry had a prayer, since he wasn't riding on FDR's coattails this time. The polls showed Truman losing by a landslide. Once more, our radio show didn't go on the air that Tuesday night in November. Everybody preferred to listen to the election returns and hear Harry lay an egg instead of me.

It was so close, the *Chicago Tribune* came out at midnight with that famous headline, "Dewey Elected!"

The next morning we discovered Harry had won by such a narrow margin he might not have made it if Bess hadn't voted for her husband.

I wired Truman a one-word telegram: "Unpack."

I was told he kept that wire on his desk in the Oval Office, right beside the sign that said, THE BUCK STOPS HERE.

We had a lot of fun with the election

results on the radio show. I said, "I phoned Elmo Roper, whose poll predicted Dewey's victory, and asked how he could be so wrong. He said, 'The prognostication is always subject to political prestidigitation.' When I asked what that meant, he said, 'Where can I get a job? . . .' And what a reception Truman got when he came back to Washington. From every window people were throwing confetti and old cabinet members . . . and the world will long remember Truman's historic words when he returned to the White House. He said, 'It's okay, Bess, you can send the laundry out now.' "

I've always had a soft spot for Give-'em-Hell Harry. Right after he was elected vice president on the FDR ticket in 1944, I was visiting the White House for a picture-taking session for a war relief drive. I was posing my best side, between Mrs. Roosevelt and Edward Stettinius, the secretary of state, when I noticed a little guy trying to get into the shot. I was a little annoyed until Stettinius said, "Bob, do you know the vice president?"

"Oh, I'm sorry, Mr. Truman," I apologized. "I didn't recognize you."

"That's the best part of this job," the little man said, and that was the start of a friendship that lasted his lifetime. The next time I met him in the White House, Harry said, "Drop in anytime." He was everybody's next-door neighbor.

Not only is the vice presidency a thankless position, but after a while the V.P. becomes almost invisible. Years later, I flew with Vice President Spiro Agnew to a Super Bowl game in Miami, and when we got off the plane everybody was yelling, "Bob! Bob!" and nobody knew who the hell Agnew was. He might have preferred to keep it that way when he got into trouble later and had to resign, but at that moment I felt sorry for him. Imagine me feeling sorry for the Vice President of the United States. He and I got along very well, and he didn't mind some of the jokes I told about his golf game. I guess he and Gerald Ford were in the same league. I told the story about Alan Shepard walking on the moon and finding a golf ball with Ford's initials. But Agnew's tee shots were so wild, he missed the moon.

The vice presidency was summed up best in *Of Thee I Sing*, the Broadway musical in which Victor Moore played the newly elected vice president, a meek little guy named Alexander Throttlebottom. In the opening scene, Throttlebottom meets the politicians who got him elected, and tells them he wants to quit the job of vice president because he's afraid his mother will find out. They assure him no one will tell her; in fact, he'll forget it himself in a couple of months.

I couldn't have imagined, when I met Truman at that picture-taking session, that in a few days he would be President of the United States. Neither could Harry, who later told the press he felt as if a bale of hay had fallen on him.

The next time I was in Washington, he invited me to the White House for a dinner he gave the senators. They had bleachers set up in the East Room, filled with people, and when I walked in I said, "This looks like Independence, Missouri, already." Then I did a few lines like "As an old haberdasher, Truman will gladly fit you for a suit. Of course, if you're a Republican, don't let him measure your inseam."

After the show, Truman said, "Every year, the President shows the senators through the White House and gives them all the history. Follow me and I'll show you how he does it." It was an unassuming line that mirrored his straight-arrow personality. He showed us all through the White House and taught us more history than I had learned in four years of high school, including the three days I went to class.

Just before Truman died, I was playing a

horse show in Kansas City — don't laugh, some horses make more money than I do — when a friendly, redheaded politician I had met asked if I would like to see The Boss?

We went down to Independence and Give-'em-Hell Harry and I exchanged some reminiscences in his living room. There wasn't a Secret Service man to be seen. I learned Harry and Bess wouldn't allow one in the house, and the Secret Service was going out of its mind, worried about his safety and the possibility of fire. None of that bothered Harry, and we had a wonderful time.

When I left, he came out to see me off, and I have a picture I treasure of Harry Truman and Bess and myself on his front porch. It was the last time I saw him.

For some reason, Give-'em-Hell Harry had agreed to have the U.S. Army stage an elaborate funeral when he died.

"It'll be a damn fine show," he said, "I'm just sorry I'm not going to be around to see it."

But don't go looking for him at Arlington Cemetery. Bess Truman vetoed the whole idea, as she had so many things in Harry's life. He was buried, simply and quietly, in his own hometown of Independence, Missouri, the thirty-third President of the United States.

The world knew who he was then.

You can understand why I was happy to do him a favor that Christmastime of 1948, when Stuart Symington, the secretary of the Air Force, called me and said Truman wanted me to get a show together and go to Berlin. That city had been cut off from all rail and road traffic by the Russians, who were trying to shove the Allies out. American airmen were getting bleary-eyed, flying in supplies around the clock to feed a city filled with Germans. Only a couple of years before, some of these same Berliners had been trying to blow them out of the sky with Messerschmitts and a solid wall of flak. Peace makes strange bedfellows.

Berlin was far inside the Russian zone of occupation and completely surrounded by the Red Army. There were three Allied zones, American, British, and French. Later, the G.I.'s who moved in said the three zones were blonde, brunette, and redhead. I never had time to check.

The Allies had a treaty guaranteeing free access by air, road, and rail. Uncle Joe Stalin didn't like that arrangement. And he wasn't going to let anything as foolish as a treaty he had signed stand in his way.

On March 31, he closed the frontiers.

Perhaps, at an earlier time, the shooting

might have started on April Fool's Day; but they knew we had the Bomb, and we suspected the Russians had one by now. That changed all the odds. Both sides realized the situation was like an old Colonna line, "Whatever happens, you lose!"

The Allies did not try to fight their way through with armed convoys, or I might not be here writing this book. There wouldn't be much point. There wouldn't be any bookstores.

By June, it seemed likely that two and a half million Berliners would starve to death.

And then came the Berlin airlift. No one had considered it possible to supply an entire city with food and fuel by air, but that's exactly what happened.

The best part of the airlift was not only that it helped raise the morale of the German people, it helped lift the smog of hatred that had existed between Germany and the U.S. since World War I.

Maybe the easing of tensions was a little overdone. The American Army issued an order that there should be no fraternization between G.I.'s and the Fräuleins. That caused a lot of confusion. One of our enlisted men asked an officer, "What does 'fraternization' mean?" The officer told him, "It means, when you stay on for breakfast."

On Broadway. *Red, Hot and Blue!* with Ethel Merman and Jimmy Durante. They promised *me* the girl.

With my first real partner, Lloyd Durban.
Now you know what killed vaudeville.

With my wife, Dolores. The longest-running act in show business.

Europe, 1943. Look at those Pepsodent
smiles on the troops. *Photo courtesy NBC*

Korea, with 12,000 guys who couldn't go home when I did.

Holding off the IRS in Jack Benny's vault.

Road to Bali. Looks like it ran through Scotland.

1951. President Truman, just before he sat down at the piano.

Vietnam. Looks like I just made a hole in one.

The truth, of course, was that the girls were starving, too. A Hershey bar got you further in Berlin than soft lights and Sinatra records.

Our plane through the corridor was loaded with ammunition. Show business ammunition. We brought Berlin to Berlin, Irving that is, and beautiful Jinx Falkenburg and her husband, Tex McCrary, who did a morning Mr.-and-Mrs. radio show out of New York that I guested on when I could get up that early.

In addition, there were our announcer, Hy Averback, our guitar player, Tony Romano, and Irene Ryan, who was on our show and later became "Granny" on the "Beverly Hillbillies." And Jane Harvey, a lovely singer, who had a strange allergy to going on stage. She would break out in a rash and have to rub up against somebody to stop the itching. At least, that's the story I told Dolores, who was making the trip with us. I think she believed me. Dolores had decided to come along when she found me packing my bag with fourteen dozen Hershey bars. She wanted to be sure I didn't overeat. The G.I.'s loved her; even today, she's kept her singing voice and her figure better than I have. And I still have fourteen dozen Hershey bars in that bag.

The group also included the secretary of the Air Force, Stu Symington, and a fellow named Alben Barkley, who admitted he waś the vice president of the United States. No Throttlebottom here.

Barkley and Symington didn't have an act, but they got more applause than any of us. On the way over from the States, we landed to refuel at a U.S. base in England, at Burtonwood. The war was over and the guys there had been forgotten. They were living in Quonset huts, eighteen to a hut, with one small stove in the middle. No hot water. No decent furniture. Almost no medical personnel. And it was cold. Barkley and Symington ordered two thousand coal stoves and extra doctors and dentists. Central heating for all the mess halls. And Stu and the veep ordered the entire base cleaned up, no matter how much it was going to cost the U.S. taxpayer.

That last was good basic training for Symington's next job: U.S. senator.

The soldiers gave them a standing ovation when they left the base. They had to. There weren't any chairs.

Burtonwood looked like the Waldorf-Astoria compared to conditions we found in occupied Germany. We landed first in bombed-out Wiesbaden. Dolores was unpacking the bags and starting to throw away the tissue paper when one of the hotel help shouted, *"Nein! Nein! Nein!"* and took it away from her and carefully folded it up. Nobody had seen tissue paper in Germany since Adolf had used it for the Munich Pact.

On Christmas Eve, General Lucius Clay threw a party in Wiesbaden and in the middle of it I was asked to leave. I couldn't figure out why, I hadn't even started the monologue. But the Army insisted. The weather was so bad, they were afraid I wouldn't get to Berlin for the Christmas Day show for the troops unless I left immediately. The others would follow when the fog lifted.

That didn't exactly give me a feeling of confidence. They were still singing Christmas carols at the party when Irving Berlin and Jinx joined me on a plane filled with sacks of coal. We knew we were the least important part of the cargo when they strapped the seatbelts around the coal.

When we took off, I shakily told the crew chief, "It looks a little soupy out there."

He said, "Soup I'd settle for — but this stuff has noodles in it."

There were no MIG's buzzing the corridor that foggy night; the Russian pilots were on the ground, drinking vodka and dancing the kazotsky. Somehow we found Berlin's Tempelhof Airport and came in on a wing and a prayer — mine.

Christmas Day dawned brutally cold, but at least it dawned. For a while, I had doubted it. We went on before a shouting audience of G.I's at the huge Tatania Palast theater. I felt right at home. It was an old vaudeville house, with plenty of places to duck behind. I had a new sponsor in the States, who made soap, which, I was told, was even more popular than Hershey bars in certain circles.

"How do you do, everybody. This is Bob 'Here in Berlin to Entertain the Men in the Airlift' Hope, saying I'm here with Swan Soap in wholesale lots. . . . Meet me tonight in Potsdamer Platz. . . ."

There was a yell. These guys were so hungry for entertainment, they were a pleasure. Of course, they were also hungry for other pleasures, but you couldn't blame them. They were cold, unhappy, lonesome, and unappreciated.

I continued with some gags like "When I landed, General Clay came up to me, shook my hand, and asked me for my autograph. What a sneaky way to get enlistments. . . . This certainly has been an unusual experience, flying into Berlin. It's the first time I've been in a corridor and didn't have to worry about the house detective."

To close the show, I introduced a little guy with a terrible voice who brought down the house.

Irving Berlin was a genius. His own contemporaries, when asked what Berlin's place was in American music, say, "He has no place. He *is* American music." But they don't deny that Irving had a singing voice that sounded like a hoarse tomcat with his tail in a clothes wringer. We had earlier become good friends, and I always kidded him about it. Once, some years ago, I was MC at a big benefit at the Mocambo in New York when Berlin got up and sang. The audience cheered him. I was afraid he'd consider that a tribute to his singing, so I said, "Irving, if you hadn't written that song, they would have stoned you."

Berlin pretended to be insulted and said something about me I won't repeat. It didn't even rhyme. Then Irving smiled at me, and continued to collect his royalties of a couple of hundred grand a week.

I remember once at Paramount, when Bing was making *Holiday Inn*, Der Bingle called me into Irving's office to hear Berlin play one of the songs he had written for the film. Irving had imported his own personal piano. As he played and sang in that tiny, rusty-hinged baritone, every time he wanted to play a flat or a sharp, he pressed a pedal under the piano and the entire keyboard shifted. That way, he could just keep playing the white keys. Irving had never had time to learn to read music. He was too busy writing it.

That day, for those thousands of soldiers at the Tatania Palast, Berlin sang the song I had heard him murder at Paramount, and it didn't much matter what his voice sounded like; those homesick guys shouted their approval until they were as hoarse as Irving.

Yeah. It was "White Christmas."

On the white keys.

After the Tatania Palast, we played a lot more shows for our airmen, but when we finally flew out along the devastated Berlin corridor, we didn't really know if the guys could hold out, if the city could hold out, or if Uncle Joe would win the battle of nerves and swallow West Berlin along with East Berlin as if it were a bowl of borscht.

The answer came on the night of May 11, 1949. The lights went on in the city of Berlin for the first time in nearly a year. There was only one place the current could be coming from; all the generators were in the Soviet zone.

At a few seconds after midnight, the iron

gate at Helmstedt, the crossing point from the British zone to the Berlin autobahn, was thrown open, and the first car from Berlin, driven by an American, drove through. A cheer went up as if he had found an open lane on the Hollywood Freeway.

The blockade was kaput. Berlin had been kept supplied even through the dead of winter.

Fifteen years later, Jack Kennedy, President of the United States, addressed a huge crowd in the center of the city and said, proudly, *"Ich bin ein Berliner!"*

He didn't have to repeat it in Russian.

When we got home, it was still 1949, but the contrast with what was going on in Berlin was almost too much to take. You could now buy strange things like gasoline, and you could get meat and butter without ration coupons. I told one radio audience, "I was really glad to be back from Berlin. I kissed my wife, I kissed my kids, then rushed out and kissed the street cleaner. He said, 'You don't have to do that anymore. The cigarette shortage is over. . . .' "

Bikinis were introduced. Never had so little done so much for so many.

Lawrence Olivier won the Academy Award for *Hamlet*. I was going to protest, until someone pointed out the writer didn't complain, and he didn't even get a nomination.

I made a few movies, including *My Favorite Brunette* with (who else?) Dorothy Lamour, and *Road to Rio*, with the walking tonsil, B. Crosby, and *Sorrowful Jones* with seven-year-old Mary Jane Saunders. If my leading ladies got any younger, I'd have to shoot my next film in a maternity ward.

We were all much too busy getting back to peace to worry about what was going on in a place called Korea. Most of us had never heard of it and didn't care that after Japan had surrendered, Uncle Joe had been allowed to stay in the northern half and organize — surprise! — a Communist government. Nobody thought they'd want to grab the rest of the country and have to put in all those voting machines. South Korea didn't seem to have anything anybody would want. Of course, that was before we learned they could make hi-fi's, TV's, VCR's, and CD players better than we could.

But then, who can't?

A very few of our soldiers had been left in South Korea after the war ended. It was so lonesome, one guy was going steady with his tattoo. And his friends kept asking him if she had a sister. The G.I.'s weren't officially allowed to think about girls. At night, a sergeant walked through the barracks and woke up anybody with a smile on his face.

On June 25, 1950, without any advance publicity, North Korea declared war on its neighbors in South Korea and ordered its army to cross the border, the 38th Parallel. In four days, Seoul, the capital of South Korea, fell to the Communist troops.

It was north versus south without Rhett Butler and Scarlett O'Hara. In a few weeks, North Korean troops had taken all of Korea except the port of Pusan. They moved faster than Sherman marching through Georgia. And almost as fast as Ted Turner.

The U.S. and its allies rushed in almost 50,000 men. General MacArthur, who had been given command of all the U.N. forces, decided to walk on water again. He launched a daring amphibious assault on the port of Inchon and recaptured Seoul so quickly, MacArthur gave thanks by lighting a candle to himself. Then he ordered the troops to continue north. They went all the way to the Yalu River, the border with China.

That country of almost a billion people had recently gone Communist. The Chinese Red Army had driven Chiang Kaishek to the island of Formosa, now Taiwan. Chiang sent Madame Chiang and a delegation of Chinese diplomats to Washington to establish diplomatic relations. On their way back, they made the mistake of stopping at Warner Brothers Studio. Jack Warner sent them on the studio tour and then invited them to lunch in his private dining room.

J. L. stood up to make a speech of greeting and noticed all the Chinese faces at the table. With his customary tact he said, "That reminds me, I forgot to send my laundry out this week."

Taiwan would have recalled their ambassador to the U.S., but they didn't have one yet.

Meanwhile, back at the ranch on the Yalu River, nobody knew if the Chinese Red Army would get upset and launch a human-wave attack. It could happen at any moment. The lines were shifting all the time. Nowhere in Korea was considered safe.

This seemed to be the ideal moment to send in the Hope Gypsies. I don't know who gave the Army that advice. Crosby didn't have that much influence.

I got together all the protection I could find: Marilyn Maxwell, Jimmy Wakely (the country and western singer), an acrobatic dancer named Judy Kelly, the Tailor Maids (three beautiful chanteuses), and the High Hatters, two tap dancers who allowed me to dance with them when things got nervous in the combat zones. When we did an "Off to Buffalo," we meant it.

En route to invade Korea, we landed in Tokyo. Colonel Leyden, the Special Services officer assigned to see we didn't escape, stood up in our plane and announced, "You're now in General MacArthur's command, the best damn command in the world. From now on, you're going to be treated like VIP's. Your rooms will have the smallest rats."

In Tokyo, a few of us were invited to have lunch with General and Mrs. MacArthur. I had four writers along, Larry Gelbart, Fred Williams, Charles Lee, and Chet Casteloff. The invitation couldn't cover all of them — writers are big eaters — so they drew lots and Larry and Fred won. Chet was so disappointed I finally offered to stay home and let him take my place, but he was afraid he might be mistaken for me. So we left him behind.

The rest of us got to the luncheon and when we all sat down at the big table, I noticed that one colonel was standing up; he couldn't find a chair.

And then I saw that Chet was sitting next to General MacArthur.

I never found out how he got in there. Chet would only say that his mother told him he would one day sit at the left hand of God.

Afterward we went to the Ernie Pyle Theater and put on our show for a big G.I. audience, with some of the gems the writers had thought up on the way to lunch. Honest. They learned to work fast on that trip. Once we were in the middle of landing at a small base and when I saw it didn't have a paved landing strip, I hollered to them, "Quick — give me some unpaved-landing jokes!" and by the time the wheels hit the ground, I was ready to greet the soldiers with "I want to thank all the guys who mowed the runway for me."

I opened the show at the Ernie Pyle with "Well, here we are in occupied Japan. And let me tell you, it's really occupied. At least, every nurse I called said she was. . . . At first I thought the Japanese people knew me when we arrived, but then someone explained hissing is a national custom. . . . And the Japanese people are so polite. I'm not used to all this bowing. I've been here five days and I haven't seen anyone's face yet."

After a few more shows, we headed across the Sea of Japan for the war zone. Korea might have been the forgotten war today if Larry Gelbart hadn't been with us. What Larry saw, and what he later wrote, became the beginnings of a decade of the best in American television on a series called "M★A★S★H," based on the film written by

Ring Lardner, Jr., and the novel by Richard Hooker. As head of its writing staff, Larry had that wonderful touch that made war a source of bitter laughter, and brought a whole new dimension to the little screen.

America now remembers the Korean War best as the setting for the warmth and fun of characters like Hawkeye and Radar and Hotlips Hoolihan. The real thing wasn't that way.

We weren't prepared for what we found when the Hope Gypsies landed in Korea. The battle lines were changing every day. We were staying at an Army hospital in Pyongyang when I heard that the 1st Marine Division was coming into the port of Wonsan. I remembered them and Pavuvu (how could I forget?), so I called headquarters in Tokyo and said I wanted to go down and do a show for them. Headquarters arranged for our whole gang to fly in. As our plane started to leave Pyongyang, all the G.I.'s on the airstrip hollered for us to give them our brand-new parkas — it was bitter cold, and they deserved them. We stopped the plane and threw fifty parkas to them and took off for Wonsan, colder but happier.

When we landed at the Wonsan airport, there wasn't a soul around. Just one guy in a jeep who took us over to the hangar. We were there about ten minutes, wondering what was happening, when General Almond, Admiral Struble, and the marine commander and a lot of other officers walked up and stared at us.

General Almond said, "How long have you been here?" And I said, "About twenty minutes." There was a short pause, and the admiral said, "Are you kidding? We just made the landing!"

We shook a little bit, realizing that when we got out of the plane, one of the retreating North Koreans could have taken his last pot shot and bagged his first comedian. If we hadn't stopped the plane before takeoff to throw out those parkas, we would have invaded Wonsan before the marines.

At the show we put on, I told the men of the 1st Marine Division to be sure they were in front of us in their next landing.

That evening, Admiral Struble invited us to come out to the "Big Mo," the battleship *Missouri*, which had backed up the invasion forces. We did a show for the sailors out on deck, in the middle of a gorgeous bay. It was so beautiful out there, we could have forgotten the war if it hadn't been for those 16-inch guns above our heads. And the history beneath our feet. It was on that deck that Douglas MacArthur had accepted the

Japanese surrender that ended World War II. That night, I slept in MacArthur's suite on the "Big Mo." I felt very heroic.

After that, we worked our way as far south as Pusan and then all the way back north and across the 38th Parallel. The girls and the music and the dancing were an odd contrast to what we saw all around us, but the weary G.I. audiences came to life and cheered every show. We could always tell how well things were going by their reaction. One unit didn't laugh very much. I started looking forward to retirement, until one of the officers told me their C.O. had been killed in battle the day before.

We hopped into a C-54 and were flown back to Pyongyang, which had been the capital of North Korea — and soon would be again, although fortunately we didn't know it — where we were to do a show in front of what had been Communist headquarters only a short while before. We didn't realize how short a while until we passed a dead horse and some dead people with straw tossed over them. And a kid twelve years old who had been shot.

It wasn't much of a warm-up for the show.

Our audience was made up of thousands of men from the 1st Cavalry and the 1st and 11th Marine divisions, who had come down from the Yalu River line. I told the men, "I really didn't intend to perform so far north but the First Cavalry went through and the suction pulled me with them. . . . Some of these towns are changing hands so fast one soldier bought a lamp with three thousand won and got his change in rubles. . . . Seoul has changed hands so many times the towels in the hotel are marked 'His,' 'Hers,' and 'Who's sorry now? . . .' I asked a G.I. here how to tell a North Korean from a South Korean, and he said, 'Turn your back. . . .' And there are no psychiatrists in Korea. They know you're nuts or you wouldn't be here."

When we left Pyongyang, all the guys who had come down for the show went back up north into the lines. Fifteen thousand of our men were lost when the Chinese Red Army stormed across the Yalu and took every town the Hope Gypsies had played, including Seoul. I don't think it was anything personal, I didn't do any Chinese laundry jokes. But that was only the first step in a long and grinding war that continued back and forth until 1953. And it was only the curtain raiser for the show in Vietnam.

I always had the feeling that if the U.S. had used the air power it had standing by in Japan and the Philippines to bomb across the Yalu River line, a lot of American lives would have been saved. But it would have meant attacking Red China, and that was a political no-no.

That had a lot to do with the big fireworks that began in Washington. MacArthur wanted to bomb and invade China; Truman felt that was a bad idea.

The Truman-MacArthur battle came to a head when MacArthur ordered the Chinese to a conference Truman hadn't authorized, and Give-'em-Hell Harry fired the most popular military commander the U.S. had ever had. It gave MacArthur the chance to return to the U.S. with flags flying and his medals polished. By the time he reached the Big Apple, seven and a half million people turned out to cheer him; Ike had only drawn four million when he returned from World War II.

MacArthur delivered a great exit line to a joint session of Congress:

"Old soldiers never die, they just fade away. . . ."

There wasn't a dry eye in the House . . . or in the Senate, either.

As soon as the general started to fade away, cries rang out to impeach Give-'em-Hell Harry, who was accused by Joe McCarthy of being a Communist agent for daring to disagree with God. There was enough made of this and other problems to persuade Truman not to run for reelection again.

The Democrats nominated Adlai Stevenson in his place. Adlai had wit, charm, and a hole in his shoe, which he carefully showed to the cameras in one famous picture. It worked against him, though. The Democratic party had been in office so many years, the voters felt that if one of its politicians still didn't have enough money to fix his shoes, he hadn't really been working at it.

Many historians have traced the progress of the campaign through my monologue jokes. Others are still employed.

For the record, then: "The big news was Eisenhower saying he'd accept the nomination. Imagine a five-star general waiting to be drafted? . . . But Ike has a very personal reason for running for President. It's the only way he can get out of the Army. . . . The day Eisenhower made his announcement was quite an event. The minute he threw his hat in the ring, an M.P. arrested him for being out of uniform. . . . But it might be interesting to have a general for President. I can't wait until he puts Congress on K.P. . . . Stevenson's pretty confident. I can tell because he just had his shoes resoled. . . ."

And after Ike was elected: "It's been an exciting week, hasn't it? The Republicans celebrating on Tuesday. . . . the Republicans celebrating on Wednesday. . . . the Republicans celebrating on Thursday. . . . Don't get impatient. Remember, the *old* needle was stuck for twenty years. . . . And they exploded the H-bomb the other day. When it exploded Ike said, 'Gee, I didn't think the Democrats would take it this hard. . . .'

The H-bomb was almost a throwaway in that situation. This was long before Three Mile Island and Chernobyl, and I could get laughs with lines like "I don't know how big the H-bomb explosion was, but in the Pacific islands they thought Sadie Thompson was back. . . . The last time I looked, the man in the moon was waving a white flag."

I would have thought you were crazy if you'd told me that in a few years, I'd have Neil Armstrong on my show after he'd walked on the moon and driven a golf ball. Shows you how far a guy has to go to get to tee off at a decent hour.

Science was amusing and not frightening in those days. We would have laughed if some Gypsy fortune-teller had predicted that an actor was going to be President of the United States, and would spend a few billion dollars developing a ray gun to shoot down incoming nuclear missiles. We would have taken away her crystal ball and called for a saliva test.

Ike had made a lot of progress in his campaign against Adlai when he said, "I will go to Korea." He didn't mention what he would do when he got there, and as a matter of fact when he did win the election and went to Korea, he didn't do anything at all. But he made the trip, and that was enough for the American public. It was the first time they could remember a politician keeping a campaign promise.

After that, the Korean War degenerated into a "peace conference" that deadlocked for two years over the prisoner-of-war issue, while the fighting continued. It was the reports from the North Korean P.O.W. camps that were later the inspiration for Sinatra's film *The Manchurian Candidate* about American prisoners who were brainwashed, hypnotized, and programmed to kill the President of the United States.

The Manchurian Candidate was a good movie, but Frank had it pulled from the theaters just after it opened. Jack Kennedy had been assassinated in Dallas.

Let me take a moment to tell a story to help show why Frank was so shaken, even more than the rest of us. When Kennedy was elected in 1960, the Democratic party was some three million bucks in the hole. Frank volunteered to bail the party out by staging an inaugural show in Washington the night before Kennedy took office. I was asked to be part of it, along with a bushel of other Hollywood entertainers. The inauguration is held in January, during the coldest part of Washington's frigid winter. The show was called the Democratic Gala, until it actually went on in the convention hall outside the capital and all the "Gala" went into the deep freeze. That night, Washington was hit by the worst blizzard in its history. No one could get to the hall for hours, not even the new President and Jackie, who finally arrived close to midnight. By that time, the frostbitten audience — who had paid a fortune to attend — had long ago turned Republican. When the stars, from Sidney Poitier and Leonard Bernstein to Fredric March and Uncle Miltie, performed, they took the brunt of the crowd's hostility. Not a laugh. The crowd was sitting on its hands to keep them warm. The only enthusiasm was shown around 2 A.M., when Frank sang "Let's Get Away from It All," and the audience agreed and left.

Frank was upset; everyone had worked long and hard on the show, and deserved better. Kennedy, too, was disturbed, but didn't mention it at the time. To make amends, Frank, whose personal fortune was a little low (he voted Democratic in those days, remember?) decided to blow whatever dough he had left and threw a big feed at the Statler-Hilton for those who had prepared the Gala.

In the middle of dinner, Peter Lawford came in and told Sinatra, "The President is downstairs at the inaugural ball and he said if everyone who worked on the show would come down, he'd like to thank them and shake their hand."

Frank said, "Tell him we're eating."

Lawford gulped. "I'm only his brother-in-law. *You* tell him."

So Frank said, "Okay, I'll tell him," and left.

There was a hush in the room, and then Freddie March said, "In ten minutes there's gonna be one skinny Italian nailed to that wall."

Everyone silently agreed.

Ten minutes later, Frankie was back.

"Ladies and gentlemen," he announced, "the President of the United States!"

And Jack Kennedy, looking young and handsome and apologetic, came into the room and said, "I didn't know you were eating."

And made a point of shaking everyone's hand.

Frank was so grateful he didn't turn Republican for four years.

I met Jack Kennedy many times during the

thousand days of his presidency, including the time he presented me with a medal at the White House. I wouldn't have missed that one. We had first met years earlier, when we both received degrees at a little college in Illinois. Kennedy was a senator at the time, and my college education had been limited to what a three-hundred-pound tackle bothers to learn in class the week before the big game. We kidded about my getting a diploma, and had kind of lost touch after that. Over the years, I didn't get as many honorary degrees as Kennedy did, but then my father didn't own most of the colleges.

After his election, I was at another college, Georgetown University, in Washington, speaking at my son Tony's graduation — funny how I get invited to speak at all the schools that wouldn't let me in when I was younger — and I said I didn't like the idea of our President going to the Army-Navy game without a hat or coat on, and I'd be glad to buy them for him if he couldn't afford them. There was a little depression going on, and AT&T stock had started to go way down. I mentioned the fact that when I got to Washington, I had put a dime in the phone and a voice had said, "God bless you." I guess Kennedy heard those laughs in the White House, because the next day Pierre Salinger, who was his press secretary as well as Secretary of Eyebrows, called me and said, "The Boss wants to see you."

I went over to the White House and got a warm welcome, and discovered that all JFK wanted to do was exchange jokes. He said to Dave Powers, one of his assistants, "Tell Bob my favorite joke." Powers told the one about an Irishman who died. His widow walked around the coffin and said, "He looks so good. And his toupee is on so straight. How did they do that?" And someone answered, "With a nail."

When I heard that one was Kennedy's favorite, I offered him the use of my writers.

All the Kennedy jokes, of course, are tinged with sadness today. But I can't forget that he had the quickest wit of all the Presidents. Laughter was part of the Kennedy image. He wasn't afraid to trade ad-libs with the best of comedians, or even with me. And, of course, we could do lines like "Did you hear about President Kennedy saying we should drink milk. Milk! Maybe he's younger than we think. . . . Milk! Is he really Irish? . . . He served milk at a cabinet meeting, but it didn't turn out too well. They spent a half hour just burping each other."

He enjoyed them all. It was a loss for the entire world when so much warm laughter turned so soon to tragedy.

Where were we? Oh, yes, Korea. No wonder I'd rather forget.

A lot of the U.S. was afraid MacArthur was right about Korea being the start of a Red attempt to take over the world, and from those fears came the McCarthy era, when everybody was told there was a Communist under every bed and another one in it with your wife.

Hollywood shelved a picture on Hiawatha because it was thought to be Red propaganda. Congress started investigating Hollywood looking for Reds, and even Shirley Temple was suspected. When I was in Washington I complained, "I feel slighted. I haven't been investigated by anyone except the credit manager of the Statler."

Show business was an easy target. Ten writers and directors were sent to jail for refusing to name names. Even Lucy Ball was investigated, probably for having red hair. One actor admitted to joining the Communist party because he was told it was a good place to meet girls.

Tail gunner Joe McCarthy, the senator from Wisconsin who claimed to be a war hero (it turned out later that the war wound he proudly showed off happened when he fell off a ladder with a bucket tied to his leg), rallied millions of voters with his red-neck appeal. The whole country was frightened by his attacks accusing everyone from General George Marshall to Truman himself of being Communists. McCarthy was making noise about running to be President, or maybe emperor, when we discovered the emperor had no clothes on.

To explain that, I first have to explain about a writer named Mort Lachman, which isn't easy. Mort was low man on the totem pole when he was hired to work on our radio show in 1946 for seventy-five dollars a week, which to him was a fortune. You have to know that Mort was from Seattle, where seventy-five dollars a week was what they paid the mayor. Mort went on to become my producer and director on all those overseas Christmas shows and eventually became my highest-priced writer. He was a real talent. I got my money's worth.

Mort, like Larry Gelbart, went on to greater glory and greater gold. He did such TV shows as "All in the Family," "Gimme a Break," and "Kate & Allie," the last two as a profit participant. Now I occasionally go to him when I'm short of cash.

Back in the fifties, Mort was shepherding all our writers. He was the one I called in the middle of the night when I had an emergency we called a NAFT — a word Mort invented meaning "need a few things."

In the spring of 1954, the radio season was over. There wasn't a good war to be found anywhere. Two days of inactivity was about all I could take before I booked some personal appearances in the Midwest.

Mort handed me the material the writers had prepared to make me sound brilliant, and I almost threw it back at him.

"Why are all the fellows writing jokes about McCarthy?" I asked him, indignantly. "They just sent ten guys up for a year! Do you want your boss to rot in a federal pen?"

There was a long pause reminiscent of Jack Benny while Mort considered his chances of keeping his job if he answered honestly. He decided against it. Instead, he merely read me some of the McCarthy jokes, which were pretty funny, and said, "Bob, honestly now, what is more important to you, staying out of jail or getting a laugh?"

"Forget it!" I told him. "If they find me with those jokes, I could be shot for treason!"

"*Now* you're talking!" Mort said, and hopefully slipped the material into my luggage.

Two nights later, he was jolted out of bed by a NAFT at two A.M. I shouted at Mort over the phone to send more McCarthy zingers.

"I did a few at the state fair tonight and they were terrific! The audience went crazy!"

I guess it's true I'd go to jail or worse for a good laugh. I felt a little like the Hollywood agent who found the devil sitting on his desk and promising him deals with Sylvester Stallone, Eddie Murphy, and Barbra Streisand, if the agent would just sell him his soul, his wife's soul, and his mother's soul.

And the agent said, "What's the catch?"

I had tried a few lines like "I almost didn't get to the fairgrounds tonight because of the jam-up of cars. Ever since McCarthy started that investigation, the traffic lights have been afraid to turn red. . . . And I have it on good authority that Senator McCarthy is going to disclose the names of two million more Communists. He just got his hands on a Moscow telephone book."

The laughs were almost frightening. It wasn't just because the jokes were funny, it was something deeper, a sense of relief that somebody had finally said out loud what the whole country had been thinking.

"What state fair are you at?" Mort asked.

"Wisconsin," I told him.

"Wisconsin! That's McCarthy's home state! You've got more guts than I have — they could ride you out on a rail!"

I thought I detected a note of wistful hope in Mort's voice, but I didn't care. We had found a surefire monologue topic. Humor is the greatest weapon in the world against demagogues and tyrants. How long would Genghis Khan have lasted if Woody Allen had done a number on him? Come to think of it, how long would Woody Allen have lasted?

For a while, I wondered how long *I* would last. One of the Wisconsin newspapers ran a headline: BOB HOPE IS A COMMUNIST! I wrote the publisher a long letter, reminding him that we made jokes about everyone, including the President. McCarthy, too, was allowed to say what he wanted to in this country. He might not say the right thing, but he was allowed to say it. Didn't the Constitution give me the same right?

The next edition of the paper carried a headline: BOB HOPE IS NOT A COMMUNIST!

It was about this time that Ed Murrow stuck his chin out and took McCarthy apart on CBS. Joe had also made the mistake of attacking the Department of Defense. He learned you don't fight city hall. The Army pulled him in front of the entire nation. The Army-McCarthy hearings on live TV proved a bigger hit than Gomer Pyle. McCarthy was undressed every session by a gray-haired Boston lawyer named Joseph Welch, who calmly let him hang himself by exposing him to laughter.

An era was over. Tail gunner Joe had become a NAFT.

Demagogues can't survive humor. Truly great men, like Roosevelt, Truman, Eisenhower, Kennedy, and the other Presidents I have known, thrive on it.

I could do jokes about any of them. "I first knew President Eisenhower in Algiers. He'd come in to replace Charles Boyer. . . . I've played golf with him at Burning Tree. He used a short Democrat for a tee. . . . It's hard to play a guy who rattles his medals while you're putting. . . . And Lyndon Johnson. When Charles de Gaulle got upset about the devaluation of the British pound, he wired Lyndon, 'Lower your dollar,' and Johnson wired back, 'Up your francs.' "

At the time when Richard Nixon was first running for President, I said, "His hometown of Whittier is so sure Nixon will be elected President, they're already building the log cabin he was born in."

After Nixon made it, the jokes changed a bit.

"President Nixon is always working. Even when he's supposed to be relaxing on the beach at the western White House, he always has the phone right there beside his sand pail. . . . His plan for settling Vietnam is to let Howard Hughes buy it and move it to Las Vegas. . . ."

Jimmy Carter's peace efforts, bringing Anwar Sadat of Egypt and Menachem Begin of Israel together, opened up another area for kidding a President.

"Carter deserves a lot of credit for getting Begin and Sadat together at Camp David. It was a million-to-one shot, like getting the Pepsodent commercial for Leon Spinks. . . . The first night, Sadat's water bed leaked and almost drowned Sam Donaldson. . . ."

Reagan? He was the easiest. Almost anything Ronnie did called for a line.

"Did you see where President Reagan finally got a hearing aid? People have been telling him to get one for years, but he couldn't hear them. . . . I was relieved when I found out it was a hearing aid. When I first saw him, I thought he was bugged. . . . When the doctors examined his ear, they were surprised to find nerve damage. They thought it might just be a jelly bean stuck in there. . . . The news that Reagan volunteered to be the first in his administration to undergo drug testing was voted the week's best government leak."

That's a good note on which to wind up almost a decade of war and hate — presidential laughter. And to get ready for the next couple of decades, when the longest war in America's history almost tore our country apart.

But through it all, there was always the safety valve of jokes.

Even about our Presidents.

If they hadn't had a sense of humor, I'd probably be writing this book on Leavenworth stationery.

Of course, there are a lot of people who might get a bigger laugh out of it that way.

CHAPTER SIX

1954-1958

"Tonight we're broadcasting from Moscow, ladies and gentlemen, for the diplomatic corps of America, Britain, and Canada, in this wonderful ballroom . . . or gymnasium . . . or . . . what kind of a garage is this, anyway?"
— *American embassy, Moscow, February 1958*

None of us suspected, early on in the carefree fifties, that something called the Cold War was about to begin. We didn't even realize that the drive-in hamburger joints, the neon Coke machines, the over-chromiumed convertibles, and the deafening music and the poodle skirts would one day be called "Americana" and be fondly revived in the eighties as symbols of the era of happy fifties innocence. The unvarnished truth is that the drive-in joints were greasy spoons, nickel Cokes had soared to a dime, poodle skirts were being worn by fat, middle-aged ladies, and the nation's innocence had been shattered when Marilyn Monroe divorced Joe DiMaggio.

I was on TV for Minute Rice and Jell-O Instant Pudding, and if only I could have gotten a deal with Hebrew National frankfurters and Maalox, I would have represented the typical American diet.

Of course, I wasn't exactly going hungry. As I told one audience, "It's starting out to be a busy year for me. Between television, my daytime and nighttime radio shows, pictures, and personal appearances, I'm also working on a plan where, when you close your eyes, I appear on the inside of your eyelids."

Then I went on to world affairs: "I wanna say hello to one of our viewers who's never had a chance to watch me until now. Welcome, Joe DiMaggio! . . . I was amazed when I heard that Joe had left Marilyn. I've heard of men giving up smoking, but this is ridiculous. . . . It could set Wheaties back ten years. . . ."

I also had a new movie to plug, and managed to slide in a few free commercials. "I've been busy over at Paramount, finishing my new picture, *The Seven Little Foys*. I work with a lot of kids in this picture. Theater screens are so wide nowadays, actors have to work in bunches."

The *Foys* picture was born when "the Boys," Jack Rose and Mel Shavelson, came over to my house in Toluca Lake one day to present me with a quart of vanilla ice cream. Never being able to resist a bribe, I called off the dog and invited them inside, where they soon revealed their real purpose. They wanted me to do a picture about Eddie Foy, one of the big stars of vaudeville days. After his wife died, he had been forced to take his seven hyperactive kids into show business. It seems he couldn't find a sitter with enough life insurance to take his children on. "The Seven Little Foys" promptly became the worst act in the history of vaudeville.

I'd seen the Foys onstage many times. When Eddie introduced the kids to an audience, he'd always say, "I'm not in this act. I'm just here to defend 'em. If these weren't my kids, I'd leave the theater. Why don't you?"

I worked my way through half the ice cream while they were telling the story, and when they figured I was softened up, they told me there was a catch. Jack wanted to produce the picture, and Mel wanted to direct it. Neither one had any experience for the job. In those days, there were no film schools;

you learned how movies were made by peeking into the leading lady's dressing room.

"That's okay," I told the Boys. "I've made lots of pictures with producers and directors who didn't know what they were doing. This is just the first time they had the guts to admit it."

Then they hit me with a real zinger: Since everyone would be taking a chance, Paramount wanted us all to make the picture for nothing. Instead, we would be paid a percentage of the picture's profits. And Paramount would keep the books. We had to trust them.

While that sounded like trusting a barracuda with your herring — ask Art Buchwald — I finally agreed. It was too good a story to pass up. Besides, I had Doc Shurr to check Paramount's books. It would be one barracuda against another.

I'm glad I made the film, because it gave me my only chance to work with one of the true greats of the movies, a guy named Jimmy Cagney. He was at Paramount at the time, and when we went to him and asked if he'd do a cameo as George M. Cohan — Cagney had won the Oscar for playing Cohan in *Yankee Doodle Dandy*, but I didn't hold it against him — Jimmy said, "I'll play the part on one condition — that you don't pay me."

I thought perhaps Paramount had started an epidemic, actors working for free, but it wasn't that serious.

"When I was a starving chorus boy on Broadway," Jimmy explained, "Eddie Foy would take me to his home in New Rochelle every weekend, and feed me up so I could get through the next week. I never said thank you. I'd like to say it now."

The Boys wanted to be sure he understood this was going to be work. "You're going to have to dance," they told him, "a challenge dance at the Friars Club against Bob."

"That's no challenge," said Jimmy, "I could dance Hope into the floor playing hopscotch. When I dance, I come out fighting, and I take no prisoners."

I reminded him I had been taking regular dancing lessons from Barney Dean, the Jewish Fred Astaire, but that didn't frighten him at all. When the Boys asked Cagney when he would find time to practice, Jimmy said, "I've got my dancing shoes in the car. Is this afternoon soon enough?"

After I watched Jimmy rehearsing, I got out my own tap shoes and went to work to lose ten pounds, all of it from the south forty.

That scene at the Friars Club is one of my all-time favorites. Everyone says my dancing was sensational, especially after I had the sound man dub in my taps. And Cagney? Well, Jimmy was known as a tough guy in pictures, but he always said, "I'm a song-and-dance man. Never wanted to be anything more, never thought I was."

He was a song-and-dance man in spades. Cagney danced a wonderful thank-you to the memory of Eddie Foy and helped make the film a very large hit.

While we were shooting the picture, we were terribly saddened to hear of the passing of Al Jolson, one of the true giants of show business. Jolie had three careers, one on Broadway where he wowed them in everything from the Ziegfeld Follies to the bill at the Palace; a second in movies, where he played the lead in the first talkie, *The Jazz Singer*; and a third when he made a comeback dubbing his own voice in the songs for Larry Parks to lip-sync as Jolie in *The Jolson Story*.

He had made his reputation getting down on one knee to sing songs like "Swanee" and "When the Midnight Choo Choo Leaves for Alabam'," quite a stretch for a kid from New York's East Side who had never been south of Lindy's Delicatessen. I once got a big laugh when I remarked I'd dropped in on one of Bing's radio shows and found Jolson on his knees in the rehearsal room.

I said I went in and got down on *my* knees and bet two hundred dollars before I found out Jolie was just rehearsing "Sonny Boy."

Jolie was once on the Pepsodent show with me. He was the original of "the ham what am," and proud of it. He enjoyed his fame. Someone got into a foolish argument with him over a joke in the script and Jolie told him, gently, "Don't argue with me or I'll hit you over the head with my bankbook."

The Seven Little Foys was the first film in which I was officially called on to do some serious acting. The seven kids were being taken away from me, and I had to appear in court and admit I had been a poor father to them. I instinctively shy away from showing emotion, but this scene demanded a lot. I wasn't sure I could carry it off. I was rehearsing my big speech to the judge when I was told that Barney Dean had been taken to the hospital. It happened so suddenly, I couldn't believe it, especially when they told me the book on Barney was 10 to 1 he would never see the hospital bill. He had two days at most.

I rushed down to Cedars of Lebanon Hospital as fast as I could and walked into his room. Little Barney, the world's slowest bald-headed whirlwind dancer, was lying, white-faced and weak, in a hospital bed six sizes too big for him.

"Were you sick before?" I asked him, "or did you see my show?"

Barney tried to smile, but I could see he wasn't worrying anymore about having his option picked up; he didn't try very hard.

And then I told him the doctor said he'd be out in no time. What's a little lie between friends?

Barney just looked at me, and I knew he knew, and I knew he knew I knew. Finally he said, "Anything you want me to tell Jolson?"

Yeah, Barney. *You* were the real star.

I didn't break down until I left the room; he would have been embarrassed.

The next day, on the set, I played that difficult scene. With Barney's help, as always. I just kept thinking of him, and the emotion came naturally.

Afterward, someone asked me, "Did you use the Stanislavsky Method?"

And I said, "No, unless that was Barney's real name."

With the movie behind me, it was time to start looking for monologue topics again, and the presidential campaign provided several in the fall of 1956. Ike ran for reelection, with Richard Nixon for his veep. The Democrats nominated Adlai Stevenson again and for his vice president, Estes Kefauver, whose main claim to fame was that he wore a coonskin cap. It did him about as much good as it did the raccoon who used to be in it.

The monologues I did on TV for Chevrolet mirrored a lot of the events that were going on that year, so don't expect laughs; look on what follows as a history lesson:

"Here I am again. I'll wait while you pay off your bets. . . . The TV shows are fighting it out this season with big guest stars. Steve Allen is having Anthony Eden and Charles de Gaulle doing a mambo with Nasser. As an added attraction they're flying in the Suez Canal. . . ."

To explain that last joke (I have to do a lot of this sort of thing), let me remind you that in 1956, Gamal Abdel Nasser, not a relative of Kareem Abdul Jabbar but president of Egypt, decided to take the Suez Canal back from the British and French. But those countries had built it, and Eden and de Gaulle refused to let go.

"Ike is going to do something about that canal. He's gonna have Stevenson step in. He's waiting for high tide. . . ."

There were lots of good campaign jokes. "Nixon says every American family will soon have two cars, three TV sets, and work only four days a week. But Stevenson's gone him one better. He's trying to fix it so the Republicans won't have to work at all."

There's no way I can explain American politics, so from here on you're on your own.

Ike won reelection by a landslide, the first Republican to do so since McKinley in 1900. But the Democrats won Congress, so it didn't do the Republicans much good.

Nobody's ever figured out how to get both parties together. Democracy is like a marriage made in heaven; that's the only place it might work.

Every spring, regular as taxes, I'd get a call from the Air Force telling me it was time to get out of the country. I said, "Okay," in 1957, since nobody was shooting at Americans that year. I'm like the guy who tried to sign up with the marines for the duration, and explained to the recruiting sergeant he meant the duration of peace.

So when I was asked to hit the trail for Okinawa, Japan, Korea, and points West — or East, depending on which way you're pointed — I grabbed my chopsticks and Jayne Mansfield and got ready to take off. Until Mickey Hargitay stopped me. Mickey used to be an Olympic weightlifter, so I listened carefully as he explained that Jayne was his

little." There was a big argument until finally Norman Morrell, one of the NBC people who had come along to watch us, said, "You might wear that dress, but you'll never get on the network with it." For the next show, Jayne put on a dress that went right up to her chin. But it was very tight, and when she turned sideways to the G.I.'s, the whooping and hollering could be heard for miles. What God hath given, no man can take away.

Our troops were then spread out all across the Pacific. Japan was still occupied by our forces, Korea had just finished a civil war, the French had been driven out of Vietnam, and China had gone Communist. If this was peace, it was pretty messy.

The Hope Gypsies were old hands at gypsying by this time. Most things went smoothly on this trip because I had sent our advance guard — Sil Caranchini, our associate producer, and Johnny Pawlek, our sound man — off a month in advance to make all the arrangements and see if the natives were friendly. Mort Lachman, whom we called the Owl because of his black-rimmed glasses, directed the show and placed the cameras, and Barney McNulty had the most important job. He held up my idiot cards. Of course, Barney had a warped sense of humor. When we did one show aboard a ship off Okinawa, the first card was lettered in Japanese. I had him show the cards to the audience and got a big laugh, and then I pretended to read them and said, "A funny thing happened to me on the way to the geisha house," and got an even bigger laugh.

Also along with us was Erin O'Brien, a lovely young singer, and, of course, the Mad Professor, Jerry Colonna, and his mad moustache.

All of our crew and the band didn't have to do this sort of thing for a living. But whenever the first Christmas decorations started to appear on Hollywood Boulevard around November, I would get hesitant phone calls asking if they could be included in this year's trial by fire, mosquitoes, K-rations, frostbite, and occasional sniper fire. If they showed up when the doctor gave those shots with the horse hypodermic, you knew they were sincere.

The crew and the band always went, I suppose, in part for the excitement, in part because we all like to be appreciated, and the men and women we entertained always gave us more appreciation than we deserved.

And then, of course, maybe we all felt we owed something to the place all those guys and girls wanted to get back to.

After a pineapple stop in Honolulu, we

arrived in Okinawa, which had been captured in bloody battles in World War II. It was soon to be given back to Japan by the U.S. Okinawa is the island made famous in *Teahouse of the August Moon*. You may remember Marlon Brando in the movie, playing an Okinawan native (I hate type-casting like that) delivering the famous opening:

We have honor to be subjugated in fourteenth century by Chinese pirates.
In eighteenth century by Japanese warlords.
And in twentieth century by American marines.
Okinawa very fortunate.
Culture brought to us. Not have to leave home for it.

I don't know if we brought culture, but we certainly brought girls, music, and a few laughs to seven thousand marines gathered in the blazing sunshine at the Okinawa ballpark. We had movie cameras with us now, and for the first time we could bring the faces of the boys overseas back home to their families.

Their faces were always the best part of the show.

Barney McNulty held up cue cards in English and I could start being brilliant.

"I've just come from Hawaii. It's the most difficult spot in the world to leave. Everywhere else they wave good-bye with their hands. . . . It's pretty rugged out here on Okinawa. I hear one marine rolled out of his lean-to this morning and shaved three times until he realized he was staring into a bear. . . . And you think you got it tough? We all had to take shots before leaving home. In fact, Les Brown and his band got seconds."

It was about then that I noticed hundreds of ragged Okinawan children plastered against the chain-link fence around the ballpark. They weren't watching me. Their eyes were on the box lunches being eaten by members of the cast, who sometimes tossed aside half an uneaten sandwich. Some of the cast noticed and gave the children what they could, but it was never enough. I sometimes wonder what those hungry children thought of our show: the beautiful girls, the beautiful costumes, the beautiful music, and the beautiful ham sandwiches being thrown away by the American visitors.

Okinawa very fortunate. Culture brought to them, instead of food.

The contrast was brought home when we got to Tokyo and were billeted in the Imperial Hotel. It was hard to believe that only a few devastated years ago, the city had been almost burned to the ground by fire-bombing B-24's. The Imperial had been rebuilt into a hotel so luxurious, soon only Japanese could afford it.

I told 2,500 servicemen at Itazuke Air Base, while some screaming F-100 jets roared out of the skies and ruined half the punch lines, how impressed I was with the hotel:

"There's a button next to my bed marked 'room service,' and a girl to press it for me. . . . The bath in my suite is big enough to float a Buick."

In contrast to Japan's new economy, in 1957 America was showing signs of running low on ready cash. Congress had slashed the budget for the armed forces.

"We're going to have to let all our generals go who are over twenty-five," I explained to the airmen, "and you'll have to cut down on many essential services. From now on, a bomber will carry only one stewardess. . . . And that reminds me, nobody's allowed to send telegrams anymore. Commanding officers are cautioned to check through their Christmas cards carefully. War may have been declared."

After another show for a few thousand men at Johnson Air Base, we took off from sushi land and headed for Korea, a different

Korea than the one we had visited before. The Korean War had ended in an uneasy truce. The country was divided again at the 38th Parallel, and the boundaries were enforced with antiaircraft fire.

We were some six thousand miles from Hollywood and Vine, flying over the China Sea, when the crew brought out the Christmas tree they had stashed in the baggage compartment. It was tiny and a little scraggly, but it had shiny ornaments and even some tinsel. Erin O'Brien started singing "Silent Night." Suddenly it was our own private Christmas, and we felt closer than we had at any other time on the trip.

If it meant that much to all of us, we knew what Christmas must mean to the guys we were heading for, standing guard in a desolate country which was stumbling back from a grinding war that no one had won. Those who had really lost were the Korean civilians, living in caves and mud hooches, trudging back along muddy roads with stacks of wood branches on their heads, looking as if they were all wearing Hedda Hopper hats. The wood was to keep them warm during the freezing winter.

It had been seven below zero a few days before we arrived at Kimpo Air Base, but a heat wave had driven it up to minus two.

In spite of a cold winter wind that would have frozen whale blubber into popsicles, we couldn't resist when we saw that the entire base had turned out in the snow to greet us. The gang climbed up on a flatbed truck and Jayne Mansfield melted the icicles just by standing there and taking a deep breath. I told the panting soldiers, "I was surprised at the crowd Jayne drew when she got off the plane. I didn't think a couple of extra hills would be a novelty in Korea. . . . And I've figured out why the Koreans wear those weird-looking double-decker hats. The upper deck has a rock in it to keep the man under it from blowing away."

The girls and Colonna did a brief routine, and then we were off for Seoul, which we had first visited when it had been recaptured from the North Koreans. We had left before it was taken again by the Chinese Red Army. It had now been taken once more by U.S. and Republic of Korea troops, and made the South Korean capital; but nobody was signing a long-term lease. Seoul was the kind of city where you lived in a trailer park and kept the motor running. You didn't bother to give the post office your address; your mail came marked "To whom it may concern."

Things are still shaky over there today.

When they held the Olympic Games in Seoul in 1988, there were student riots and threats of invasion. The South Korean athletes never threw the javelin very far. They were worried that a North Korean would throw it back.

Their track team ran the 5,000 meters carrying their furniture.

When we got to Seoul, we ran into the "slicky boys," the most accomplished little sneak thieves in the world, tough kids who could shake your hand, swipe your gas cans, and steal your tires in the same motion; but the average annual wage in South Korea then was ninety-two dollars. The slicky boys had to steal or starve.

It took years before the South Koreans discovered how to build Hyundais. Now Detroit is trying to figure out how to swipe *their* tires.

In 1957, of course, things were pretty shaky all over the world. The U.S. suddenly had to give up its belief that Russian scientists were just a Polish joke.

Sputnik 1 beeped its way around the world 560 miles above the earth, and sent a couple million American school kids back to arithmetic class. The U.S.S.R. had gotten an "A" in science. The Space Age had dawned, and it had a Russian accent.

The joke was on *us*.

Of course, it wasn't long until we had our own little sputnik in orbit, thanks to some captured Nazi rocket scientists led by Wernher von Braun. The Russians had captured some of the same group. There was a famous cartoon at the time, showing the Russian and U.S. satellites orbiting the globe together. One satellite leaned over to the other and said, "Now we can speak German."

But we were worried. Like Avis, the U.S. was going to have to try harder.

That's why I opened our show at 1st Cavalry Division headquarters outside Seoul like this: "What with the sputniks and the international missiles flipping around in space, the people back home are so nervous it's a pleasure to be here in this rest area."

We had already done a Christmas Eve show at Seoul's new, plush International Theater for General Decker and the U.N. forces. After that, we boarded some big twenty-passenger twin-rotor helicopters to the Bayonet Bowl, near the 38th Parallel. Our pilot pointed out the border on our right, and remarked that if we strayed over it, we'd probably be shot down. I leaned to the left all the rest of the way, and it must have helped because we got to the bowl safely. Seven thousand G.I.'s of the 7th Infantry Division were perched on a snow-covered hillside that made Erin O'Brien's singing of "White Christmas" sound like a news bulletin.

It was even more so when we got to the Wallenstein Bowl, 1st Cavalry headquarters. The thermometer hit five below and gave up. But waiting for us were thousands of soldiers, huddled in their seats under their parkas. Some of them had been there since dawn.

The snow stretched for miles all around us. Any minute I expected to see Admiral Byrd and his dog teams mush by on their way to the North Pole. Or the South Pole, whichever came first.

This was our last stop in Korea; we were to leave for Japan immediately after the show, and the choppers remained close by, their rotor blades turning; if they stopped, they might never start again.

Our cast were all troupers; no one complained. But when they were offstage, I noticed they huddled about the coffee urn for warmth, and I could see them eyeing the choppers hopefully. The pilots had warned us that the fog tended to roll in thick and fast when the winter shadows grew longer. And the weather was closing in.

When the cast tore themselves away from the coffee long enough to come back onstage, the dancers danced a little faster, Hedda Hopper answered questions about Hollywood with one word or less, and Jayne Mansfield kept most of her assets hidden under a shawl. There was a brief heat wave when she removed it; then she ran offstage to refuel at the coffee urn while the wolf whistles froze in the air.

Jayne had brought five costumes along for the tour. She confessed later she was wearing all of them that day.

Then it was my turn onstage. I started to race through a few monologue jokes and made up my mind to quit halfway through, when I saw that the men weren't looking at me; they were looking, wistfully, at the members of the cast being hustled off behind me into the waiting choppers, some of which started taking off for warm beds, cocktail lounges, and steak dinners as the G.I.'s watched.

I pretended I didn't notice.

"How about this weather? All day long my undies have been creeping up on me looking for a place to hide. If they find one, I'm gonna crawl in myself."

Vroom. Chug chug. Another chopper took off. The shadows started creeping in.

"They don't bother with roll call here. No sense counting noses. Nobody's got one."

311

Laughter, mixed with another *vroom*. I was getting nervous. I started talking faster than Walter Winchell.

"In a climate like this, you don't need a marriage ceremony. You just wet your lips, kiss the girl, and freeze till death do you part. . . ."

One of the chopper crews was coming out onstage for me. The shadows were turning blue and violet on the snow. The fog started rolling in. But the guys out front were watching me like a little kid watches his parents when he knows they're leaving on a long vacation without him. Sure, there was no war on. In some ways, that made it tougher.

I couldn't leave them. After all, they were still laughing.

I went into another routine. Finally, someone almost pulled me off the stage as I shouted, "Merry Christmas!" to a few thousand guys and girls who weren't going to have one, and in a couple minutes I was warm and safe in the belly of a Huey chopper, on the way back to make-believe land again.

We lifted off into the gloom, and down below I could see those kids forming into squads outside the stadium and the squads forming into lines, looking like tiny toy soldiers as the lines marched off into the chill blue twilight of a Korean winter.

It was a Christmas card Grandma Moses might have painted if she'd been drafted.

That was the worst part of the Christmas tours. It was always Christmas.

Getting back to the U.S. was like walking into Disneyland. Hollywood was still romanticizing the last war, and *Bridge on the River Kwai* had won the Academy Award for "best picture." *West Side Story* and *The Music Man* had opened on Broadway with songs that could be sung by adults. We didn't realize how rare that was soon going to become. Robert Strom won $192,000 on a program called "The $64,000 Question." And Robert Strom was ten years old. Every father started snarling at his kids to stop wasting their time at school and get on some quiz shows and support the old man.

And then "The $64,000 Question" was knocked off the air when the government found out it had been rigged.

Of course, that was before we found out some parts of the *government* were rigged. I did a line on one TV special that went "I'm happy to see so many evangelists getting into politics . . . at least it keeps their hands out where we can see them." And then I learned some TV evangelists were themselves dipping into the collection plate, and sometimes their secretaries.

And you have to be careful with religious jokes at my house, because Dolores takes her Catholicism very seriously. As a matter of fact, there was later a rumor that the only reason I went to Vietnam every year was so I could have meat on Friday. Not true, but Dolores passed her feelings on to the children. When Linda and Kelly were small, Kelly once asked, "Is everybody in the world Catholic?" And Linda answered, "Everybody but Daddy. He's a comedian."

Later, the kids thought I was an airline pilot, because I was away from home so much. I remember once calling the writers and telling Norman Sullivan I was going to Alaska instead of Japan, and Norman said, "Okay, Bob, we'll move your pin on the map." I recently had someone check up on my schedule and found out that in 1989, I was on the road for 153 days out of 365. I must be slipping. I used to be on the road 365 days.

What I was getting at is that today, it sometimes seems that the whole world is on the take, including all our childhood idols. The toughest blow was to learn that Pete Rose may never make it into Cooperstown. It's enough to make a kid start burning his baseball cards.

But back in the fifties the United States

still considered itself to be Mr. Kleen. The Cold War came along and the Russians went from being "our heroic wartime Allies" to becoming our favorite heavies.

"I just heard that they've allowed commercials on Russian radio now. I saw a Russian ad for a cold cream. It had a picture of a beautiful girl, and underneath it said, 'She's lovely, she's engaged, she's gonna be shot in the morning. . . .' They've been copying our method on breakfast cereals, too. Of course, the Russians have it a little mixed up. They've been putting the cereal in the bowl and shooting the people out of guns. . . . The other day Uncle Joe fired Molotov, who was in charge of Russian relations with other countries. Stalin didn't like the way he was handling the job. There were still other countries. . . . A lot of people think Molotov was the victim of purge. . . . Purge . . . that's 'Break him in two, and put half in Minsk, half in Pinsk.' "

There was a grim joke going around about those purges: One rainy morning, a Russian peasant was being led off to be executed by one of Stalin's firing squads. The peasant said, "What brutes you are to march me through the rain like this." And the soldier leading the squad said, "What are you complaining about? *We* have to march back."

Our attitude toward Stalin was not based on fiction; after Uncle Joe died in 1953, a coal miner's son named Nikita Khrushchev took his place. Nicky was tough, bluff, and outspoken. The first thing he did after being elected — by secret ballot, all of them *his* — was to start the "de-Stalinization" process. Khrushchev had statues of Stalin torn down in every city in the country, which left a lot of Russian pigeons with nothing to do all day. The feeling then was a little like what is happening now in the Gorbachev era. Everyone was hoping something good was around the corner, that we and the Soviets were going to be pals.

In 1958, I was in London for the opening of *Paris Holiday*, a film in which I had co-starred with the great French comedian Fernandel. Arthur Jacobs, the demon press agent, came to me with the idea of originating my next television show from Moscow. I would be the first American comedian to do it.

And possibly the last, I told him. *Nyet*. Not a chance. Too tough in too many ways.

I mentioned Arthur's crazy notion to a few people and they got so enthusiastic, I started to like my idea.

Besides, I had to get out of London fast. I had decided to produce *Paris Holiday* myself, with United Artists putting up the money. With my firm hand on the controls and my eagle eye on the schedule, we only went a million dollars over budget. UA was starting to ask questions. I didn't know how to explain Fernandel to them.

This great performer was sometimes known as the French Bob Hope. I was flattered until I started to talk salary with him. I found out Fernandel lived in Paris, but he had a flat in Marseille. Therefore, he claimed he really lived in Marseille, and I would have to pay his living expenses in Paris. I asked him, if he was making a picture in Marseille, would he claim he lived in Paris?

Fernandel looked me in the eye and asked, "Wouldn't you?"

He got the deal.

When the picture started, I found he didn't read English, except for dollar signs. I would greet him every morning with, "*Bon jour*, Fernandel," he would say, "Good morning, Bob," and we wouldn't understand a word either one of us said after that.

After we wound up the picture, I brought him over to London for a television show. Fernandel brought ten friends with him and they drank the Dorchester wine cellar dry. *Vive la France!*

Being a producer gave me a fast insight

into how Paramount must have felt when we were making the "Road" pictures and Bing and I took a day off to play golf. Comedians are notorious for their disregard of shooting schedules. Once Jerry Lewis was directing a film of his at Paramount called *Ladies' Man*, and Jerry had a basketball basket set up at the side of the movie set. When he was called to direct a scene, he would pick up a basketball and wouldn't go on the set until he had made a basket.

Jerry quickly proved he would never have made the Boston Celtics.

Although Paramount started hoping he'd try.

Besides Fernandel, we had other unforeseen expenses in Paris, like lunch for the French crew. In Paris, you must give them a seven-course lunch, with a different wine at every course. The picture doesn't start shooting until noon and work finishes at seven. The food is served on the set and the crew keeps eating and drinking all the time. It's what is known as a "rolling lunch," and believe me, by the time they finished, they all were.

There was to be a big benefit performance for French war orphans that year — we sometimes forget the real victims of war are too small to protest it — and Ingrid Bergman asked me if I would perform. Of course, with Ingrid, I couldn't refuse anything she asked. Although she never asked me the question I was really waiting to hear.

There was a tremendous French audience in the theater we played. Eddie Constantine, the American actor who has become a cult figure in French films, translated my jokes for them. My French isn't very good, but I started to get worried when I heard him getting louder laughs than those jokes got in English.

I would say, "It's very frustrating making a picture in Paris. We work hard all day to get a love scene just right and then, on my way home, I see couples on every street corner doing it better."

Eddie translated it, and I knew something was wrong by the size of the laugh. Only later did I find out his French version went, "Three French kids saw a French couple making love in the grass in the Bois de Boulogne. The five-year-old said, 'What are they doing?' The seven-year-old said, 'They're having sex.' The nine-year-old said, 'And badly, too.' "

I never argue when they're laughing, even when I don't understand why, so I went on, "Our progress on the picture has been slow. We were held up three days on production.

Somebody lost the corkscrew. . . . At present we're three weeks behind on the film and six weeks ahead on the wine. . . . Now I know what they mean in France when they say labor is high."

Eddie must have translated those jokes perfectly, because when I got to the set the next day to take bows for my performance, there was no one to bow to. The union felt I had degraded the French worker and called the crew out on strike.

There were some frantic moments until I called a meeting with the union leaders and apologized. Everybody knew the French worker didn't drink.

We shook hands and had four bottles of champagne on it.

As I mentioned, we wound up a million dollars and four corkscrews over budget. The picture became known in the trade as *Around the Bank of America in Eighty Days*.

So Russia sounded more and more inviting. It never occurred to me that the Russian winter might be more difficult to handle than Fernandel. Nobody had found a happy ending to the road to Moscow yet. Even Napoleon went over budget on the way. So did Adolf.

But I had made up my mind. In London, I brought a small group from our show to the Soviet Consulate at 5 Kensington Gardens and we all filed for Russian visas. When I asked how long they would take, I got a shrug and a few bars of a Russian song that translated as

How deep is the ocean?
How high is the sky?

I guess they didn't realize whom they were dealing with. I had made powerful friends during my career, friends who owed me favors, important government friends I played golf with, friends whose influence went all the way to the White House.

I called Ursula Halloran, my public relations person in New York, and told her to go to Washington and call in some of my due bills.

A week later she called back, reporting success. She could get me a golf date at Burning Tree with a guy in the Department of the Interior, but I'd have to pay for the caddy.

I changed direction and called the NBC representative in Moscow, Irving R. Levine, whose regular broadcasts gave me the impression that he lunched every day at the Kremlin with Khrushchev. I asked Irv to push things from there.

He pushed it for three weeks and nobody pushed back. It turned out he never had lunch at the Kremlin. The food was lousy.

I had to show the Russians they weren't playing with children. I dialed the American embassy in London and asked for my good old friend, Jock Whitney, the American ambassador. I only had to spell my name three times before I got through to him. Then I had to spell it again. Jock explained that he couldn't do anything officially, but he was seeing the Russian ambassador, Jacob Malik, at a cocktail party that evening, and after a few vodkas he thought he might be able to mention my name.

He told me the next day that he did, and Malik had said, "*Nyet*. What does your Bob Hope want to do — entertain our troops in Red Square?"

At least Ambassador Malik had heard of me. I wanted to call him right away and tell him I had entertained a few of his troops, when the loudspeakers had carried my voice across the 38th Parallel, but I decided he didn't have any sense of humor.

By this time I was back in New York. I called Irv Levine in Moscow again, and told him they couldn't push me around anymore. I was going to fly to Copenhagen, buy a ticket on a Russian jet to Moscow, and climb aboard without a visa. After all, what could they do to me?

Irv spent five minutes explaining what they could do to me. It didn't sound encouraging. I spent the next five minutes telling him what I thought of Russian bureaucracy.

Irv said, "They'll be glad to hear that. My telephone is bugged."

A Russian voice on the line said, "That's another capitalist lie!" and my phone hung itself up.

The press found out what was going on and kept pressing me to explain how Moscow could ignore such a famous personality. I think they were talking about Levine. But I told them, "I can't understand it. I gave the names of two Czars who could vouch for me."

After months of delays and red tape, I got a call from Julian Goodman, of NBC Washington. My visa was waiting to be picked up at the Russian embassy.

"What took so long?" I wanted to know.

"They told me to tell you it was a technical problem. Your passport is okay, but some of your jokes have expired."

I guess it took them two months to think of that line, but I didn't care. I was going to Moscow. Only then did I start to get worried. Remember, this was over thirty years ago, the Iron Curtain was real. Khrushchev had just ordered the U.S., Britain, and France out of Berlin again. You wouldn't say it was a good time for an American to go to Russia to get laughs.

And I was worried about a more immediate problem: there had been all this hoopla about my doing the first big television show from Moscow, and I had no show. I had no script. I didn't really have an idea. But I had the tickets and the publicity and what Barney Dean would have called the chutzpah, so I had to go. It reminded me of the first time Jerry Lewis was called on to emcee the Academy Awards show, and he told the writers not to give him any jokes. "I won't need a script," he explained. "When I step up to the microphone in front of an audience, something happens to me."

A few weeks later, he frantically phoned the writers from Las Vegas, where he was playing, and asked them what had happened to his jokes for the Academy Awards show.

"We're awfully sorry, Jerry," they told him, "but when we sat down at the typewriter, nothing happened to us."

Of course they'd written the show, and Jerry went on and was great, but he never used that line again.

I was faced with a more difficult situation:

If I got up in front of an audience in Moscow without a script and laid a Russian egg, my sponsor would see that something happened to me when I got home.

So I made sure that the Owl, Mort Lachman, and his writing partner, Bill Larkin, were flying in from Prague chained to their typewriters, and would meet me in Moscow with a completed script. All it required was an Idea.

That sounds simple, but it reminds me of a story I heard from Harlan Ellison, the science fiction writer who left his little green people to go out and play the lecture circuit. Harlan was always being asked by audiences where he got his ideas.

He had a stock answer: "There's a little company in Schenectady. For forty dollars a month, they send you six ideas." Invariably, he told me, one of the newspapermen covering his lecture would sidle up to him afterward, ask him questions about his latest book, and then casually say, "Oh, by the way, can you let me have the name of that place in Schenectady?"

I knew Mort and Bill would arrive with some ideas. I've forgotten now why they were flying to Moscow by way of Czechoslovakia, but Mort had been playing golf in London and might have sliced one into the rough.

Ursula Halloran and Arthur Jacobs, the PR representatives who had suggested Russia in the first place, accompanied me on the flight from New York to Copenhagen, where we boarded a TU-104, Russia's first commercial jet airliner. You must remember, in 1958, Pan Am had just put the first U.S. jet in service across the Atlantic. The Soviets were right up there with us in aviation technology.

I thought the CIA might be able to use any information I could get them on this new jet, so I put my keen mind to work gathering secret intelligence. The TU-104, I managed to discover, was an airplane. It had swept-back wings that made it look as if it was breaking Mach 1 when it was still on the ground. I figured this was to fool a lot of enemy pilots into shooting it down when it was parked at the terminal. The interior was done in Russian style with material that looked as if it was from Mrs. Khrushchev's old shower curtains. Of course, this was assuming they had a shower in the Kremlin, and Mrs. Khrushchev wasn't wearing the curtains. I was to learn more about her wardrobe when I met Mrs. K. later in Hollywood, but you'll have to stay with me a few more pages to hear about it.

The TU-104 took off vertically. At least,

that's the way it felt. We got to Moscow before my stomach could put down its landing gear.

Our hostess was dressed in a uniform right out of *Vogue*: black jacket and a babushka. But she had a winning smile. Her teeth seemed to be made out of the same stuff as the fuselage. Lunch, though, was great. They had loaded it aboard in Copenhagen, delicious Danish beef and vegetables. We never saw real beef again until we left Moscow.

Our passports were taken away from us before we left the plane. I never felt so naked in my life. There we were, up the Volga without a paddle.

In the Moscow airport we went through customs, which turned out to be a complete surprise. They didn't even bother to open my suitcase. They had a dog sniff my luggage and it turned up its nose.

An MVD man, a tough-looking Soviet official wearing black riding boots, approached me. I looked to see if he was still carrying a cossack whip, but apparently he'd recently given up pogroms as a hobby. What he was carrying was my passport. He handed it back to me and remarked, in a booming Russian basso, that he was very sorry to hear that Detroit was all closed down. I was startled that the Russians had already heard of the strikes then going on in our auto industry, but I realized the story had probably appeared in *Pravda* under "There's Good News Tonight."

The Russian workers have recently taken a 180-degree turn under *glasnost*. The miners went out on strike in 1989 and invited U.S. TV cameras into their homes, to show how inferior they were to the homes of American workers they were now allowed to see on Russian television. The miners also asked for a piece of the profits of the coal mines, showing that some of them must read *Daily Variety*.

It's becoming one world, all right. Next thing, they'll want to direct.

Thirty years ago, conditions in the Soviet Union were much more primitive. We stepped out of the airport and saw empty parking spaces. We were driven in our Ziv limousine to our hotel and didn't see one car get rear-ended. This may have been because we didn't see any cars. Moscow was full of broad boulevards with no automobiles. It was frightening. You could breathe the air without coughing.

Recently, there was a Russian picture shown in the U.S. called *Moscow Does Not Believe in Tears*. Now I understand why. No smog.

Today, I've heard, more and more cars are on the streets and parking space and oxygen have started to disappear. Soon Russians will learn to cough like real capitalists.

Our 1958 Ziv limousine was a copy of a 1947 Lincoln Continental, the first luxury limousine to be produced in the U.S. after World War II. One arrived in Moscow for the American ambassador. Stalin was so impressed, he ordered it copied for himself and all the commissars he hadn't liquidated yet. When he died, nobody dared to cancel the order. So the Russian auto factories were still building 1947 Lincolns.

I go into this detail because back then, we knew so little about Russia and its people, items like that were hot news. So was the fact that our hotel, the Hotel Ukraine, had been designed to look like the Waldorf-Astoria, if you'd never seen the Waldorf-Astoria. The main difference was that at the Hotel Ukraine, a tough Russian matron was stationed on every floor at a desk in front of the elevators. She gave you the gimlet eye and took your room keys away from you when you left and gave them back to you when you returned. I suppose this made things a lot easier for the KGB, but I always expected to come back at night and find her wearing one of my suits.

The lobby looked as if it was five stories

high and was very impressive, but I don't know what the furniture was like. They kept it covered with sheets, because it was the property of the people, who weren't admitted to such a plush hotel. At the Georgian Restaurant, where we occasionally ate, the food was so good they kept the doors locked so Russians couldn't get in. It was strictly for foreign VIP's, who were admitted through a side door, like the old speakeasy days. They served vodka there in round-bottomed glasses. You couldn't set them down, you had to swallow that firewater in a single snort. One shot of that explosive Russian vodka knocked all the Republican out of you. After a few rounds, Communist society took on a rosy glow and nobody minded drinking a couple of rousing toasts to Lenin, the Little Father whose portrait looked down on us from the wall. And occasionally winked.

At least, he winked at *me*.

When we checked into our rooms at the Hotel Ukraine, the first thing we did was look for the hidden microphones. We had been told that the thirteenth floor of the hotel was filled with recording equipment, and that every word we spoke was being monitored.

I don't know if the rooms were really bugged, but whenever we entered we'd talk to the doorknob, we'd talk to the chair, and to the pictures on the wall. And when we left, Mort and Bill and I would face the wall and shout, "That concludes our broadcast for this evening. Be sure to stay tuned for Lawrence Welk."

There was a joke the Russians told on themselves a couple of years later, when Moscow proudly announced its third TV station. On Channel 1 you always found Khrushchev, making a speech. On Channel 2 was Molotov, making a speech. On Channel 3 was a KGB man shaking his fist and saying, "Go back to Channel One!"

I don't know if we were tailed or not. We didn't have to be. We suspected the KGB was part of our group. First there was a Russian who took us to dinner, and he started with the vodka, and I thought, "Here we go. He's trying to pry some secrets out of us." We started to drink toasts to each other, and he went out first and fell under the table. The KGB immediately took him away from us for further training.

Then we had an interpreter, a charming girl of about twenty-two named Larissa Sorobova. She always wore boots, a sheared beaver coat, and, on her head, her crowning glory, a blue angora babushka. In all the time she was with us, she never took it off.

We all figured there was a radio transmitter inside so the KGB could hear everything that went on. If Larissa had a sex life, she probably had to turn off her babushka before she turned herself on.

She was hardly what we had expected, some hard-core propagandist who was going to sound like a meeting of the Politburo. Larissa was a shy, quiet girl, proud of her country and her job, which was probably why she kept it. She had previously been assigned to Adlai Stevenson, John Gunther, and Mike Todd. In fact, Mike was the one who gave her the blue babushka. This was before he met Elizabeth Taylor, and learned that diamonds are a girl's best friend.

Larissa showed absolutely no interest in the United States or our stories about Hollywood. I'm not sure if this was a pose or not, but she never let her guard down.

I heard of another group of American visitors whose interpreter was an English teacher in a Russian high school. She never showed the least interest in America until she was alone with one member of the group on the way to the airport, on the last day of their visit. She handed him a pad and pencil and asked him to write down every four-letter word he knew. She told him she had learned her English from books and the Voice of

America; she knew that wasn't the way American high school kids spoke. She needed a few colorful, teenage expressions so she could bring her students into the twentieth century.

The guy wrote down four pages of dirty words. I don't know what happened to that pad, but they turned up later as the plot of *Porky's II.*

With Larissa guiding us all the way, we started to make our frontal attack on Soviet bureaucracy. Mort and Bill had come up with a great idea for the show. All our talent would be Russian, and our leading lady would be the city of Moscow itself. All we needed was permission to go wherever we wanted to go, and photograph the real Moscow.

Like all great ideas, it had one small flaw. It wouldn't work.

We learned that the first aay, when we were taken to see Igor Rachuk, deputy chief of the cinema section of the Ministry of Culture. We drove through the streets in snow so deep we sometimes had to get out of the car through the windows. I think our Russian driver had filled the radiator full of vodka to keep it from freezing. He was in no danger, himself. But every time he hiccuped, the windshield fogged up.

He drove us to the Soviet Film Export building, the kind with walls so thick you can't hear the screams through them. There were stern, silent, uniformed Red Army guards in fur hats, who stared at the American visitors as if wondering how we had broken out of Lubyanka Prison.

Inside, the rugs were threadbare and the stairs creaked. Wherever we went, silent faces turned to watch us. They looked like a Rasputin family reunion.

After passing through five offices and seven doors, we finally got to Comrade Rachuk's inner office, where he sat backed up by what looked like five heavies from various James Bond pictures.

His first words were "You are seven and one half minutes late and, according to Soviet law, must pay a penalty."

I didn't know whether to leave Mort or Bill as a hostage. Maybe it would be better to leave both and a typewriter. We had to get the script finished somehow.

After a look at our white faces, Commissar Rachuk laughed out loud. When he got himself under control he said, "The penalty is, the men must drink this wine to the bottom of the glass and the women must eat these chocolates to the bottom of the bowl." And, still chuckling, he set out a bottle of wine and a bowl of candy.

The real Red Menace isn't the Russian

army. It's Russian comedians.

We all laughed heartily as soon as our blood returned, and drank the wine and ate the chocolates as we matched wits with Comrade Rachuk for over an hour. All we wanted from him was permission to shoot on Moscow streets, and the use of a theater, with an audience that understood English.

You would think that would require only a simple *da* or *nyet*. Not in Russia. Rachuk had not gotten to be deputy chief by making decisions. We were told the matter would be discussed "at the highest levels." I could just see them calling Khrushchev back from building the Berlin Wall to find me a theater full of good laughers.

There's a story — you knew there would be, didn't you? — about a network executive at CBS in Hollywood whose decisions were always made by the brass in New York. He was called as a witness in an important legal case, and the bailiff held out a Bible and said, "Do you promise to tell the truth, the whole truth, and nothing but the truth, so help you God?"

And the executive answered, "I'll get back to you."

Rachuk never got back to us. Time was running out. We decided to go ahead without permission.

I'd always wanted to see Siberia, anyway. The Russians had already informed us we would have to use a Russian camera crew. We knew that wouldn't work. We had brought a great British cameraman along with us, Ken Talbot. He immediately put Mort, Bill, and me into training as his assistants. It must have been like teaching three chimpanzees to fly the space shuttle. We had brought an Arriflex camera and plenty of film. Black-and-white film, of course. In those early days of color TV, my sponsors didn't think it worth spending the money to tint my jokes. It didn't make them any funnier, did it?

There's no answer to that one, especially if you want your option picked up.

So Mort, Bill, and I learned how to change film magazines every night when we returned to the hotel. Only once or twice did I reload a magazine with film that had already been shot. It made an interesting effect when it was developed.

The extreme cold made the film very brittle, and it would sometimes break in the camera while we were shooting. We lost a lot more good shots that way. Everything and everybody seemed to be working against us. Walter Mirisch, the producer of many great Hollywood films, once said, "They ought to give you an Academy Award just for getting the picture made."

I'm willing.

In those days, Moscow was almost an unknown city to Americans. Nearly everything we did was a first. We decided to open the show with shots of me walking out into Red Square, the largest open city square in the world. So we just marched out there with the camera and waited for somebody to stop us.

It's a magnificent view, the huge square with the golden-domed buildings of the Kremlin behind the wall at one side, and at the end of the square the crimson and gold of St. Basil's, one of the most beautiful cathedrals in the world. The Communists have kept it just as it was in the days of the czars, as a lesson to the people on how the church squandered their money on useless gold and silver ornaments.

It's the kind of cathedral Donald Trump might build in Atlantic City.

St. Basil's was built in the sixteenth century by Ivan the Terrible. He lived up to his name when he had the Russian genius who designed it put to death so he couldn't build another like it. I've heard of people who got mad at their architects, but Ivan carried it to extremes. When St. Basil's was finished, he had his enemies locked in cages in front of it and set them on fire. It's said that's how shish kebab was invented.

No, it isn't really funny. The Russians have a long history of oppression under rulers like Ivan the Nasty and Peter the Great. Possibly that's why they didn't rebel at the repression and cruelties of the Stalin era. After Ivan and Peter, life with Uncle Joe must have seemed like Easter vacation at Hollywood High. We have to keep that in mind in these days of Mikhail Gorbachev. It's difficult for the Russian people to decompress after all their centuries of suffering.

If *glasnost* happens too fast, the whole country is likely to get the bends.

Near the Kremlin wall is a low, modern building that was built as Lenin's tomb. When Stalin died, he was placed in it beside the Little Father. Uncle Joe was still there when we visited. Long lines of Russian people shivered in the freezing cold, lines eight abreast and a mile long, waiting to get in to view his body, possibly to make sure he was really dead. I guess it must have annoyed Khrushchev, because later he ordered Stalin removed.

Lenin's lease didn't include boarders.

We wanted to get shots of the people in the line, but there was a cordon of police around the whole area. So we just marched through them with our camera and pretended not to speak Russian, which was easy. They paid no attention to us, which I found a little annoying. Ten thousand people in line, two hundred police, and not one request for an autograph. I felt as if I'd never left home.

Things were a little different when we got to Sovietskaya Square to shoot film in front of one of the monuments, with yours truly in the foreground. In a little while we had over a thousand spectators, half of them interested in our equipment and the other half waiting to see us get arrested.

For a while, nobody tried to stop us. We decided the police had been given orders to ignore our camera. The KGB must have secretly observed Mort, Bill, and me in my room, trying to load the film cartridges, and figured we'd never get anything on the film but thumb prints.

We fooled them. We managed to get some good shots of the faces of the children watching us, by pretending to be shooting in the other direction.

There is something in the faces of innocent children that is truly universal. They could have been kids anywhere, bundled up against the cold, out for a walk with their parents, too young to understand grown-up hates and prejudices.

Of course, you have to catch them before they're old enough to start reading newspapers.

We were congratulating ourselves until we saw a Soviet policeman turn from directing traffic and start toward us, blood in his eye. He probably had missed the morning KGB briefing. I quickly told Ken to turn the camera on him, and pantomimed to the cop that we wanted to photograph him directing traffic.

He hesitated a moment, then he straightened his uniform, threw out his chest, and stepped out into the street blowing his whistle, glancing over his shoulder to see if we were shooting his good side.

We got out of the square while he was taking bows.

Ham, too, is universal. It takes one to know one.

During the next couple of days, we kept negotiating with the Russian bureaucracy for permission to do what we were already doing, and finally got a direct answer: It was still being considered by higher authorities.

So we kept on doing it.

I was trying to round up Russian talent for the show, and was doing fairly well. We went to the Russian circus and got the great clown Popov to appear, as well as a couple of dancing bears. I was a little hesitant about signing the bears. They reminded me of that scene I played with Crosby in *Road to Utopia*, when that supposedly tame bruin tried to chew my arm off. The bear finally paused while he looked around for some ketchup, and the trainer finally got him off before he started on dessert.

There was one act in Moscow I wanted to get on film, an all-girl orchestra that one of the newspapermen, Serge Fleigers of International News Service, told us was a riot. We went to see it at the Leningradskaya Hotel one night, and I had Ken tuck the Arriflex under his coat while Serge bribed the headwaiter for a ringside table. I don't know what you use to bribe a headwaiter in Russia, possibly a herring, but we got the table.

The music started. It was an all-girl orchestra, all right. All girl and each one about two yards wide. They swung into an arrangement of "When My Tractor Smiles at Me" loud enough to frighten the kulaks off a collective farm. Ken pulled the camera out from under his coat and started to film them, while I tried to shield him from view.

Immediately, a maître d' descended on us and shouted that it was forbidden. I guess any photographs of those "girls" could be considered enemy propaganda.

Serge spoke fluent Russian and started shouting back, telling him we were guests of the Russian government, and anyone who stood in our way would be the first to disappear in the coming purge of maître d's.

The fellow blanched a little and invited Serge to go with him to the hotel manager.

The minute they left, Mort grabbed the lenses, Bill took the tripod, I lugged the battery, and Ken operated the camera as I acted as lookout and yelled "Chickie!" whenever a waiter came near. We photographed the girls from every angle without finding their good side.

By the time Serge returned with the news that the whole matter would be taken up with the highest authorities, we had all the film we needed.

But we still didn't know what we were going to do with it. Until you've tried to deal with a Communist bureaucracy, you don't know how red red tape can be. Maybe there never would be a show from Moscow.

I was feeling pretty low that night when I got my key from the female Rambo at the elevators and let myself into my room. I stopped short. Someone had opened my suitcase and spread all the jokes that were in it on the bed. I couldn't figure who would want to steal them; Milton Berle was at least four thousand miles away.

Then I realized these jokes were the ones supplied by the writers we had left behind in Hollywood, who didn't care if we got back. I had pulled them out of the monologue before they got us in trouble.

"The workers love Khrushchev very much. He hasn't got an enemy in the entire country. Quite a few under it.

"Following doctor's orders, Nikita has cut his drinking in half; he's cut out the water. . . .

"They have a national lottery in Russia. It's known as living."

If these ever reached those "higher authorities," I would probably spend the rest of my life defrosting.

I still don't know who broke into my room. At the time, it didn't seem to matter. Everything was looking hopeless. We still had no place to do the show. We couldn't get a theater, we couldn't get anything except *"Nyet!"*

I didn't know what to do. I heard they were having a cocktail party at the American embassy, so I went over there and met Ambassador Llewellyn Thompson, better known as Tommy. He was as unbureaucratic as they come, and in ten minutes he had offered us Spasso House, his official residence, where we could do our program from a large hall, which during a more festive era had been used as a ballroom by the czars before they went out to hunt peasants. He understood, if the Russians didn't, how important a broadcast like this could be during these trying times. The Eisenhower Administration was truly looking for some sort of accommodation with the Russians. Only a month or so later, Vice President Nixon would have his famous live television encounter with Khrushchev in the kitchen at the American Trade Show in Moscow. They both traded blistering arguments about the merits of their competing systems. Nixon came off well enough to start eyeing the Republican nomination for President.

Khrushchev didn't have to worry about getting nominated.

But at least the U.S. and the U.S.S.R. were talking to each other, and in public.

Our show didn't compare to "Breakfast with Dickie and Nickie," but we felt it might help, in some small way. It was a victory just to be standing on the hastily constructed stage at Spasso House. Neither snow, nor sleet, nor "highest authorities" had been able to stop us.

"From Moscow, Russia, the Bob Hope Show! Featuring Popov the clown, comic

David Ryiken, prima ballerina Galina Ula-
nova, Uri Durov's Bears, violinist David
Oistrakh, and the Ukraine state dancers!"

The orchestra that played "Thanks for the
Memory" made it sound more like "The
Volga Boatman," but who cared? We had
made it. Our Russian camera crew had shown
up four hours late, but they had shown up.
They had insisted on using Russian film,
which could only be developed in Moscow,
but that didn't seem important at the time.

Nobody had thrown us into jail. It was a
tremendous victory for capitalist ingenuity,
even if we didn't get laughs.

Of course, if we didn't get laughs, I would
kill myself. Maybe I could get Lenin to move
over.

In addition to the Canadian, British, and
French embassy staffs, the American embassy
had invited most of the English-speaking diplomatic community, but they could only
round up two hundred chairs from the neighbors. Three hundred guests showed up, of
every nationality. Our audience was a mixture
or turbans, top hats, fezzes, burnooses, and
loincloths. It looked like a San Francisco
paddy wagon after a drug bust.

I didn't know how many spoke English
and there was only one way to find out. I
took a deep breath and plunged in.

"Good evening, tovarich and tovariches . . ."

When that got a laugh, I knew they must understand English. It couldn't have been my Russian.

"Well, here we are in Moscow, broadcasting to a large group of Democrats. . . . You must be Democrats or they wouldn't have sent you here — "

That got a yell from the American diplomatic corps. Russia was not considered a prize post in the State Department. It was so cold in Moscow that day, I tripped in my hotel room that morning and broke my breath.

The laughs were thawing me out. And they kept getting better.

"But really, I'm thrilled to be here in Moscow. Quite a switch for me, entertaining our civilians overseas. . . . I'm happy to be working for the State Department. Now I'll get even for that passport picture. . . . I'm here on a cultural exchange. You know, we sent *Porgy and Bess* and they sent the Moscow Ballet. I'm here for Mike Romanoff and four cans of caviar. . . ."

For the yuppie generation who never heard of him, in those days Mike Romanoff ran a fancy restaurant in Hollywood and claimed to be part of the Romanoff royal family. But he spoke Russian with a Brooklyn accent, and that kind of spoiled the act.

"I flew in from Copenhagen to Moscow and I got a wonderful tribute. At the airport, they fired twenty-one shots in the air in my honor. It would have been nicer if they'd waited for the plane to land. . . . The Russians are overjoyed with their sputnik. It's kind of weird being in a country where every ninety-two minutes, there's a national holiday. . . . Anybody without a stiff neck is a traitor. . . . And I'd like to congratulate the Russian scientists, but I can't speak German."

I didn't know that last line was going to get us in trouble with the minister of culture, who called me the next day to come see him. He was no one to fool around with. It was rumored he had helped kill three million peasants in the Ukraine. What was one more peasant to him?

Sputnik had military implications for the Soviets, and wasn't considered a joking matter. I didn't really understand that at the time, and just plunged ahead with the jokes.

"They're starting to show American movies here. The Russians may find some of our historical pictures a little hard to take. For instance, when they see *War and Peace*, it may come as quite a shock to them to learn that Napoleon was really chased out of Moscow by

Audrey Hepburn. . . . It's amazing how Russians can get the wrong impression of America. An official here showed me a picture of starving Americans, people without shoes and nothing to eat, absolutely desperate. And I couldn't argue with him. It was a picture of the bus station in Las Vegas. . . . One good thing, though, I'm not really having trouble with the Russian language. Nobody talks to me."

I was surprised at the laugh that last line got. Then I realized I had touched another nerve, just as I had with our G.I.'s when I brought their gripes into the open. Relations were still strained between our diplomatic personnel and the Russians. I talked with State Department people who had been in the country for years and had never been invited to a Russian home. Part of it was the language barrier, part of it the lack of housing, which made Russians sensitive about their living quarters, and part of it that most Russians were afraid to talk to foreigners. Only now is that starting to ease up, although there is still suspicion. Russians aren't sure how long the Gorbachev era will last, and they know the KGB is still taking notes, if only from force of habit.

In those naïve days of 1958, we all thought the suspicion was temporary. Especially later that year, when Khrushchev came to the United States with Mrs. Khrushchev, and she persuaded him to visit Hollywood. Stalin's wife had never visited Hollywood. Mrs. Stalin hadn't visited anyplace. Nobody ever saw her. It was rumored that Uncle Joe kept her and a bottle of vodka in a closet in the Kremlin, so he wouldn't have to go out of the house if it rained. We knew there *was* a Mrs. Stalin, because later her daughter Svetlana came to the U.S. and married an American. Svetlana became so Americanized, she divorced him and wrote a book.

I was at 20th Century-Fox Studios when Mrs. Khrushchev and Nikita were given a welcoming luncheon by Spyros Skouras, who was head of Fox. Spyros was Greek and still had an accent. Khrushchev spoke nothing but Russian, which helped him understand Spyros's English.

Skouras wasn't as bad at English as his brother Charley, who was also an officer of 20th-Fox. Once, when the two were conducting a delicate negotiation with Paramount's top brass, trying to buy Paramount pictures for television, Charley glared at the Paramount people, jumped to his feet, and shouted, "No palookas! No palookas!" and hurried out of the room. Spyros ran after him to find out why he had insulted such important executives by calling them palookas, and Charley looked indignant and informed his brother that what he was saying was, "No Paul Lukas! No Paul Lukas!" Paramount had been trying to sell them some Paul Lukas pictures, which Charley happened to hate.

Paul was a fine actor, but maybe Charley had seen him with me in *The Ghost Breakers* and got the two of us mixed up. It was easy to make a mistake. We were both so strikingly handsome.

At the luncheon, Mrs. Khrushchev was seated between me and Frank Sinatra. I could see she was absolutely thrilled when she turned away from Frankie and looked at me. That was right after I spilled my ice water in her lap, but I'm sure that had nothing to do with it. Mrs. K. had been all gussied up for the occasion, a new hairdo carefully done in the latest style, if this had been 1923, and wearing the new trendy dresses designed for her by Moscow's leading cement bag manufacturer. She loved Frankie, and through an interpreter told him she often listened to his records. Then she was very complimentary to me, I think, although at that point the interpreter refused to translate.

Like most of America, Frank and I were hoping that this visit by Stalin's replacement signaled a new era of friendship between old World War II allies. We generously decided to do a job our State Department obviously needed our tremendous diplomatic ability to bring off. We didn't expect any reward, outside of perhaps a building next to the Lincoln Memorial containing our statues.

Taking my cue from the fact that Mrs. K. looked like the typical tourist wife from Nebraska, I suggested that she and Mr. K. might get a kick out of a visit to Disneyland. We saw her eyes light up when the interpreter got to, "Disneyskilandsky," and Frankie jumped right in and said, "Yeah, you gotta make that crazy scene. I'll take you and we'll dig it together."

We could see Mrs. K. was thrilled by that idea, after the interpreter figured it out. She was so excited, she forgot to ask if I was coming along. She told the interpreter, "I must ask Nickie," and scribbled a hasty note and passed it down to her husband, the ruler of all the Russias, successor to Josef Stalin, Nicholas II, and Ivan the Terrible, none of whom had ever been to Disneyland. This might be Nickie's best chance to upstage them.

Khrushchev was seated at the head of the table with the two Skourases and Henry Cabot Lodge, representing the State Department.

Frank and I hoped Lodge was paying attention so he could learn how to do his job right.

We could see Mr. K.'s eyes light up as he read the note. Disneyskilandsky! He knew Mickey was an international mouse. Khrushchev realized the worldwide propaganda value of being seen as Mr. Nice Guy, taking his wife on the Mr. Toad ride. Even if she fell off, it would make headlines. Khrushchev knew how the whole thing would play in the West, which still didn't know too much about him. Could this kindly old Communist tourist want to blow us all off the map? What a silly idea!

It didn't seem so silly a little while later, when Khrushchev promised the U.S., "We're going to bury you," and tried to sneak those nuclear firecrackers into Cuba to start the funeral off with a bang. But we didn't know that, then.

Frankie and I watched, happily, as Khrushchev whispered to one of his top aides, who hurried off to arrange for the free tickets.

And then everything hit the Russian fan. The aide came back and reported to Nickie that the Los Angeles Security Police would not let him visit Disneyland. Steam came out of Khrushchev's ears and he started to pound the table with his shoe, but decided to save that part of the act for the United

Nations. Wasn't America supposed to be a free country? Couldn't a guy take his wife on the Whirling Teacups without some patriot calling out the National Guard? This sort of thing could never happen in Moscow, where citizens were free to do whatever they wanted to do, as long as the KGB didn't catch them doing it!

It made front pages all over the world. Nickie Khrushchev had seized the attention of the press, who were all there to advance the cause of international understanding and get a free meal on Spyros Skouras at the same time. Mr. K. quickly switched to another topic. Spyros had earlier made the mistake of taking Mr. and Mrs. K. onto the set of *Can-Can*, the musical Frankie was shooting with Shirley MacLaine and Maurice Chevalier. Khrushchev claimed he was outraged when he once actually caught a glimpse of Shirley's bloomers. This would never happen in the Soviet Union! In the first place, Russian women didn't wear bloomers.

Poor Mrs. Khrushchev by that time was trying to slide under the table, but I almost beat her to it.

Mr. and Mrs. K. never got to see Disneyland.

And that's how Frankie and I started the Cold War.

★ ★ ★

Of course, it had really started for me some months earlier, during the sputnik jokes at Spasso House. I mentioned that the Minister of Culture was not pleased; let me now go back and fill you in on our adventures.

The next day, we got a call from our old pal, Comrade Rachuk. A couple of other comrades wanted to speak to us.

Immediately.

We couldn't refuse. It seems they had developed our film and didn't want to give it back.

I wasn't very happy marching into the building with walls so thick you couldn't make your screams heard through them. I was planning to try.

Commissar Rachuk marched me in to see Commissar Fadeyev, deputy director of Soviet Film Export. Commissar Fadeyev marched me in to see Commissar Aleksander Davydov, head of Soviet Film Export.

There was a picture of Lenin on his desk. Frowning.

Fadeyev got right to the point, that line, "I want to congratulate the Russian scientists, but I don't speak German."

The official verdict: censored! Insulting to the Russian government! Out! You would never be allowed to say such things about the United States military!

What an opening. I got slowly to my feet and delivered a monologue to the toughest one-man audience of my career. I told him we *always* did jokes about the U.S. military. We also did jokes about President Eisenhower and the Secretary of Defense.

The commissar sat back in his chair and glared at me. But that didn't frighten me; I've played Cleveland.

I started with "I guess you've heard the good news from Cape Canaveral. Our government has launched another submarine."

I saw the commissar fighting hard not to smile. Obviously, the fact that a couple of American missiles had recently gone in the drink had hit the front page of *Pravda*, although they hadn't hit anything else.

"Actually, our test firings of missiles are going very well. They land on the target every time. As a matter of fact, there's hardly anything left of Bermuda."

Had I heard a Russian snicker? No time to waste, hit 'em before they recover.

"We have nothing to fear. With a ten-second warning, our Army can launch a missile that would completely wipe out our Air Force."

Comrade Fadeyev finally laughed. It was a bigger victory than winning the Academy

Award, I keep telling myself. I started to laugh with him, until he handed me a bill for stock film clips, the Russian camera crew, and processing the film they had forced us to use. At the same time, he assured me the matter of the jokes would be promptly acted upon by the highest authorities in the U.S.S.R.

I thanked him and assured him I would immediately have the bills acted upon by the highest authorities at NBC.

We're both still waiting as you read this.

Then he shook my hand and said, "I will send you the film in America."

I told him, "You can't *send* me the film. My people are going to wait right here in Moscow until you deliver it." I knew that was the only way I could get it out of the country without the Russian censors spending a lot of time cutting polka dots out of it.

I went back to the hotel and told Mort and Bill I was leaving them there until they got the film. I had to get to Copenhagen. They both glared at me, knowing I was going to Denmark to eat real food.

"You mean," they said, "you'd sacrifice two writers for a lousy piece of film?"

Fortunately, there was no real problem. They got the film out of Russia, and the first — and last — Bob Hope Show from

Moscow went on the air in the United States on April 28, 1958.

With all the sputnik jokes still in.

The broadcast included my closing, a plea for *glasnost* before I ever heard the word:

"You know, when we were in Korea at Christmastime, looking across the Thirty-eighth Parallel into Communist rifle barrels, little did we dream that three months later, we'd be wandering around the Kremlin, un-escorted . . . I think. . . . I felt right at home when I saw the kids on the streets there. Fat kids, thin kids, kids who love to skate, kids who are just kids. I found out the little kids with the fur hats and the sticky faces have no politics. Twenty years from now, will they be violinists, shopkeepers, teachers, or will they be the ones at the countdown who push the button which shakes the crust of the earth?

"It would be nice if somebody could work out a plan for peaceful coexistence, so that human beings like these kids don't become obsolete."

More than thirty years have passed. No one has pushed the button yet.

Those sticky-faced kids I saw in Red Square are all grown up now.

Let's hope our world has grown up with them.

CHAPTER SEVEN

1958-1963

"I'm happy to see so many of you
here today. As a matter of
fact, I'm happy see *anybody.*"
— *Ankara, Turkey, 1963*

Things were pretty good stateside now. These
were the years of Eisenhower and Kennedy,
a time of prosperity and hope, when musicals
like *Gypsy* and *The Sound of Music* were
born and life was filled with melodies you
didn't have to bang your head against the
wall to keep time with.

My movie career was on a roll; I went
from *Alias Jesse James* with Rhonda Fleming
to *The Facts of Life* with Lucy Ball, and
from there to *Bachelor in Paradise* with Lana
Turner. Talk about paradise; I wouldn't have
traded places with Saint Peter.

Even with television specials every month
or so, and a trip up north to entertain the
troops in Alaska with Jayne Mansfield — I
asked one group if they'd like to hear her

sing, and they hollered back, "We just like to see her breathe" — I found time to stay home. There was another trip to warmer climates, the Caribbean, but we took Zsa Zsa Gabor along and that's almost all I remember. We had made just a short flight from the States, so she hadn't married anybody on the way.

On our tour, she was a blond sensation with the men at Guantanamo Bay, although she wasn't as big a hit with the other girls in the group, because she'd stolen our makeup man and hairdresser and was holding them hostage until she was finished with the show.

"Hello, dahlings," she called to an audience of thousands of panting men at the base, every Hungarian hair in place, her makeup perfect. I could hear the other girls growling backstage, but it didn't bother Zsa Zsa. She was facing the largest male smorgasbord she had ever seen and made the most of her opportunity. She blew kisses to every one of them and called out, "Are you married? Well, never mind, call me when she's not home!"

There was a howl that rocked Guantanamo and she turned to me and said, "Bob, where are these handsome boys from?"

"Some are Air Force, Zsa Zsa, some Army, those over there are Coast Guard, and those sailors there are off the battleship *Utah*."

"Why are their uniforms wet?"

"It docks tomorrow. . . . Zsa Zsa, I don't know how you do it. You seem to get more beautiful every year."

Of course I knew how she did it. Our makeup man and hairdresser were still missing.

"Dahling, I'm so happy to hear you say that. I was afraid I was losing my touch."

"What gave you that idea?"

"Well, I walked back to my quarters last night and I had the strange feeling I wasn't being followed."

Zsa Zsa was great, so was Anita Bryant, so were Andy Williams and Colonna and the band, but the adrenaline of the shows we did for men in combat was somehow missing. Zsa Zsa supplied a different kind of adrenaline, but you had to be a millionaire to afford it.

After the tour with Zsa Zsa, I needed to relax and took every opportunity to hang around with the family in Toluca Lake. Milton Berle once said that I had four children, two of whom I'd met personally. I felt it was time to learn to relate to human beings who hadn't stood in line to see me. It was tough. I'll never be the typical father, but at least we found out we liked being around one another.

These were pleasant days in politics, and in politics, where monologues are born, Ike was at the peak of his popularity. He had had a rematch with Adlai Stevenson and won by an electoral vote of 457 to 73. The campaign was as exciting as sitting around watching concrete harden.

I knew both Ike and Adlai personally, but I knew Ike better because we played golf together. I could say things like "Ike is all Army. He loves golf, but if you lose, you not only have to pay him, he makes you eat K-rations. . . . And sometimes Ike cooks. I once played nine holes with one of his meatballs."

I think history underestimates Ike the President, in contrast to Ike the general. Eisenhower helped bring the war in Korea to a finish, and we had years of good times in America because there was a strong and honest hand at the controls. In 1958, he sent U.S. marines into Lebanon to restore order, and they did. We didn't realize how much of a miracle that was at the time. It was like telling your mother-in-law to shut up and having her listen. Vietnam was only a minor irritant then, and Ike went along with the established U.S. policy of trying to contain communism by supporting the government in the south.

Ike also had to face the beginning of the Space Age. In 1959, the Russians hit the moon with a rocket, and planted a bowl of borscht. America had to do something fast, but our Pioneer IV moon shot was only partly successful. The rocket stayed down but Cape Canaveral went up. The second shot got off the ground, but it missed the moon and went into orbit around the sun, giving NASA a cosmic headache.

I told my TV audience, "The first stage of that rocket was a Thor. The second stage was a Vanguard. And the third was a five-foot Bufferin. . . . But this is the first time an earthbound object has ever floated in space freed from the forces of gravity. The only thing comparable to it is a woman who has just taken off her girdle. . . ."

When the Russians put their first chimpanzee into space, the chimp did a good job. He was supposed to go around the world three times, and he made it twice. That was pretty good for a pilot who ate bananas with his feet. But America finally put a man in space. Alan Shepard rode a Mercury missile capsule 115 miles above the earth. After Yuri Gagarin and a lot of other Russian cosmonauts, it was nice to have a spaceman whose name we could pronounce. The whole nation got a lift from it. We were now only two years behind the Russians and ten years behind the comic books.

It all proved that Russia's Germans were better than our Germans, but not for long. When Jack Kennedy became President, he promised we would land men on the moon in the next decade. Nobody believed him. But JFK's prediction came true, although, tragically, he wasn't around to see the "Eagle" module land at Tranquility base. But he did live to watch John Glenn orbit the earth three times on his way to Congress. Alan Shepard, who became the fifth man to hit a golf ball on the moon, almost immediately became a guest on my show. One small step for mankind, one giant leap for Buick.

The whole idea of space travel soon became commonplace; the Bomb had made major wars unthinkable except in the movies, the moon landing made us realize we were, in Wendell Willkie's phrase, "one world."

But Khrushchev wasn't quite ready to recognize that fact. During the Eisenhower Administration, the U.N. held an important meeting in New York and invited Khrushchev, Castro, and Nasser to discuss how the world could get rid of people like Khrushchev, Castro, and Nasser. They invited Eisenhower, too, and I couldn't figure out why; he was *elected* to office. I told my TV audience I didn't think it was a good idea to restrict Khrushchev to his hotel while he was in New York. I thought they should let him go out and take his chances in traffic like the rest of us. Castro was very active. He made a speech at the U.N., had two meetings with Khrushchev, and auditioned to be Santa Claus at Macy's. At one time during his visit, Khrushchev tried to send a message home by pigeon. But it didn't work. Castro caught it and cooked it.

By that time, Eisenhower's second term was drawing to a close and his veep, Richard Nixon, won the Republican nomination. But by 1960 the country was swinging away from conservatism, and when the Democrats nominated the young, liberal, and handsome Jack Kennedy, the GOP had a real fight on its hands.

It was going to be tough for me to choose in November. I'd never voted for a candidate with hair.

The television season and the political season started at the same time, so there was plenty of comedy material. I opened our first show saying, "Here I am, starting another season in television. What else can I do, I'm too old to be a candidate. . . . A few months ago Kennedy's mother said, 'You have a choice. Do you want to go to camp this year or run for President?' "

I liked giving youth a chance, but did we really want a President who rode for half fare on the bus?

Nobody paid much attention to Kennedy's choice for vice president, some senator from Texas named Lyndon B. Throttlebottom or something, but it wasn't long before we all knew who Lyndon was. One thousand golden days, and "Camelot" had ended its run, to be replaced by "Dallas."

The 1960 presidential campaign came to a climax with the TV debates between Kennedy and Nixon. Lighting and makeup may have been the deciding factor, just as they kept ruining my chances for an Academy Award. After the first TV debate, one commentator remarked, "Nixon looked for all the world like a man with shaving and perspiration problems, glumly waiting for the commercial to tell him how not to offend."

But it was still a toss-up. Nixon was getting more confident. He went back to shaving only once a day.

In spite of his five-o'clock shadow, Dick Nixon turned the election into one of the tightest in history. He lost the popular vote by a margin of only .3 percent. Talk about close shaves. He might have won if he had used blue blades.

As President, Jack Kennedy became fair game. We laughed about his youth, about the rocking chair he used for his bad back, about Jackie, about his little daughter, Caroline.

"Did you read where Kennedy's asking for two billion more for the budget?" I asked one TV audience. "We expected *some* breakage in the White House, but Caroline's too much."

Kennedy hadn't thrown out Ike's budget; he was using it for petty cash. He started worrying about a recession, so he called the unemployment bureau to get the statistics and they asked him if he could call back. They didn't want to keep General Eisenhower waiting on the line.

JFK enjoyed the ribbing and gave as good as he got, as I've mentioned before. He was one President who could ad-lib with you on equal terms. I never talked to him without idiot cards. After he appointed his brother Bobby to the post of attorney general I kidded him about hiring a relative. Kennedy answered, "Bobby's going into private practice soon. What's wrong with his getting a little on-the-job training at the taxpayers' expense?"

There was some bigger comedy waiting in the wings: "The Bay of Pigs," written and directed by the CIA. A group of Cuban exiles was trained in secret by the Agency and was supposed to land and capture Cuba with 1,500 men. Nobody explained to them you couldn't capture *Bloomingdale's* with 1,500 men, even when it was in receivership. It turned out to be the biggest fiasco since my first screen test. The whole invasion force was wiped out in three days and the CIA retaliated by booby-trapping Castro's cigars. Honest. Just their luck, his lighter didn't work.

After the Bay of Pigs flopped on opening night, everything continued to go wrong with Jack Kennedy's New Frontier. We were still behind in the space race, and there was still trouble in Cuba, Laos, and Vietnam. Nixon was starting to get the feeling he had won. Things got so bad, even Norman Vincent Peale said a discouraging word. For the first time I started to worry if Kennedy had enough hair to last out the job.

JFK was a Harvard man, and to be part of his administration you had to be one hundred percent Ivy League. You couldn't get into the cabinet if your alma mater had ever beaten anybody at football.

Bobby, of course, had gone to Harvard. Jack's kid brother, Teddy, was also a Harvard alumnus, so quite naturally he decided to head for politics, too. Teddy ran for senator from Massachusetts. Imagine a Kennedy willing to start at the bottom.

The Kennedy Administration started to look like "All in the Family."

In 1963, all the Kennedys were in the news. Ted and his wife were expecting their third child; Bobby and Ethel had seven and were expecting their eighth; and the press announced that Jackie was pregnant. It looked like JFK might win the next election without leaving the White House. It just went to show that the President could really get things done when he didn't have to depend on Congress.

I said that it proved what the Republicans had been saying all along: Occasionally, our President was off his rocker. Anyhow, I was glad his back was better. There was talk of redesigning the flag again. Fifty stars and a diaper.

The whole country was happy for the Kennedys, except for some Republicans, who didn't like the idea of another Democrat in the White House.

And then JFK's very Irish luck started to run out. Jackie's baby, Patrick Bouvier Kennedy, died two days after he was born. It was only the first tragedy. In the snake pit that South Vietnam was becoming, Kennedy had at first backed President Diem. Diem's beautiful sister-in-law, Madame Nhu, came to the U.S. on a goodwill tour and instantly became known as the Dragon Lady. I called her Vietnam's answer to Zsa Zsa. She spoke her mind so openly she got more time on television than stomach acid. But you couldn't help liking her. She was tiny and charming and about as fragile as Sonny Liston.

The Dragon Lady returned to Vietnam, and some generals overthrew President Diem and murdered him, along with Madame Nhu's husband, in the back of an armored personnel carrier in Saigon. There was a lot of talk in the United States about what a vicious, primitive society they had in Vietnam.

Then, three weeks later, in the good old U.S. of A., Jack Kennedy drove down a main street in Dallas with Jackie and Governor John Connally of Texas at his side, and ran into sniper fire.

For quite a while, there wasn't anything to be funny about. The lights had blown out in Camelot and the whole nation was stumbling around in the dark.

LBJ was sworn in as the thirty-sixth President of the United States in the cabin of Air Force One and took off for Washington before he could figure out what he was going to do when he landed. Harry Truman had said he felt as if a bale of hay had fallen on him; Johnson must have felt as if he'd been hit by the whole barn.

We all know now this was far from the end of the Kennedy family's bad luck. Some years later, I was in Los Angeles the night Bobby Kennedy won the California Democratic primary for President and was gunned down in the kitchen of the Ambassador Hotel by Sirhan Sirhan, two names that will live in infamy. Dallas had had an unwanted rerun.

It took a long while for the country to get over the tragedy of Jack Kennedy's assassination, but finally LBJ was back in the saddle and political business continued as usual. It became open season again on anyone unfortunate enough to be getting free rent in the White House.

"President Johnson says he wants to get started on his 'Great Society.' I don't know exactly how it's gonna work, but I think he wants Texas to adopt the rest of us. . . .'Great Society' — it's the New Deal, with spurs. . . . "

It was the honeymoon period for LBJ, especially since it was a healing period for the country. The healing got a boost when the Beatles arrived in the U.S. on their first overseas tour. They came from England by plane and were forty pounds overweight, and that was just their hair. They looked like a barbershop quartet that couldn't get waited on. There was a popular movie out that year called *Mr. Ed*, about a horse that could talk, and on television we now had Beatles that could sing. I started thinking of getting out of show business before they started to fumigate. I couldn't believe their first record. To me, it sounded like Yma Sumac and Jerry Colonna on a barbecue spit.

I'm obviously not much of a music critic. What they were singing on that barbecue spit eventually brought them over a billion dollars. The Beatles finally could afford a haircut, got a good look at each other, and split up. But in the meantime, they had changed popular music forever. I think the split between the generations dates from that time: the kids who could understand the new rock music, and their parents who went deaf trying.

I figured the music would drive a lot of people out of their houses and into the movie theaters, so I went back to making films. I did one about the United Nations that starred Adlai Stevenson in a Cary Grant part. At least, that's what I told him to get him into the movie. Stevenson was then our delegate to the U.N. Yasir Arafat had just spoken to the membership and waved a pistol to help make a point. After that, the U.N. made everyone pass through a metal detector if they were going to talk about peace.

Adlai just had to do a cameo in our film, but it was a very tough acting role. He had to walk out of the U.N. building and look as if he was enjoying it.

The picture was called *A Global Affair*, originally titled, *Gidget Dates Dean Rusk*. It featured a dozen international beauties. You remember — where they had to dub in my blood. It was sort of an adult picture. Very adult. The ushers were blindfolded.

About the time the film came out, the Democratic convention of 1964 opened and was dominated by President Johnson. The delegates didn't have tickets. To get in they had to show the LBJ brand, and that wasn't easy when it wasn't on your arm.

The convention nominated LBJ and Hubert Humphrey on the first ballot. I said, "It had all the suspense of a Russian election."

You can tell that's an old line I've had to rewrite several times since I started this book. Gorbachev has ruined all my Russian jokes. I used to be able to get laughs with lines like "They fired Khrushchev because his agricultural plan failed. None of the people he planted came up." No more. Gorbachev has opted for a kinder, gentler Russia. He's made sure of it. He watered down the vodka. Still, as this is written he's having trouble holding the country together. Maybe he should have put an olive in it.

The Republicans nominated Barry Goldwater, and that was good for laughs, too. Barry was the darling of the military because he was in favor of going all out in Vietnam: more planes, more bombs and more Agent Orange. Barry flew his own jet in the campaign. LBJ didn't make speeches at airports because he was afraid Goldwater would land on him. The country wasn't ready yet for Goldwater's hard-line conservatism. The Supreme Court had just gone the other way, banning praying in schools. Now kids were going to have to study to get good grades. I don't understand why they won't let children pray in schools, but they put Bibles in motels. Who has time to pray in a motel?

When LBJ won the election everyone was afraid the Supreme Court wouldn't okay the use of a Bible at the Inauguration.

When Christmas started rolling around again, I got another call from the Department of Defense. There was no chance of getting into Vietnam that year, they were having a little trouble themselves getting out, but all was peace and quiet in the Mediterranean around Italy, Sicily, Greece, and would I go? I wasn't too enthusiastic until I realized that Turkey was the land of exotic belly-dancers, half-naked harems, and tasty halvah. I agreed to do it. A fellow can never get too much halvah.

We put a great troupe together: Tuesday Weld, Anita Bryant, the Earl Twins, Michele Metrinko, who was that year's Miss U.S.A., a fine actor named Peter Leeds, and John Bubbles, of the famous black dance team of Buck and Bubbles; and of course Colonna and Les Brown.

And then everything began to go wrong. I became a casualty. After all the close calls I'd had on unfriendly foreign shores, I was ambushed five blocks from home. I started seeing double on the golf course at Lakeside, and with my golf score, once is enough. The story got out that I might lose my sight, and I suddenly discovered how many real friends I had. I was swamped with sympathetic mail, and among the letters, an offer from an ex-marine to give me one of his eyes. I still haven't gotten over that one. Of course, by that time in life I could have used other replacement parts, but nobody offered any of *them*. It reminds me of a line in *Same Time, Next Year*. A married woman is spending a weekend with her lover and he asks her how good her husband is in bed. She tells him, sadly, "When I married a public accountant, I always thought his *eyes* would be the first to go."

My eye problem couldn't have begun at a worse time. I couldn't take time out for anything as foolish as my health. It was the first time anything like that had happened to me, and I've been playing golf since guys signed their score cards with a feather. If they threw me into a hospital I would have to go over the wall, dragging my I.V. bottle behind me so I could join the Gypsies.

By the time I got to my eye doctor, the whole world looked like a split screen. Dr. Biegelman, my Beverly Hills ophthalmologist, stared into my eyes for five minutes. If a girl does that, you usually expect her to blow in your ear and invite you up to her room. What Doc Biegelman did was invite me to get on a plane immediately for New York.

"This is a job for Dr. Reese at Columbia Presbyterian," he said. He didn't blow in my ear once.

When I arrived in New York, Dr. Reese stared into my eyes for five minutes and said, "This is a job for Dr. Pischel at Stanford University. Get on a plane for San Francisco."

I could have gotten a better diagnosis from my travel agent. Larry Gelbart once told me he was having a suit fitted by Dick Carroll, who runs one of the famous men's stores in Beverly Hills, when Larry mentioned he was going into the hospital for some minor surgery. Dick asked to hear all his symptoms and told him he was crazy to go through with the operation. Larry said, "Do you mind if I get a second opinion from Mr. Guy?"

I guess word of my problem got in the papers, because as I was spending an uneasy night at Columbia Presbyterian before leaving on the plane for San Francisco, the night nurse woke me up and handed me a quart of vanilla ice cream. There was a note on it, "The dogs wouldn't let us in. Get better. The Boys." I was so touched I almost offered the nurse some of the ice cream.

When I arrived at Stanford, Dr. Pischel examined me carefully and said, "You'll have to check into Children's Hospital."

I couldn't figure out what part of me he had been examining, but before I could get insulted he explained Children's Hospital had the latest equipment for the treatment of detached retinas. Something called the Schrecker Beam. The laser beam was too powerful. I was to be Schreckered the next morning, at Children's. I sent out for a pair of Dr. Dentons and went over to the hospital.

I didn't sleep much. The cast and crew were getting ready to take off for Turkey. The doctor had warned me that if I tried to join them, I might wind up as the white Stevie Wonder. I knew I didn't have the voice for it.

Doctor Pischel and his crew Schreckered me the next day. They lock your head in a vise and clamp your eyes open, then they aim the bright, electronic Schrecker beam at you. It reminded me of the scene where Dr. Frankenstein creates the Monster. When it was over, I expected to see Boris Karloff bending over me, complaining like Durante, "Everybody wantsa get into da act!"

When you start breathing again, they put two sandbags on your head to hold it still. Did you ever lie on your back with sandbags on your head and a bandage over your eyes for two days? It's like living in Pacoima.

Later, I had one more shot of Schrecker, and then the doctor told me, "Your eye is going to be all right. You can go to Palm Springs now."

"No, I can't!" I told him, "I've already got a tan! I have to be in Turkey tomorrow — I've missed one show already!"

He stared at me as if I were crazy.

"You can't go to Turkey in this condition," he said. "You shouldn't have any excitement or any rapid movement!"

"I won't even touch the halvah," I promised him, "but I have to go. I'll fly SAS direct to Copenhagen, and an Air Force plane will pick me up and take me right to the air base at Ankara."

"Are you crazy?"

"Listen, all I'll do is walk out on the stage and show the guys I'm there."

"It's on your head," he said.

"Better than two sandbags," I told him.

I went, trying to hold my head still all the way. SAS over the pole to Copenhagen, military transport to Ankara. The Air Force asked Sil Caranchini, our associate producer, if he could hold that day's show from two o'clock in the afternoon to 6 P.M., in the hope that I'd get there in time at least to take a bow.

When Sil and Johnny Pawlek, our audio guy, got a look at me when I dragged myself off the plane, they rushed me to the hotel and told me to sack out for a couple of hours; I think they planned to carry me onstage and prop me up with a microphone up my jacket. At least I think that's where they were going to put it.

At six o'clock, Jerry Colonna went on in my place. I tried to get out there on time, but couldn't. The cast was twenty minutes into the performance when I finally got onstage. If I thought I'd gotten an electric jolt from the Schrecker, it was nothing to the million volts I felt when I heard that yell from six thousand lonely guys gathered in an old Turkish trolley-car barn.

I went into the monologue I had memorized because I knew I wouldn't be able to read idiot cards for a long time.

"I'm happy to see so many of you here today. As a matter of fact, I'm happy to see *anybody*. . . ."

They cheered. Another million volts.

"After I got to Ankara this morning, I visited twelve mosques. Not that I'm so religious, I'm just trying to get my shoes back. . . . And I smoked my first Turkish cigarette. It's part of basic training here, I understand. Talk about stunting your growth — I took a second drag and had to reach up for the ashtray. . . ."

They were laughing. That's much better than cheering.

"And for lunch today we had some of the famous shish kebab. That's a meat popsicle. . . . It's an ingenious dish. When the meat's tough, you have a stick to poke it down."

More laughs.

I felt I could go on for hours, and I would have, but my gang wouldn't let me. I called everybody out for another bow, and that night I sacked out happily, still hearing those laughs. What a lullaby.

From Ankara we went on to the air base

we shared with the Turks at Incirli. You probably never heard of Incirli, because it was a well-kept secret until a pilot named Francis Gary Powers flew a U-2 spy plane from there over Russia, and unfortunately got shot down. Ike was President at the time and denied the whole thing. The United States would never — horrors! — spy on our wartime allies, the Russians. Then Gary Powers blew the whole scam by being alive. Eisenhower had to apologize by sending Khrushchev free tickets to Disneyland.

There were Turkish troops mixed with the Americans at Incirli and by this time I was feeling well enough to speak their language. Well, sort of. I said it was wonderful working at bases with exotic names like Karamursel, Incirli, and Diyarbakir. In case of war, I hoped we didn't have a phone operator who stuttered. Even the Turks laughed, whether they understood the jokes or not. That's the kind of audience I respect.

My eye was feeling so good, I went on the whole tour after that, Crete, Athens, Naples, and the aircraft carrier *Shangri La*, which I called the U.S.S. *Crapgame*. I never saw such action. In the mess hall, even the sugar cubes had numbers on them. And I've never seen a chaplain wearing a green eyeshade before.

By the time we got to the big auditorium in Naples, I decided to ignore the doctor's orders completely. I had to test the job he'd done before the guarantee was up. I went to John Bubbles and dared him to go out onstage and do a challenge dance with me. John had played the Palace, done a command performance for George VI, and George Gershwin had created the role of Sportin' Life for him in *Porgy and Bess*, so you know he was no slouch as a dancer. When we got out onstage, I started throwing ad-lib steps at him and he never missed a beat. Neither did I. I kept going faster and faster. When we finished he was puffing hard. "Man," he said, "You're crazy! You musta done five finishes! Let's forget the fancy stuff next time. You may be auditioning, but I'm established."

It looked like the eye was okay. Another victory for Medicare.

The challenge dance played even better in the hospitals in the Mediterranean area, where even Tuesday Weld showed up when she didn't have to. For the first time in her carefree life, she realized there was more to the week than Tuesday. She discovered she really did care about other people.

When I got home I found all those letters from people who cared about me, including the marine who wanted to give me that Christmas present. His eye.

He had added a postscript:

"P.S. Would it be possible to get an autographed picture of you? If so, how much would it cost?"

I sent him my picture.

I didn't charge for it.

I was healthy again. And just in time. We got another message from the Pentagon.

Our next gig would be Vietnam.

CHAPTER EIGHT

1964-1974

"This is my ninth trip to Vietnam,
and my last. It has to
be. . . . The chicken with my
blood type died."
— *Tan Son Nhut air base,
Christmas, 1972*

I know I've been accused of being a hawk
about the Vietnam war; but I was only a
hawk when there was a chance that we could
win and get out of Vietnam quickly. To
win we would have to use the full military
power of the United States; I knew if we
didn't, a lot of the guys laughing at the
jokes would soon, needlessly, stop laughing.

There are some cynics who say I never
met a war I didn't like. They're the ones
who haven't smelled it close up, in the hospital wards. It's also said I never discussed
Vietnam with anyone below the rank of five-
star general. That's not true. Every time I
walked out on a stage, I was face-to-face

with the kids who were doing the actual fighting. Their cheering and whistling told me one thing: They were very much alive and preferred to stay that way. I was only interested in doing what I could to see that most of them did just that.

Politics didn't matter to me. I never saw a 75mm shell wearing a Willkie button.

Toward the end in 'Nam, when the G.I.'s at Lai Khe started booing the jokes, I knew it was finished. This wasn't vaudeville, where you could always get a laugh by taking a pratfall. America had just taken a big one, and no one was laughing. It wasn't World War II, either, where we could proudly insist on unconditional surrender from Adolf & Co. There wasn't going to be any surrender in Vietnam. We had to get our men and women home any way we could, and pretend we won. It was years later before we could bring ourselves to face what happened. Hollywood went from John Wayne and *The Green Berets* to Oliver Stone and *Born on the Fourth of July*.

We slipped into the whole mess in 1954, almost by accident. Rocky Marciano had kayoed Ezzard Charles, everybody was dancing the mambo, hamburger had skyrocketed to forty cents a pound, Ike Eisenhower was at the height of his popularity, and I had just made a film called *Casanova's Big Night*, in which I played the world's greatest lover, so you could see that America would stand for anything. In that mood, Ike thought it wouldn't do any harm to send a few "observers" over to Southeast Asia. The Communists in North Vietnam were trying to take over South Vietnam, and having just been through that song and dance in Korea, Ike was getting tired of reruns.

Vietnam had been a problem over the years. First the Japanese, then the French, had occupied the country, and been driven out. Eisenhower thought the Communists could be stopped easily with a little good old American know-how. So he sent in the CIA.

That was like sending your Aunt Emma to seduce Ivan the Terrible.

The agency secretly stationed undercover units in Saigon and went to work. Among their more daring operations, they loused up the oil for the Saigon buses so they stopped running, and they hired astrologers to predict hard times in the North and good times in the South. This was supposed to encourage the Communists in North Vietnam to become capitalists in South Vietnam. However, since the buses in the South weren't running, they couldn't get there.

If history had gotten any funnier, I might

have had to go to work for a living.

When Jack Kennedy took over from Ike, he followed the lead of every American President since FDR when he said, "South Vietnam is the finger in the dike against the red tide of communism." He didn't know that one day the North Vietnamese would overrun the dike and give us the finger. During his administration, Kennedy sent more "advisers" to put out the little brushfire war. By 1962, we had over nine thousand personnel in Vietnam, supposedly "advising" the ARVN, the Army of the Republic of South Vietnam. In some of our later Christmas shows, I could always get a howl from our troops when I opened with "Greetings, advisers!"

The American public didn't pay much attention to what was going on in those days. There never was a declaration of war. The closest our government came to it was in 1963, when they finally invited the Hope Gypsies to go over. We were all in a hurry to do our bit. We were afraid the North Vietnamese might surrender before our group had a chance to give them an excuse. We didn't know this was the start of the longest vaudeville tour since Sarah Bernhardt made fourteen farewell appearances.

For our first Christmas show from Vietnam,

we got together Lana Turner, Janis Paige, Anita Bryant, Colonna, Les Brown and the band, and the new Miss U.S.A., Amedee Chabot. Zsa Zsa wanted to come but she was either on a honeymoon, or getting engaged, or filing for divorce, I forget which. I was sorry she couldn't make it, because since our last trip together I'd put together a whole routine. I was going to introduce her and say "Zsa Zsa got married again. I think that's great. Everybody should have a hobby. . . . This time she wanted to do it Saturday morning so if it didn't work out, she wouldn't blow the whole weekend. . . . When it came time for the wedding march, Zsa Zsa tapped the organist on the shoulder and said, 'Play it again, Sam. . . .' This is her seventh, I think. Her towels are marked 'Hers' and 'What's his name.' "

Zsa Zsa laughs at all the jokes; she is not only beautiful but smart, and she knows she survives on publicity; she doesn't care, as long as the newspapers spell her name right. Her first name, that is — even Zsa Zsa can't remember what her last name is at any given moment.

The rest of us boarded a MATS (Military Air Transport Service) cargo jet in California and headed for that little disagreement in 'Nam. Three hours out over the Pacific, we were suddenly jolted out of our complacency. The Defense Department radioed the plane and canceled all our shows. The little brushfire was too much for the South Vietnamese army. U.S. helicopters had to be ordered into the battle zones for the first time, roaring in over the treetops to transport ARVN troops to the front lines. The Viet Cong (the VC, who were the Communist forces of South Vietnam; the Communist North Vietnamese Army was known as the NVA) were battling back furiously, and Washington felt a group our size — and with our tremendous talent — would draw so many soldiers, we'd all become an obvious target. Of course, we had drawn larger audiences from Sicily to Korea, and no one had worried; but this was our introduction to a new kind of war, where there really wasn't any front line. The enemy could be anybody. Even children might be "Charlies" — after the military shorthand for VC, "Victor Charlie."

Trying to defeat Charlie by normal means, one of our generals later said, was like trying to sink a floating cork with a sledgehammer. It just kept bobbing back up.

After we were canceled, the Hope Gypsies were detoured to Japan, Korea, Taiwan, Okinawa, Guam, and the Philippines. No use wasting all that aviation fuel by letting us go home.

Tokyo was a revelation. Wherever we looked, new skyscrapers were going up. All the matchstick buildings that had burned to the ground in World War II were being replaced by a reasonable facsimile of midtown Manhattan. I felt a little twinge the other day when the Sony Corporation bought Harry Cohn's old movie company, Columbia Pictures. Columbia's logo on the front of every film is still the Statue of Liberty. I didn't know that was for sale.

We spent two days gypsying all over Japan by helicopter. Tachikawa air base, the Iwakuni marine base, and the Atsugi naval base, all occupied by U.S. troops. When we withdrew our forces from Japan some years later, we ordered the Japanese not to build up their army and navy again. So the poor Japanese government had nothing to spend its yen on except new automobile and television factories.

Some years later, I could tell the G.I.'s, "We defeated the Japanese into prosperity. The next war we've got to lose. . . . Some people are saying that if the Japanese continue the way they're going, they'll buy the world. They don't have to worry. Fortunately, Donald Trump won't sell."

After leaving Japan, the Hope Gypsies flew off for another visit to Korea, which was an entirely different story. No new skyscrapers. No old skyscrapers, either. Nothing much had changed since our last visit except the temperature. The snow had melted and Korea was now one big mud puddle. I had to change all my cue cards from, "It gets so cold here they use brass monkeys as hand warmers," to, "We stepped off the plane into mud so deep, only Lana Turner didn't need water wings."

We played mainly to Air Force personnel and some Army personnel who had come from as far away as Pusan, Unsen, and Taegu. Lana was the big hit. Just having her there was enough for most of the men, but I still put her to work as my straight man.

"Bob, if you're an officer like you said and I have to polish your shoes every night . . . why don't you wear a uniform?"

"Well, Lana, I don't want this to get around, but I'm with Central Intelligence."

"Oh? What are you investigating?"

"You."

We held our annual Christmas Eve dinner for the cast and crew late on night in Seoul. Onnie Morrow, our production girl, had heard that a Salvation Army warehouse had burned down, destroying a tremendous amount of clothing intended for Korean war orphans. We all played Santa Claus when Onnie passed the hat. It made it a better Christmas for everyone. It was a small gesture, but later when we returned to Uncle Sugar we received a wonderful letter of thanks, signed by all the kids.

There was still a little mud on it.

On Christmas morning, we got a surprise, and it hadn't come down the chimney. The Korean War was long over and a cease-fire was in effect, but North and South were still divided — as they are to this day — by a demilitarized zone. I had wanted to get up to Panmunjom, truce headquarters on the 38th Parallel, to see if the U.N. needed my diplomatic skills. Finally our special badges and passes came through and we flew north in an American helicopter that zigged and zagged all the way up. I couldn't figure out why, until the pilot explained he had to follow the white line in the middle of the highway; if we had to make an emergency landing, the fields on both sides of the road were mined.

I advised him not to make an emergency landing. My goose pimples were pooped.

At U.N. headquarters, which was surrounded by barbed wire, we were shown one revealing item: the North Korean flagpole. It was one quarter inch higher than the United Nations flagpole. The North Koreans had insisted on it, for the same reason, I suppose, that my agent, Doc Shurr, used to wear Adler elevator shoes. Well, not exactly the same reason. Doc wore them so his eyes would come up above the neckline of the tall girls he dated. He liked to see what he was getting into.

We started to walk back and forth across the line that marked the exact middle of the demilitarized zone, like kids stepping on a crack in the sidewalk to see if the sky would fall. Two Red sentries started down the hill toward us. I quickly told a few Khrushchev jokes, and they retreated. The sentries were followed by a Czech general with a dozen medals on his chest. I was about to execute a snappy about-face when he called out in English for us to stop. I stopped. It turned out all he wanted to do was shake hands.

The general seemed so friendly, I asked him if we could take a look at their sentry box. That ended our peace conference. He turned and went back to Czechoslovakia.

There was a small Christmas tree nearby that had been decorated and lit by the U.N. troops. The North Koreans had said it was a capitalist symbol (I guess they thought

Christmas was invented by Macy's) and asked that it be removed. The U.N. had refused and it was still there, bravely glittering in the Korean mud. Like the flagpole that was a quarter of an inch taller, the battle over the little Christmas tree was another sign of mankind's foolishness.

We proceeded to island-hop home by way of Taiwan, Guam, Okinawa, and the Philippines, where we visited a Negrito village where the fierce native fighters, carrying spears and blowguns, paraded for us wearing nothing but loincloths. One optimist tried to get Lana to try on one of their uniforms, but she wouldn't listen to me.

Some of the men we played to were litter patients back from the fighting in 'Nam, the first evidence we had seen of what was really going on over there. They didn't look like "advisers," but we still weren't very concerned. It would be over soon, wouldn't it? What was more important to our audiences was that the Dodgers had just moved from Brooklyn to Los Angeles. Now L.A. had both the Dodgers and the Angels. With the traffic, you had to be one or the other.

The laughs came easily, but we did so many shows we were all pretty well worn out by the time we were ready to head home for a Happy New Year. As we were about to board our C-135 jet for the U.S., the project officer, Major Ed Swinney, whispered to me that the starter on the Number Four engine was broken, and that they would have to transfer the starter from engine number one to get it going. He was telling me because he didn't want to upset the others. He did the right thing. He knew I would get upset enough for all of us.

We finally managed to take off and found ourselves flying in the teeth of a tremendous storm. We caromed among the thunderheads all the way back across the Pacific and I started to turn green. I felt like George Bush going to meet Gorbachev off Malta. I wasn't too happy about the way things had been going, anyway. We had started out to be the first troupe into Vietnam, and wound up playing for the blowgun-and-poisoned dart battalion. My biggest thrill came when I was made an honorary pygmy. By the time we landed in Los Angeles, where some of the airsick cast and crew were held up for two and a half hours in customs, I was weary enough to pop off to the press at the airport.

But later, in the car riding home to Toluca Lake, I remembered our last show in Okinawa. The audience had been filled with patients off the ambulance planes from 'Nam.

When I looked down at the first row, I noticed one of the guys laughing at some joke I was telling. That wasn't unusual. Except that he was getting a plasma transfusion at the same time.

The memory quickly stopped my complaints.

After we were home, the Vietnam situation changed quickly. Just before the political conventions of 1964, North Vietnamese P.T. boats were reported to have attacked the U.S. destroyer *Maddox* in the Gulf of Tonkin off the Vietnamese coast. President Johnson authorized U.S. jets to bomb the P.T. boat bases, and Congress approved. The mood of the country was solidly behind LBJ, and he won a landslide victory over Barry Goldwater.

During the campaign I said, "There's no animosity between the candidates, but if Johnson wins, I hope Arizona enjoys being a part of Mexico. . . . Before he went into politics, Lyndon ran a little ranch; he called it 'Texas.' . . . You can tell he used to be a rancher. He squeezes Republicans like he's milking a cow. . . ."

LBJ was determined to be a strong and forceful President and teach the Vietnamese Communists a lesson, without interference from Congress or anyone else. Under his orders, what had started as a little exercise for the CIA to give Saigon buses a fast oil change became a shooting war for the United States. Undeclared, so Congress couldn't stop it. But using real, undeclared bullets.

Once they were certain we could get killed, the powers that be told the Hope Gypsies to start packing again. This time we were promised it was no false alarm; we were finally headed for our first Christmas show from Vietnam. The Defense Department also told me they were hoping it would be my last. I believe they meant the war would be finished before the next Christmas, but thinking it over, I'm not sure. There are a lot of wiseguys in Washington.

I made certain we had enough ammunition. We brought along Ann Sydney, who was that year's Miss World, our old friends Anita Bryant and Janis Paige, Peter Leeds again to help in the sketches, Anna Maria Alberghetti to sing "White Christmas," and Jill St. John just to stand there. As for Colonna, I always had to plead with him to make a trip to a battle zone. I'd phone him and say, "Hello, Stash?" And he would say, "I'm packed." The same goes for Les Brown and his Band of Renown. They seemed to enjoy it.

We kept our geniuses in the baggage compartment: Mort Lachman, Bill Larkin, Charlie Lee, and an old typewriter. It was Charlie who later suggested, when the crew served us our box lunches, that we hijack the plane and fly it to a delicatessen.

Lighthearted and ignorant, we took off from March Field never realizing this was the beginning of an annual television event that would last for more than a decade of American history and create a little of its own. There were eighty of us. Our transport was a C-141 Starlifter, which could carry an incredible 47,000 pounds, almost enough to lift my idiot cards. No wonder. It had six engines and a truss.

Our destination in Vietnam was kept secret, even from us. We didn't know what kind of a war it was, how many troops we had over there, or how tough the fighting might be.

The enemy? We only had a fragmentary idea of what Charlie was like, and why he kept fighting. We also didn't know how many Charlies there were, and how well equipped and determined they were. In that respect, I found we had a lot in common with the Pentagon and U.S. intelligence. We were all flying blind.

It was to be a strange war, a war without victory or victory parades. Nobody marched into a conquered city with banners flying and bugles playing. We weren't fighting the war to end all wars. We had already fought that one several times.

In Vietnam, the front lines never really moved very far. The best most units could achieve was a change of mud. We found ourselves playing the same bases year after year and the jokes started to have a familiar ring:

"I'm happy to be here at Cu Chi" — or Cam Ranh Bay or Da Nang. "This place has changed hands more times than Liz Taylor. . . . I was here last year and I had to come back. It's mating time for my scorpion. . . . When I played here two years ago, the Cong had the best seats. I held out my hand to see if it was steady and Ho Chi Minh shook it."

On that first Christmas tour, we quickly discovered the war was not somewhere on a distant front; the front was sometimes behind us, sometimes in front of us, and sometimes to the right or left. Once in a while, so we wouldn't get bored, *we* were the front. The girls often had to put on their costumes in armored personnel carriers and be driven to the stage under armed escort. Even in Korea during the worst of the shooting, we had never seen anything like that. It was a tip-off to the kind of war our soldiers had been ordered to fight: a war where the object was not to gain territory, but to destroy the enemy by attrition.

The problem was, attrition worked both ways. Body count became a mutual pastime.

On our first trip we made a short stop to get in the mood. We touched down for twenty-four hours in familiar territory: Korea. This time it really was a white Christmas; snow everywhere, falling so thickly it forced down one of our helicopters. We men could all bundle up in our parkas, but the girls had to go onstage wearing sleeveless gowns, while the snow swirled around them. A few of the girls wound up with extremely frozen assets. I worked in a coat, a hat, and long johns. I didn't know which trap to open and which trap to shut.

I told our soldiers, who gathered by the thousands in spite of the snow, "This is my fifth trip to Korea. The first four times, I didn't believe it. . . . I asked Secretary of Defense McNamara if I can go to Vietnam this year, and his answer was, 'Why not? We've tried everything else.' "

That was the first mention of our country's growing frustration in 'Nam, but it was only a joke then. Most of the officers we met assured us that next Christmas, all of our troops would be home.

After Korea, we thawed out in the warmth

and color of Bangkok, where we were wined and dined by a king who did most of his ruling while playing the saxophone. King Bhumibol had been born at Harvard, while his father was a student there. Presumably his mother was in the neighborhood, too. Being born in the U.S. made him eligible to be President of the United States, but he was looking for a steadier job. Bhumibol became king of Thailand when it was still called Siam. He was two years old and they had to put the royal crest on his diapers. The king was educated in Switzerland and France, where he became interested in American jazz, and when we met him he was nineteen, a teenage king with a teenage queen. She was beautiful. I could understand why, for the first time in history, a king of Siam renounced polygamy and limited himself to one wife instead of the six to which he was entitled. It gave him time to practice his saxophone. But I don't think Yul Brynner ever forgave him.

Thailand became a staging area for U.S. forces, with huge air bases for American B-52's. But they weren't allowed to do much actual bombing. Stuart Symington was with us on the trip and said, "I'm disgusted. They're using a two-million-dollar plane to bomb a five-dollar bridge."

As Brynner put it in *The King and I*, it was indeed a puzzlement. We couldn't figure it out, so we just went on with the show.

"Here we are, at Camp Usarthai in Korat, Thailand, which is located between Laos, Burma, Malaya, and Cambodia. Or, to put it another way, we're lost. . . . We just got here from Bangkok by following a river. That place has more rivers and canals than we've ever seen. Families use every inch of them. On washday the whole city looks like an open-air laundromat."

When we returned to Bangkok, our two project officers, Colonel "Red" Beasley and Colonel Larry Glaab, told us that our upcoming schedule in Vietnam was being changed to confuse the Viet Cong, who might want to make international headlines by attending our performances. We were to fly secretly direct to Saigon the next morning, and they didn't want the VC to know where we were billeted or where we were going from there. The two officers gave me a revised itinerary, which they told me to be careful not to show to anyone. Bangkok had more spies in it than a BBC miniseries.

That night, our entire cast and crew — eighty, count 'em, eighty — were invited for dinner at the royal palace. The king got into a saxophone jam session with Les Brown, and the king's orchestra promptly came out of the bushes, where they apparently waited, and they all didn't run out of jam until the wee hours of the morning. All night long there were wine and music and dancing girls. I hate to think any of the girls was a spy. I prefer to believe the prettiest ones found me irresistible. I don't think they went through my pockets while we were dancing, but I doubt if I would have noticed. Even if I had, I probably would have taken it as a compliment.

So after all these years, I finally got a chance to play the Palace again, and I may have played second banana to Mata Hari.

The next morning, we took off for never-never land. Our transport flew out over the Gulf of Thailand to avoid crossing neutral Cambodia, and headed into Vietnam over the Mekong River delta. Suddenly, a fighter escort appeared to lead us to Bien Hoa, on the outskirts of Saigon, where we were scheduled to give our first show. We went into a steep dive that had my ears hollering "Uncle!" but the idea was to get on the ground before enemy gunners zeroed in and assisted our landing. We realized then that this war had new rules; there was no way we could be completely protected in this insane country. The VC were everywhere.

The Bien Hoa airport was littered with wrecked and burned-out B-52's. The Cong had staged a mortar attack a few days earlier. The runway was torn up more than the back nine at Lakeside when I forgot to replace my divots. The smell of cordite and uncertainty was in the air, and it wasn't very reassuring when our hosts insisted every member of the cast should have an armed escort. Wherever we moved we had to be in convoy, with armed drivers in every car. And remember, this was at an *American* base. We were told that terrorists were everyplace, bombing, sniping, hiding in crowds. The Cong could attack and escape quickly because half the Vietnamese were on their side. The other half were trying to get to the U.S. and open restaurants.

Twenty-three thousand armed G.I.'s were waiting for us when we stepped out on the stage at Bien Hoa. I kept hoping that would be enough.

It was Christmas Eve.

"Hello, advisers!"

A yell.

"Here I am in Bien Hoa. That's Vietnamese for 'Duck!' "

I wasn't kidding. A jeep backfired and I almost dove off the stage.

"We're going to Saigon next and I hope

403

I do as well there as Ambassador Henry Cabot Lodge. He got out."

He certainly did. My old pal Henry had been recalled to Washington. He didn't waste any time before he followed orders. There's a saying in Boston that the Lodges speak only to the Cabots and the Cabots speak only to God. Henry might have gotten information directly from a Higher Command.

"What a welcome I got at the airport. They thought I was a replacement. . . . As we flew in, they gave us a twenty-one-gun salute. Three of them were ours. . . . This is terrible country for a coward. Can you imagine my not knowing which way to run? . . ."

After the show, we were quickly loaded into an Air Force convoy for our trip to downtown Saigon. It was the kind of protection I often wished for on the Hollywood freeway — armored cars, jeeps, and guards with loaded rifles. Just let anybody try to cut in front of us.

We all got very angry at Barney McNulty, who handles the cue cards. He had printed up so many with my ad-libs, we were held up for over ten minutes loading them. Little did Barney know he was saving our lives. He would have asked for overtime.

The convoy finally started out and had to crawl through incredible traffic when we reached the outskirts of Saigon: pedestrians, cars, bicycles, pedicabs, all blowing horns and yelling at the same time, jammed in as far as we could see. This was Asia; even in wartime there was no place to park. It was picturesque, smelly, noisy, frightening, and strangely invigorating. Even so, I couldn't wait to get to our secretly changed billet, the — shh! — Caravelle Hotel, and sack out until peace was declared.

We were driving over the McNamara Bridge when it happened. *BANG!* Smoke and flame shot into the sky ahead. The Vietnamese jamming the roadway around us scarcely looked up. Just another boring day at the office.

I grabbed General Joe Moore, the Air Force commandant of the Saigon region, who was riding with us, and asked if he could book us on the next flight back to Burbank. Word came on our radio that there was a fire at the Brinks Hotel. I nervously asked General Moore where the Brinks Hotel was, and he said, "Just across the street from yours . . . if the street's still there."

Suddenly there was another *BANG!* Our windshield cracked. When I got my face off the floorboards, I spotted a half-naked five-year-old boy running away. He had just thrown a rock at our car with its U.S. Air Force insignia.

It didn't matter to that little kid that American and United Nations troops had been invited in by the Vietnamese government. In his five-year-old mind, he could see with his own eyes that we were round-eyed invaders.

Blue smoke hung in the air when we reached our hotel. All the ground-floor windows were broken, glass and masonry were strewn all over the street. There were fire trucks, people shouting, and a big hole in front of the Brinks Hotel, which had been bachelor officers' quarters (BOQ), housing some 125 people. Now every room had a southern exposure. The walls had been blown out. So had some of the bachelors.

Later, General William Westmoreland, the U.S. commander in Vietnam, told me that a disguised Viet Cong truck loaded with three hundred pounds of TNT had driven up in front of the Brinks just before we were scheduled to check into the Caravelle across the street.

"You were lucky," General Westmoreland told me, "how come you were ten minutes late?"

I swallowed hard and said, "I had to wait for my laughs." And then I kissed Barney

McNulty, who looked at me suspiciously. But I didn't care. Luck, I thought, my blind luck had held again. My Saint Christopher medal must have been working overtime. I always carry it right next to the mezuzah Barney Dean once gave me. I like to cover all bets.

It wasn't until 1967 that I learned the truth. I received a letter from the II Field Force in Vietnam:

Dear Bob:

A few minutes ago I read a translation of a document we captured several days ago, in which the VC were pointing out their weaknesses in conducting successful terrorist activities in cities. This quote should interest you: "Attack on Brinks BOQ missed Bob Hope by ten minutes due to faulty timing devices."

I'm *not* kidding.

Sincerely,
Lt. Gen. Jonathan O. Seaman

Some Charlie probably got bawled out for not blowing up my cue cards. I didn't feel a bit sorry for him.

It was one hell of a strange war if they had started to target comedians.

I couldn't figure out how the VC had known exactly what time I was to arrive, unless one of the dancing girls in Bangkok had slipped that itinerary out of my pocket. I decided to stop being so irresistible.

This was only one incident in a war where the walls had ears, in addition to scorpions, lizards, spiders, and red ants. "Hanoi Hannah" was the name the G.I.'s gave to a girl who broadcast to our troops from Radio Hanoi, much like Tokyo Rose in World War II. Hannah took special pleasure in telling our soldiers anything our brass considered top secret. Several times she told the Hope Gypsies where they would be appearing next, before we had been informed ourselves. Our soldiers used to listen to her broadcasts and then run down to get the best seats. So, we figured, did the VC snipers. We really didn't need all that publicity.

When we finally checked into the Caravelle after that over-enthusiastic welcome and tip-toed through the shattered glass to our rooms, we found the Army's demolition squads had gotten there first and were already searching our luggage. Anita Bryant was taking a shower when the security men barged in and searched her room, finally winding up in the bathroom where Anita had to drape a towel around herself as she tried to convince them she wasn't carrying concealed weapons.

One of the soldiers said, "You're Anita Bryant? I'm from Oklahoma, too. Went to school with your cousin Alfred! Glad to meet you!"

And he shook her hand, happily. Anita barely managed to hold up her towel.

It was only after they left that she remembered she didn't have a cousin Alfred.

Later in the ruined lobby, Colonels Glaab and Beasley told me it might be best to cancel our shows and get us back to Thailand as fast as possible. The danger was too great and the girls were probably too shaken up to continue.

Just then Janice Paige and Jill St. John came running downstairs. They were both terribly upset. We were all due at a Christmas party at Ambassador Maxwell Taylor's, and the girls' gowns and makeup cases hadn't arrived. If the Army didn't deliver them from the plane right away, there was going to be a *real* war.

Now it was the Army's turn to be shaken up. They'd never met *this* kind of trouper before. I think the girls were just trying to keep *my* courage up. But the situation in Saigon that Christmas Eve was serious enough for Ambassador Taylor to cancel his party. Some of us decided to go over anyway. We all sang Christmas carols and told each other lies about how brave we'd been.

Then Garrick Utley, of NBC-TV News, came in, and asked if there was any chance that I could go over to the naval hospital. He'd just received a report that the victims of the Brinks explosion had been taken there.

I grabbed Colonna and Les Brown and we headed out into the unfriendly night.

By the time we got to the hospital, the wards and operating room were swamped. It was "M★A★S★H" for real, with doctors and nurses from every hospital in Saigon. We all trouped into the emergency room. Somebody yelled, "Bob Hope!" and I turned to see a young G.I. raise his head and look at me. He was lying on an operating table while they picked pieces of glass and metal out of his back. He was smiling through the blood that was streaming down his face.

"Merry Christmas, Bob," he said.

I reached out and shook his hand.

"Merry Christmas," I said, finally, when I could talk.

Later, when I got back to the half-ruined Caravelle, a UPI reporter was waiting in the rubble to interview me. We spoke for a while, and then, as we shook hands good-bye, he saw blood on my cuff.

His story made the papers in America the

next morning: "BLOOD ON BOB HOPE'S CUFF ON CHRISTMAS EVE."

True. But it wasn't *my* blood.

I thought that night was over, but some of the crew had heard that Cardinal Francis X. Spellman was going to conduct a midnight Mass in a big field at Tan Son Nhut air base. If the rest of our stay in Vietnam was going to be like this first day, I felt a little prayer wouldn't hurt. I grabbed my Saint Christopher's medal and my mezuzah and Jack Shea, our director, and we went with them. The Army insisted on giving us an armed escort through the treacherous, darkened streets. Or maybe *I* was the one who insisted.

Cardinal Spellman was making one of his last appearances in Vietnam at that Mass, and I should have paid attention, but by that time I was so weary, I kept falling asleep. Jack Shea had to wake me.

A couple of days later I met the cardinal at the airport and apologized. I said, "I'm sorry, but I fell asleep three times during your Christmas service."

He said, "Don't worry about it, Bob. That makes us even. I once caught your act at Loew's State."

Saigon became our base for our tour of Vietnam. It's now called Ho Chi Minh City, but in those days it was Fear Alley. When you walked the narrow, littered streets at night, you would get jumpy at the sound of your own footsteps. Twice I tried to surrender to myself.

Anybody could be a Cong terrorist, an old man, a pretty girl, a little kid with a paper sack. You couldn't tell them from friendly Vietnamese until it was too late. You just had to take the gamble.

That reminds me of another story. A well-known comedy writer who used to work for me always had terrible problems with his wife. One night he woke up to find her sitting on the edge of his bed, playing mumblety-peg with a butcher knife.

"What are you going to do with that knife?" he asked her, nervously.

"Take a chance," she said, "go to sleep."

Saigon is one of the oldest cities in the world, and they had the plumbing in those days to prove it. When the French had occupied it, it was a beautiful colonial town of 400,000, but by 1964 it had become a steaming bouillabaisse of two million people, its population swollen by thousands of refugees and all sorts of military, including the VC.

The city had been playing host to foreign invaders for over a quarter of a century,

412

and a lot of the bar girls spoke Chinese, French, and Japanese. Some of them looked as if they had fought their way through every army, one soldier at a time. Others were young and pretty and existing the only way they could in a country devastated by war.

One of the most popular restaurants was called Cheap Charley's. They didn't have bar girls; if you ordered a drink they let you thumb through an old copy of *Playboy* while the jukebox played "Imagination." There was also a Howard Johnson restaurant, Sears tailors, Hart and Schaffner tailors, and the Texas laundry. The laundry had bar girls who cleaned you out while you waited.

Christmas Day, we went to Tan Son Nhut airfield to do our show. The Air Force had built a stage for us right on the runway, which was jam-packed with servicemen. General Moore looked at the mob scene and told me, "This looks like real Cong bait. Don't take too many bows."

If anybody saw that show, I wasn't bowing, I was looking for the nearest foxhole.

"Thank you, thank you! I want to thank General Westmoreland for that wonderful welcome yesterday. We opened with a bang. . . . General Moore drove me into Saigon, and just as we got to town, a hotel went the other way. I've never seen a house detective in flight before. . . . Incidentally, if there are any Viet Cong in the audience, remember I already got my shots. . . ."

From Ton San Nhut we went on to U.S. bases at Vinh Long and Pleiku. Pleiku was a chopper base high in the mountains, about forty miles east of Cambodia. At night, North Vietnamese army troops slipped down the nearby Ho Chi Minh Trail to link up with the Viet Cong. From dusk to dawn, red tracer bullets whined over the barracks and nearby explosions rocked the area. By this time, there was a growing feeling in the U.S. that we were in the wrong war, and there was already a lot of pressure on Washington to untangle us. Secretary of Defense McNamara had just announced we were soon going to start closing down some of our bases, so I started the show at Pleiku with "What a welcome! Wherever we go, we're met by thousands of cheering servicemen. They think I'm Secretary McNamara with the shutdown orders. . . . One of the bases they closed so fast, they had to reopen to get me out. I was stuck in the nurses' quarters and who needed help?"

I sometimes worried that the bases were being closed too soon. I hated to think that soon the only thing that stood between us and Russia was John Wayne.

The political situation was another problem. South Vietnam was a very democratic country. Too democratic. It seemed that everybody got to be president. And the U.S. was always backing the wrong presidential horse: first Diem, who was assassinated; later Duong Van Minh, who was ousted by General Kanh. Kanh went through the revolving door when he was shoved out by General Nguyen Cao Ky.

I understand that today, General Ky is running a grocery store in Pomona, which he considers a promotion.

Our troops never knew who was in power. Sometimes the new president made his acceptance speech right from the getaway plane. It was a toss-up whether or not the South Vietnamese army, the ARVN, was loyal to whoever was president that day, and could be depended upon for help if the VC launched an attack.

No wonder we got a big laugh at every base from this little exchange with Colonna, who played that great psychiatrist, Professor Sigmund Fraud:

"Tell me, Professor, what are the symptoms of battle fatigue?"

"Well, Hope, under fire, you'll find some men who will turn tail and run. They shake, quiver, and cry."

"Poor wretches. What do you do for them?"

"Nothing. They're the normal ones."

In our troupe the girls did the most to keep up our spirits; they never let the danger get to them, and that went for both the war and all the panting males. The ladies made up a game to bolster their morale; they laid bets on who could steal the most medals from the officers. Anita Bryant, with her innocent baby face, went into an early lead. She batted her eyes at General Westmoreland one night and asked if she could try on one of his cute little decorations. Before he knew what was happening, Anita had pinned it to her bosom and the general never had the guts to try to unpin it.

Jill St. John wasn't quite as lucky. At the officers' club in Da Nang, she walked up to a handsome captain, pointed to a medal on his collar and said, "Oh, what an adorable little medal! What is it, captain?"

The captain answered, "I'm the chaplain, madame, and that is a cross."

When we got back home and the Vietnam Christmas show aired, the American public got its first really good look at the faces of the men and women who were caught up in the fighting over there. Our rating went through the roof. There was such a demand

416

that we were forced to do an additional program using the outtakes from the first one.

"Good evening, ladies and gentlemen. I want you to know our Christmas show had the highest rating in television, and I'd feel very happy about it, except for the fact that it took a bomb to do it. . . . One reason for the tremendous audience was that my life was really in danger. Which only proves one thing: To get a rating, give the public what they want."

By that time, everyone at home was telling President Johnson what to do. Senator Dirksen wanted to step up the war; Senator Morse wanted us to get out immediately; and Defense Secretary McNamara said we should just go in and close down the country.

At that time, a lot of people agreed with McNamara. Charlie had attacked the base at Pleiku a short time after we played there. A two-hundred-man force had managed to infiltrate the perimeter and get close enough to lob mortars onto the barracks. Some of the guys who had laughed so hard at Colonna became names on the Vietnam Memorial.

The U.S. eventually sent over 500,000 men to Vietnam. And officially, we still denied it was a war.

That reminds me of the line in the Broadway musical *Jumbo*, when Jimmy Durante, who has just stolen an elephant from the circus, is tiptoeing across the stage with the huge pachyderm clomping behind him. He's stopped by the sheriff, who demands, "Where are you going with that elephant?"

And Durante, looking as innocent as only Durante could, says, "*What* elephant?"

The elephant that was Vietnam was going to be with us for a long time. We were all hoping that the ARVN, the South Vietnamese army, would become strong enough to take over the fighting and all the American troops could go home. But Christmas after Christmas, the Hope Gypsies kept going back.

Every year, the war kept heating up instead of cooling down. The U.S. was starting to split into two factions, those who wanted us to win at any price, and those who wanted us to get out at any price. If you were of draft age, it wasn't hard to choose sides.

With Joey Heatherton and Kaye Stevens added to our list of moving targets, we went back to Vietnam along with the Christmas carols. From Tan Son Nhut airport in Saigon, we were flown in three Chinook choppers to a base called Dian, in the heart of the jungle war. It didn't do my blood pressure much good when our pilot told us they always traveled in threes because while the VC might get one chopper, they knew the other two would get them. I didn't like those odds; Charlie was batting .300.

Our old friends from the 1st Infantry Division, the Big Red One, were occupying Dian. When we reached the stage they had built for us, we were told, "Be careful. We're not only surrounded by Charlies, there are liable to be some in the audience."

They weren't kidding. They hired civilian crews to work on the base, and there was no way to check them thoroughly. Before we started the show, a sergeant major stepped to the microphone and said, "I want you men to keep the aisle clear on both sides of the stage in case of mortar attack. The left side of the audience will move out to the left and the right side will move out to the right. The cast of 'The Bob Hope Show' will take cover in those foxholes adjacent to the stage." I couldn't see the foxholes from where I was standing, but I wasn't worried. I knew I could dig my own in about five seconds. Without a shovel.

Dian reflected the American buildup. It was jammed with fighting men in battle gear. There was an infantry battalion of a thousand men surrounding the base to intercept the mortars. Four armed helicopters continuously circled the perimeter with orders to shoot anything that moved. With that kind of protection, I could have opened with my original vaudeville act. And taken a bow.

The jungle heat was blistering, but this was Christmas Day. We did our best to remind them.

"In Saigon, Santa Claus doesn't have to slide down the chimney. He just waits and the building goes up. . . . And Christmas dinner is really exciting here. Did you ever stick a fork in a turkey to see if it was going to go off?"

All the troops in this area had their own Christmas displays, but they had to be continuously on their guard. One battalion woke to find their manger scene had four Wise Men.

We flew on to Bien Hoa, where seven thousand men waited for us. Just a year before, there had been only fifteen hundred and the runway had been littered with wrecked planes. Now a truce had been instituted, and it was relatively safe. But the truce was due to expire that night. I cut three jokes out of the monologue before I went on.

Our audience reflected the escalation of the battle. This was turning into a full-scale international war: the 145th Army, the 173rd Airborne Brigade, the Royal Australian Regiment, the 161st New Zealand Artillery Brigade, the Vietnamese air force, ARVN troops of the regular South Vietnamese army, and whatever Cong had managed to sneak in, even though we had announced there would be no passes for this engagement.

The U.S. was still insisting the war was winding down.

"Greetings, advisers!"

What a yell.

"Secretary McNamara just announced he's closing another hundred and forty-nine bases. Anybody at this one like to make it a hundred and fifty?"

There was a roar of approval, and I said, "Not so loud, you'll wake the sentries."

I told them I didn't realize how much the budget needed balancing until I saw McNamara riding in a Hertz Rent-a-Tank. When the Aussies didn't seem to get it, I tried harder. I said it was an *Avis* Rent-a-Tank.

Security hustled us out as soon as the girls had finished their performance, and we flew back to Saigon. I felt they'd been a little hasty until later that night, when we heard that Bien Hoa had been the first place hit after the truce ended. Charlie's mortars had plastered the soccer field where we had done our show just a few hours earlier.

One good thing about that war; it was certainly improving my timing.

When we got back home, we found that the growing casualty lists and the televised news from the battlefronts were having a tremendous effect on popular opinion, especially in the colleges, where political protests usually start, as we recently saw in China and East Germany and Czechoslovakia. Everywhere in the world, students don't seem to mind cutting classes.

There were demonstrators on both sides, with signs like "Get Out of Vietnam!"; "Don't Get Out of Vietnam!"; "Why Don't You Go Back Where You Came From?"; and "I Came From Vietnam, That's Why!" The students calmed down a little when they ran out of matches to burn their draft cards. Later they ran out of draft cards and started burning library cards.

Then they started letting their hair grow long, and it got to be very confusing. I asked one student, "How can you tell the boys from the girls?" And he said, "We can't but we use the honor system." I remembered the good old days when a student would write home, "Dear Dad, I got an 'A' in business management, send money for laundry." Now they were writing, "Flunked picketing. Send bail."

Every year when we went back to Vietnam we found that the mood over there was changing, too. I saw the tremendous concentration of air power the U.S. had in Japan.

If the military had been allowed to use it against the supply lines from Communist China, the war might have ended, but the orders never came. The G.I.'s saw themselves forced to fight on the VC's turf because of international politics, and LBJ found himself caught in the middle. He sent two aides on a special mission to Vietnam to find out if we were winning or losing, and they found out nothing. One of them couldn't find Vietnam and the other one couldn't find Texas.

On one Christmas tour, Dolores and three of the kids decided to go with me. Maybe they didn't believe I really went. I put them all to work on the show, Nora and Kelly and Tony and their mother. It was the first Christmas we'd planned to spend together in a long time, but at the last minute things heated up again on the battle fronts and we had to leave the kids in Bangkok. I could only get permission for Dolores to come to Saigon.

When she sang "White Christmas" to ten thousand battle-weary G.I.'s at Tan Son Nhut on Christmas Eve, I told her, "Sing it good or you go back by bus."

She sang it good.

I told those guys, "This is the first war that's ever been televised home in color. Aren't you G.I.'s nervous? Do you realize that if you don't get a big rating, the sponsor will get sore and the war will be canceled?"

It was the first living-room war, scenes from the battlefields reaching every home in the U.S. almost as soon as they took place. There was no sugarcoating the reality. The protesters in the U.S. were shouting louder now.

The following Christmas, it was back to Vietnam again. This was the first tour Colonna missed. He was never to make another. A chronic illness had brought the Mad Professor who used to holler, "Help! I'm in midair!" down to earth.

That year's Christmas show was memorable because Raquel Welch came with us. I told the soldiers, "I understand that everything you want is either frozen, dehydrated, or off-limits. I faced the same problem when I found out Raquel was a judo expert."

The audiences we played to were veterans now. The war had already lasted as long as America's participation in all of World War II. But the guys still greeted us with all the enthusiasm of new recruits. We still meant Home.

"Yes, here I am in Vietnam again. And you thought there was going to be a truce. . . ."

They laughed, because they knew it wouldn't happen.

Negotiators had gathered in Paris to hammer out some sort of peace settlement, but they were getting nowhere. At one base we were only eight miles from the Mekong River delta and only nine from neutral Laos. If you listened carefully, you could hear the neutral troops carrying the neutral ammunition down the neutral Ho Chi Minh Trail. Neutrality had already become a joke, and soon even the U.S. would disregard it.

In January of 1968, right after we returned home, the U.S. embassy in Saigon was attacked during the bloody Tet offensive that proved the VC were stronger than ever. General Westmoreland was planning a major retaliation, but LBJ recalled him before he could become another Douglas MacArthur and walk back across the Pacific.

The history books will note that this was the year Martin Luther King, Jr., and Bobby Kennedy were assassinated within a month of each other. The home front was in disarray, and we all started suffering from protest fatigue as the presidential campaigns started. Richard Nixon was running for the Republican nomination, and everybody expected LBJ to be the Democratic candidate. The war in Vietnam was the major issue. I said Nixon's solution was simple.

And then came the surprise. On March 31,

Lyndon Johnson went on TV to announce he was halting the bombing of North Vietnam — and withdrawing from the campaign for the presidency. The old cowboy had had enough. The war and the protesters had proved tougher to handle than a pair of maverick steers. Somebody else could have the pleasure of climbing into the blazing saddle that was the presidency.

LBJ had run out of patience, strength, and Valium. The continuing protests and his enemies in Congress, led by Senator William Fulbright, were making it difficult to continue. The sentiment in the country had swung around 180 degrees, and the compass needle was pointing toward the White House exit. I felt sorry for him, because he had been one tough cowhand, full of vigor and energy. He had absolutely floored me once by appearing unannounced to present me with an award at the U.S.O.'s silver anniversary dinner in 1965. He even told a couple of jokes I had been planning to do myself. I wondered if you could sue a President for stealing laughs.

He started out, "Bob Hope is the only frequent visitor to Vietnam who has never been asked to testify before the Senate Foreign Relations Committee. At least, not yet. . . . He was planning to testify until he learned the hearing would be covered by only one network, and in prime time. He refused to go against 'I Love Lucy' without some help.

"Bob, the courageous young men who laugh with you today in Vietnam have fathers who laughed with you from Europe to the South Pacific in World War II. This plaque says, 'Thanks for the memory from a grateful nation.' "

I decided not to sue him. I managed to say, "Thank you, Mr. President," and then was stuck. I had a lot of jokes I was going to do about LBJ before I knew he was going to be there in person. I finally decided to go ahead with them. As I've noted before, a laugh is a laugh, even if you get investigated by the IRS.

"It's nice to be here in Washington, or as the Republicans call it, Camp Runamuck. . . ."

I saw the President staring at me, so I leaned over to him and said, "I have to do that, sir — it's on the paper."

He just kept staring. The audience roared. It took me a moment to realize Lyndon was pulling a Jack Benny, trying to help my jokes. Of course, some of them could use it. I had one I really liked, though. I said LBJ had arranged a wonderful welcome when Mrs. Indira Gandhi, then India's prime minister, had come to Washington. It wasn't easy to get Senator Fulbright to lie on a bed of nails.

The President helped every joke with his reaction. I lost a great straight man when he retired, but that wasn't the only reason I was sorry. He'd had a rough time. One day he went over to the Lincoln Memorial and he looked up at Abe and he said, "You had a war; you had a civil rights problem; you had protesters; what can I do?" There was a pause, and finally a voice said, "Don't go to the theater."

The 1968 election campaign really got under way at the Democratic convention in Chicago, where antiwar demonstrators were roughed up by the police on prime-time television.

"I've been busy this past month entertaining the troops at the Democratic convention. . . . Did you see the Democrats in 'Run for Your Life' or 'How to Blow the White House Without Really Trying?' "

Nixon became the first Republican President elected by a Democratic convention. But LBJ had started a trend when he decided to move out of the Oval Office. Both Nixon and his veep, Spiro Agnew, were to resign before they served out their second terms. After them, Gerald Ford only served about half a term after taking over for Agnew, then for Nixon himself. Presidents and vice presidents were leaving so fast, the White House began to seem like a Tijuana motel. The first thing they asked a new President when he checked in was if he was staying all night.

Our annual Christmas show from Vietnam that year included Rosie Grier, the three-hundred-pound tackle of the Los Angeles Rams. When Rosie walked on the plane we told him, "Just take any three seats you want." He was a one-man security force for the beautiful, sexy Ann-Margret and for Penelope Plummer, the eighteen-year-old blonde from Australia who was that year's Miss World. This was also the first trip for the Golddiggers, a singing-dancing group of twelve girls. I thought twelve might be too many, but somebody pointed out that the ratio of G.I.'s to blondes in Vietnam was about 40,000 to 1. I handed Rosie Grier a baseball bat, and made him an unofficial M.P.

Rosie had a great time when we hit Thailand. They gave him a cut rate at the elephant wash.

One time over 'Nam, a motor on our plane caught fire en route to Bien Hoa. When the pilot told us not to worry, I whiled away the time while counting my rosary beads by telling the story of the Russian airliner that lost an engine on its way to Moscow. The navigator told the passengers, "Comrades, don't worry, we can fly on three motors." Later he told them, "We've lost another motor, but don't worry, we can fly on two motors." Then he came on once more and said, "Comrades, another one just went. Don't be alarmed, we can fly on one motor." When he finished, a comrade in the back of the plane spoke up. "That stupid pilot. If we lose one more motor, we'll be up here all day."

Fortunately, we landed safely in Bien Hoa in time to go on in front of ten thousand men, some of whom had been helicoptered out of combat after drawing straws. The losers had to see the show.

"Everything's fine back home. Nixon captured Washington and Jackie Kennedy got Greece. . . . I know you remember Nixon, Ike's caddy. . . . You know that's pretty exciting. A guy who couldn't make governor of California is going to be President of our country. . . . The bombing halt the President asked for is really working. We flew over the Ho Chi Minh Trail and nothing was moving. It was the biggest traffic jam I ever saw."

That last got the biggest laugh, because the G.I.'s knew it was the truth. All the cease-fires, all the bombing halts, all our government's attempts to get us out of the swamp we had wandered into were failing, because the North Vietnamese refused to behave like gentlemen and lose the war.

The problems of Vietnam didn't go away after Nixon was inaugurated. He brought in Henry Kissinger, who sometimes liked to write his own jokes. "We will not make the same old mistakes," Henry said, "we will make our own." And he wasn't just whistling "Dixie" — if you can whistle that with a German accent. The negotiations in Paris dragged on, the North Vietnamese promising, "We will sit in Paris until the chairs rot."

The G.I.'s knew all about the Paris peace talks; they also knew about the student protests at home. I told them, "Last year the students were burning their draft cards. This year, it's the colleges. When you muster out, keep your rifle. If you want to go to school under the G.I. Bill you may have to recapture one first."

I didn't know that kind of joke would soon stop being funny after the incident at Kent State, when National Guard soldiers fired at student protesters. Comedy was getting tougher the longer the war lasted. A couple of more years and I'd have to go back to tap dancing.

We continued our Christmas tour 'way

down south in the Mekong delta, where we had an unusual performance of *Romeo and Juliet* on an outdoor stage at Dong Tam. In the middle of a romantic love scene where I was playing Romeo to Miss World's Juliet, machine-gun and rocket fire broke out across the river, seemingly aimed in our direction. I didn't even know Shakespeare was in the area. However, it turned out to be VC, and choppers took off to quiet things down. Later, one of the chopper crews sent us a neckerchief with the company crest and a note, "Sorry about the noise. Hope we didn't disturb the show."

What was disturbing was that Charlie refused to go home. He kept insisting he *was* home.

I've kidded about Rosie Grier, but he summed up the mood in Vietnam and in the U.S. that year better than any of us:

"Even though I'm against the war," Rosie said, "I came on this trip because I thought we ought to let the soldiers know that we were not deserting them. The antiwar battle we are fighting at home is not against these soldiers and nurses; it's against the power that sent them here."

By that time, Vietnam veterans were returning home by the thousands and many of them were echoing Rosie's sentiments.

The whole purpose of the war was in question, as well as its legality. It all came to a head the next Christmas, when the Hope Gypsies flew around the world in fifteen days. After doing shows in Berlin, Italy, Turkey, Thailand, and aboard the U.S.S. *Ranger*, we wound up at a remote base in Vietnam known as Lai Khe. I couldn't believe whom we found there. The Big Red One. Our old friends of the 1st Infantry Division were still slugging it out in the same old boondocks.

The division commander, Major General Milloy, welcomed us with "We're real happy to have you with us today. I also want to take particular cognizance of our honored guests, members of November Platoon, of the Sixteenth Infantry. Last night on patrol they intercepted nine VC just seven clicks — that's kilometers to you civilians — from here, emplacing six rockets aimed at this very area. It may well be the show goes on today through their courtesy. Stand up, fellas, let people take a look at you."

I led the applause before starting with the jokes.

"Boy, what a crowd here. I gotta drop a note to the President about this. They told him you were all home. . . . I didn't really expect to be here at all this year. The Paris peace talks were going so well. . . ."

Something was wrong. No laughs. And for the first time, I heard some boos. I'd faced that from civilians all through my vaudeville days. But never from "my kids" in uniform. I didn't know quite what to make of it. I quickly went into some jokes about having had dinner at the White House, and the talk there about cutting the defense budget.

"The fighting is costing entirely too much. Wouldn't it be awful if we ran out of money and they repossessed the war?"

Nothing. The men just sat there and stared at me. There is something in show business called "flop sweat." It's the perspiration that gathers on your face when you're laying an egg. I was drowning in it. But it takes a lot to discourage me. So I plowed on.

"The President told me he has his own plan for ending the war. He's going to have you home before you know it, and then — "

I stopped. The boos had started again, only louder. I realized they weren't booing me or the jokes — at least, that was my own unbiased opinion — but they knew the show was going to be seen at home and it was the only way they had of trying to let the country and the President know how they felt. I found out later they were really in a state of shock; they had been in a firefight that day and lost a lot of friends; and then they had been rushed in to catch my show. Not the ideal warm-up. They were too worn out, too heartsick, and too disillusioned to believe that anyone had a real plan to end the war and get them out of that hot, miserable, rotten jungle.

I guess, in their place, I would have booed me, too.

As we were leaving Lai Khe, one of the worn-out soldiers came up to me and put something in my hand. A Zippo lighter. It wasn't much, but it was all he had.

Some time after the Christmas tour had finished and I was back in Hollywood, I got a call from the two writers who were preparing my next picture, costarring Lucy Ball. It was about a guy who goes to Vietnam to entertain the troops and gets involved with a group of children, both VC and South Vietnamese, and an American nurse who helps them to escape the war down the Mekong River. Sort of an *African Queen* with kids, with me playing a cowardly Humphrey Bogart. I was already dusting off a place on my mantel for the Oscar.

They had just gotten a phone call from the secretary who was typing the script. She couldn't work on it anymore. That day it had been announced that American troops had been ordered to cross the Vietnam border into neutral Cambodia. She didn't want to have any part in a film about the Vietnam War. This war was nothing to make a comedy out of.

The writers said they were quitting, too.

I told them about an incident that had just happened to me. I was outside my hotel in Washington, D.C., putting my golf clubs in my car before heading out to Burning Tree, when a convertible loaded with college kids drove by.

They recognized me. One of them leaned out and called, "Hey, Bob! We're gonna bring them home to *you* next Christmas!"

We scrubbed that picture.

But no one could scrub the war. They didn't bring them home that next Christmas. Or the next, or the next.

Catcher Johnny Bench of the Cincinnati Reds joined us on the Christmas tour of 1970. He was as big a hit at the mike as at the plate. But the symptoms of what was really going on in Vietnam surfaced, in reaction to one joke I did with him.

"It's a great sport, baseball," I told Johnny, "you can spend eight months on grass and not get busted."

It got a roar from the men, but I had no

idea of the roar that was to go up from NBC when they heard it in an advance cut of our show. They insisted I take it out. I hate to lose a laugh, but I also hate to lose a contract. Later, on NBC's "Tonight" show Johnny Carson and I reviewed a lot of the jokes about marijuana that were making the rounds; NBC said Johnny's was a news show, so it was okay. The news that he was doing a news show was news to Johnny. He thought he had been doing a comedy show for the last twenty years or so.

The whole subject of the Vietnam War had become touchy by this time. I told reporters, "Sure, they smoke pot in Vietnam. But it was never a problem until this year. That's because the guys have nothing to do. Before, when soldiers got bored, they said, 'Let's have a drink.' Now they sit around the fire and light up."

I never realized what kind of trouble you can get into by telling the truth. It was Winston Churchill who said, "In wartime, truth is so valuable it must be surrounded by a bodyguard of lies." I didn't want to lie about the guys who were over there, facing death every day. I told the truth about myself, too. "Sure," I said, "I smoked pot when I was in vaudeville. I tried it and it scared me. It made me sexier — and I thought

I was already sexy enough."

In the movie *Beau James*, where I played New York's Mayor Jimmy Walker, I told Paul Douglas, playing a tough politician, that I wanted to tell the voters the truth, and he said, "You give the public too much truth and they'll hate you." For a while after that Christmas show, it looked as if Paul might have been right. And then *New York Times* TV columnist Jack Gould wrote:

Hope told it as he found it: The troops in Vietnam did respond to quips on pot, which even the Pentagon admits is heavily used there, and everyone did want peace and want to come home. More by manner than word, he left no doubt about the war's unpopularity among the troops he encountered. . . .

In the case of the Christmas tour, Hope is not only an entertainer and his trip not just a show in the usual sense. He also doubles as a reporter, a journalist in greasepaint, and the public would seem entitled to share in what he found out. . . . Probing jokes that win a hand often can be intensely revealing of attitudes that should be imparted to those at home. . . .

Thanks, Jack, for that bodyguard of truth.

In 1971 George C. Scott was awarded the Academy Award for *Patton* and refused to accept it. Imagine refusing the Oscar. That's like turning down the male lead in *Deep Throat* because you can't stand drafts.

The U.S. blockaded North Vietnam and mined all its ports. The tremendous explosions that followed knocked three negotiators off their chairs in Paris. But it didn't end the war. So I decided to do it all by myself. I had to. I was running out of jokes like "Da Nang . . . that's Vietnamese for 'I never promised you a rose garden.' "

We were in Da Nang on our umpteenth Christmas tour and were supposed to follow the show by flying out to the U.S.S. *Coral Sea* in the Gulf of Tonkin, but a monsoon came up and we were grounded. This gave me time to think, always a dangerous pastime. And what I thought about was all the letters I was getting asking if there was anything I could do about getting our P.O.W.'s home. Everyone else had failed, and I guess I was the only one left they thought might be stupid enough to try.

In my innocence, through my publicity man, Bill Faith, I arranged to go to Thailand for a secret meeting with our ambassador to Laos, Leonard Unger, who had contacts with the North Vietnamese. That gives you an idea of the kind of war this was. You arranged a secret meeting through a publicity man.

Unger was visiting Bangkok at the time. I flew there and asked for his help. Before I knew what was happening, the ambassador had arranged for me to fly to Vientiane in Laos and meet with Nguyen Van Thanh, the North Vietnamese consul there, who might be able to get me to Hanoi.

Hanoi! A guy could get killed in Hanoi! That was like playing the Apollo Theatre in Harlem without a net! I hadn't asked to go to Hanoi! Not without the 3rd Fleet, the 101st Airborne, and fourteen infantry divisions to scout the territory. Led by Dwight D. Eisenhower and Omar Bradley. *Mrs.* Eisenhower might help, too.

The next thing I knew, I was aboard an unmarked U.S. Army scouting plane, flown by General Evans, head of the U.S. Air Force in Thailand, who carefully changed into civvies before he got into the plane. He explained that if we got shot down, he didn't want the other side to know who he was. I asked what would happen if they knew who *I* was, but he didn't think there was much danger of that. Besides, they didn't regard comedians as the enemy in that area.

We flew an unmarked route into Vientiane, where we were met at the airport by a group of civilians. At least, I thought they were civilians until I recognized one of the guys in street clothes as Admiral John McCain, Jr., chief of the Pacific command, later a senator from Arizona. I knew right away why he was there. His son was a P.O.W. The admiral was present in his unofficial rank of Father, First Class. Probably, so were most of the other "civilians." I felt a chill when I realized what a small straw these big men were grasping at: me.

We drove from the airport to the North Vietnamese consul's house with the Reverend Edward Roffee, a Canadian missionary who was going to interpret for us. The North Vietnamese spoke French.

It was a little house with a wire fence around it and a tiny living room; and into it walked Nguyen Van Thanh, the first North Vietnamese I had ever met who wasn't taking a shot at me. My jitters disappeared when he shook my hand and told me he'd seen all the "Road" pictures and thought Dorothy Lamour was beautiful and Bing Crosby the greatest singer in the world. I didn't disillusion him. After all, maybe Frank Sinatra's flicks didn't play Loew's Hanoi.

When he mentioned his favorite "Road"

was *Road to Singapore*, in which Bing and I befriend a Vietnamese child, I leaped at the opening. "Wouldn't it be wonderful," I said, "if the children of the U.S. could help the children of North Vietnam in exchange for the release of the prisoners? Our kids could raise money to help rebuild homes and schools and hospitals for your kids."

I guess when it comes to children, everyone is a human being. Thanh seemed to like the idea. Soon, over tea and cookies, I was showing him pictures of my grandson Zachary and trying to decide if I wanted to be named secretary of state or director of the IRS by a grateful President.

I decided to settle for dogcatcher when Thanh remarked, "Nixon could get the prisoners freed tomorrow if he would listen to the seven points of our negotiators at the Paris peace talks."

I knew then it was impossible; those points included the unilateral withdrawal of all American and allied troops.

But when we went outside to pose for pictures, I noticed Thanh looking at me, sympathetically.

"Perhaps," he said, "you would like to go to Hanoi and put on a show for American P.O.W.'s?"

My heart jumped. It was a Christmas show

that would do more good than all the others put together.

I shook Nguyen Van Thanh's hand and said, "Have tux, will travel." He smiled.

I never heard from him again.

Back to the real world. Flying aboard a C-130 into Hue, the ancient beleaguered city that was the home of the famous Screaming Eagles, the 101st Airborne, we watched F-4 Phantom jets streak by, strafing the VC on the ground. Smoke was rising from bombed-out vehicles. When we landed, the officers who met us told us that a Cong convoy had just been captured fifteen miles from the show site.

The men were waiting for us. They'd been waiting a long time.

"Merry Christmas! Well, here we are at the home of the 101st Airborne; they've seen more action than a towel girl in a bathhouse."

Laughs. Pretty good audience today.

"Last year our show was interrupted by some shelling; the general said, 'Don't worry about it, Bob. It's outgoing.' I said, 'How can you tell?' And he said, 'Just watch the smile on my face. When it's replaced by my feet, then it's incoming. . . .' "

Lots more laughter.

"The infiltration rate is pretty high here.

If you're sitting next to somebody in black pajamas, move. He's either one of theirs, or he's got a lot to learn about laundry."

Laughs again.

Business as usual.

We finished that tour and went home, and still the fighting and the Paris "peace" talks dragged on. The U.S. was still determined to make sure communism didn't spread to the South; and the North Vietnamese were still determined to find some way to spread it.

A lot of American troops were actually being withdrawn, and more of the fighting was being taken over by South Vietnam's army.

In Washington, the Democratic party headquarters at the Watergate apartment complex was broken into, but nobody paid much attention because we were all looking toward Paris and Hanoi. Richard Nixon and Spiro Agnew were reelected over McGovern and Eagleton by an electoral vote of 521 to 17. Notre Dame couldn't run up that kind of score against the DAR. The country was convinced Nixon was truly trying to end the Vietnam War.

The draft was about to end, but the Hope Gypsies were in for the duration. We hoped that 1972 would be the last year of the fighting and there wouldn't be any need for us, but I couldn't forget the final scene of *All Quiet on the Western Front*. Lew Ayres, playing a German soldier — I guess Erich von Stroheim was busy — is so happy at hearing of the Armistice that ended World War I that he reaches out his hand for a butterfly fluttering over the trenches, and is killed by the last shot of the war.

Fade out.

In the immortal words of Yogi Berra, it ain't over till it's over. Some guys were still there.

We went back.

We had a great show, and what made it even better was that sometimes there was no audience. The G.I.'s were being pulled out.

We played Shemya Island in the Aleutians; Yakota, Japan; Osan, Korea; Udorn, Utapao, and Namphong in Thailand; but when we flew into Long Binh, in Vietnam, we found all 30,000 men had been sent home.

I never thought I'd enjoy the sound of no applause so much.

Where there still were some American troops, the jokes still played. The guys still cheered and whistled at the girls. But you had the feeling they all had their barracks bags packed and were awaiting word from Paris that the chairs had rotted and all the diplomats had fallen on their rear ends.

You'd never have known it from the laughs and the cheering from the guys and the girls who were still in Vietnam. The jokes played even better. They were grateful that we had remembered them, when others were trying to forget.

"I'm very happy to be here at Tan Son Nhut, Southeast Asia's biggest rocket base . . . mostly incoming. . . . This is my ninth trip to South Vietnam, and I love it here. Don't laugh. That line kept me a civilian. . . . It's hard to believe. This is the last time we'll be playing this base. And this is the last time you out there will be seeing us here. Try not to cry. . . . We figured the war would be all over when we got here, but no such luck. Not only did they fail to reach an agreement in Paris, now they're fighting over the hotel bill."

The show ended, as all our shows ended, with the audience joining the entire cast in a song. Usually it was the one written by the little guy with the terrible voice I met all those centuries ago at Paramount. But Irving Berlin's "White Christmas" didn't seem quite right for our last show at a huge combat air base in a foreign land.

I told them, "Dolores is going to lead you in a song, and I want you all to join in. If you can't think of the words, just move your lips, and we'll dub something in from some other base."

And we all sang "Silent Night, Holy Night."

And it was.

That show was broadcast in the U.S. on January 17, 1973. On January 27, the delegates in Paris finally got off their keisters and signed the Vietnam peace agreement. It included a cease-fire, the withdrawal of all American troops within sixty days, and the reunification of the North and South through peaceful elections. North Vietnamese forces in South Vietnam would remain in place.

We all knew it was a phony peace. The NVA and the VC would just sit back, waiting for the U.S. and U.N. forces to get out. Then the roof would fall in. And half of Saigon would try to crawl to the top of the American embassy to be choppered out along with the last of our marines.

But by that time, the U.S. didn't care. The Watergate battle was going on and there was something else to watch on TV. Most of the country was happy to forget Vietnam.

But I'll always remember.

When that last show was broadcast I closed with "Well, that's it. That's the end of the line.

"When we made our first trip to Vietnam

in '64, we saw a lot of courageous fighting men from our country being baptized in guerrilla warfare, a very treacherous business. The 'river rats' at Dong Tam, the 'grunts' at Pleiku, the 'jolly greens' and the 'sandies' at Nakhon Phanom. We owe them more than we can ever repay.

"To them, to all the fighter pilots on the carriers on 'Yankee station' in the South China Sea, to the millions of guys we played to in every latitude and longitude around the world, thank you for Christmases I'll never forget."

CHAPTER NINE

1974-1990

BOB:
Well, George, what'll we do for a finish?

GEORGE BURNS:
At our age, do we want a finish?
— *Madison Square Garden,*
October 2, 1989

Even the Bible had to have an ending. But there is none to this rambling valentine to my adopted country. I figure I'm only beginning. After all, when I appeared onstage at Madison Square Garden beside God, God had to sit down.

We're entering exciting times, the nineties; totalitarian governments are crumbling all over the world, and dozens of politicians have been running for cover. I plan to hang around until there are no good monologue topics left.

Since this is supposed to be some sort of a history, let me take you for a fast roller-coaster ride through the Marx Brothers comedy that was the late seventies and eighties.

If you were paying attention, you may remember that the Vietnam War finally ended in an agreement neither side intended to honor. It was like one of Zsa Zsa's weddings.

I announced it by saying, "I guess you've heard the good news by now. North Vietnam has finally qualified for foreign aid. . . . The reason they delayed the peace treaty for so long was that Hanoi wasn't sure they had enough ammunition for a cease-fire. . . ."

It wasn't long before the North Vietnamese overran the South and Saigon became Ho Chi Minh City. By that time the American public didn't care; they didn't want any more foreign adventures, unless Sophia Loren was in them.

That made it tough on Presidents. After Vietnam, when we did launch a military operation, it had to be made to look as if we didn't mean it.

When Jimmy Carter was President, he had to try to rescue the Americans taken hostage at our embassy in Tehran with six old helicopters on loan from "M★A★S★H." They hardly made it to the first commercial.

During Reagan's administration he had to find a country small enough to beat up without getting Mike Wallace upset. Ronnie finally found one and sent the marines into Grenada. Estelle Getty could have handled that one by herself.

Later, President George Bush figured he was playing it safe when he declared war on only one man. Noriega took refuge in the Vatican embassy. We all figured the Catholic Church would know how to handle him; we expected them to raffle off his car. Finally, the Army played loud rock music until he gave himself up. If he's convicted, there's talk of sentencing him to the Grammy Awards.

Going back again to Reagan: He won one big victory that secures his place in history — he went to China and opened the doors to the West even wider. He found out a lot about their ancient culture. In only two meetings with Deng Xiaoping, Ronnie learned how to eat jelly beans with chopsticks.

The atmosphere became so cordial, I decided it was time to do a show from Beijing. We called it *Road to China*, and the cast was a real chop suey of international talent: Mikhail Baryshnikov; the Peking Opera; Big Bird from Sesame Street; Chinese comics Yuan, Hong, and Li; the Shanghai Circus; Shields and Yarnell; Chinese ballerina Zhong Run Liang; the Philadelphia Boys' Choir and Men's Chorale; and Dolores. The biggest item in the budget was for interpreters.

We were all bubbling over with international good will, and I had no idea how ironic some of my opening remarks were to become: "This is Tienanmen Gate. Tienanmen means, 'the Gate of Heavenly Peace.' It leads to Tienanmen Square, the biggest square in the world. It looks like Jackie Gleason's patio. . . . They can get a million and a half people in here. Of course, they're not here today. Nobody knew I was coming."

Heavenly peace didn't last very long. Only a few years later, the people were mowed down in Tienanmen Square by the People's Army. But at our show back then, we had a warm and happy audience, including Ambassador Leonard Woodcock and a lot of Chinese VIP's. I got laughs with lines like "I really can't believe I'm here, but this must be China. Last night, I went to a movie called *America Syndrome*. . . . I'm part of a cultural exchange. The State Department sends me over here and the Chinese send back a yak who can count to ten. . . . We had a great flight over but I'll tell you one thing, this is a long way to come for a Coca-Cola. . . . They gave me quite a ride to the hotel from the airport. Twice, I fell off the handlebars. . . . And can you believe the auto horns? Peking sounds like a whole city that just got married. . . . And let me tell you, I loved the Great Wall. Of course, I love anything as old as I am. . . . Service at the Peking Hotel is really fast, especially the laundry. Yesterday they washed my pajamas, and I was still in them."

And I summed it all up by saying, "What this trip is all about is getting to know each other. Talking and laughing and singing and dancing together, the way good friends should. And liking each other. The Chinese are easy to like."

But behind the scenes, there were warning signs. We had a brilliant Chinese actor, Ying Ruo Cheng, to act as interpreter and show us around Beijing, or Peking, depending on when you studied geography. You may have seen Ying in the Marco Polo miniseries, playing Kublai Khan. Later, he translated *Death of a Salesman* into Chinese and played the lead. I don't know what a Chinese salesman would sell, maybe fortune cookies, but Ying was a great performer. He used to translate my jokes for our Chinese audiences and started getting bigger laughs than I did, until he realized his mistake. He helped us do a spot from Democracy Wall, a wall in Beijing where the people could post their opinions, including opinions of the government. The deputy minister of culture got a look at it — the Chinese reviewed all our film — and said, "We don't like it. Take it out." So we rewrote it and tried it again. They still didn't like it. Too much democracy was showing up at the Democracy Wall. They finally took Ying away from us and replaced him with a member of the Communist Party. Apparently, his party dues weren't paid up, because after we shot the scene with him, they took it out again and it never reached the air.

After that, we didn't have much heavenly peace. They gave us a terrible time at the airport when we were leaving, searching our luggage for our film. They opened Dolores's bag, and she told them, firmly, "If you unpack that suitcase, *you're* going to pack it."

There's something in Dolores's voice that doesn't require translation. The customs officials closed her suitcase immediately. It was the biggest Chinese defeat since CBS canceled Charlie Chan.

We recently learned that our friend Ying was one of only two Chinese officials who refused to sign the order to open fire on the students in Tienanmen Square. I'm not certain of what has happened to him. I hope his fortune cookie was a good one.

Nixon had started our friendship with the Chinese even before Reagan, but he soon found out that Washington was his Forbidden

City. Watergate proved to the country how tough it is to find good plumbers today, and Nixon had to resign.

Gerald Ford became President and immediately pardoned his former boss. He said this was to save the nation from long hours of heartache and misery. But they made the miniseries anyway.

Jimmy Carter ran against Ford in the 1976 election, and during the campaign the two candidates stayed at a lot of the same hotels. On one broadcast I said, "Of course, Ford tried to get there first. That meant more impact, more votes, and less peanut shells in the beds. . . . A lot of people were surprised that Ford picked Nelson Rockefeller to run with him; after all, Rocky had tried to get the job of President three times himself. That's like asking Morris the Cat to watch your tuna salad."

Carter defeated Ford, and at the inauguration the new President and Rosalynn Carter walked down Pennsylvania Avenue together. They had to. By that time, OPEC had tripled the price of gas.

Jimmy Carter had the tough break of becoming President at a time when the whole world was becoming paranoid. You may have heard the latest definition of a paranoid — that's anyone who's in possession of all the facts. As I mentioned, the Iranians took the entire staff of the American embassy in Tehran hostage. They wouldn't let them go until after Ronald Reagan defeated Jimmy Carter in the 1980 election. Not that they were that anxious to see Ronnie as President; they were afraid if he didn't get elected, he'd go back to acting.

The years that followed were a merry time of hijacking, hostage taking, and terrorism. Anybody in Lebanon who hadn't been shot at wasn't really trying. The Israelis, the Syrians, the Muslims, and the Christians were all fighting at the same time. Beirut was the only town where you could get mugged at confession. So many U.S. citizens were being taken hostage, there was talk of putting the ransom on your American Express Card.

On April 18, 1983, the U.S. embassy in Beirut was virtually destroyed by a car bomb. A U.N. peacekeeping force was sent in, but there was no peace to keep. Two American marines were the first U.S. fatalities when they were hit by mortar fire near the international airport. The U.S. sent in the Navy, the French sent in planes. If this wasn't a war, why was everybody eating K-rations?

Naturally, there was a big peace conference, and a cease-fire was declared. Everybody knew what that meant. They put their fingers in their ears and waited.

They didn't have to wait long. On October 23, a terrorist drove a truckload of high explosives through the barriers of the driveway at the U.S. Marine Corps headquarters in Beirut and blew up the building and killed 241 U.S. marines. It made the explosion we escaped at the Brinks Hotel in Saigon seem like Palm Sunday at Pat Boone's.

The U.S. Department of Defense ordered the Hope Gypsies out of mothballs and into box lunches. After ten years of soft beds and home cooking, there was finally an area of the world unsafe enough to fly us into. There was more hatred in Lebanon than at an Academy Awards rehearsal.

And by that time, it was Christmas.

In ten years, of course, the Gypsies had changed, and not only around the waistline. Our producer was now Elliott Kozak, a man of infinite patience and talents, one of which was his ability to sleep standing up. That was a necessity on this tour, where our schedule was so tight you only got a chance to lie down if somebody was shooting at you. Our director was Sid Smith, and the writers, commanded by Gene Perrett, were Bob Mills, Fred Fox, Seaman Jacobs, Martha Bolton, and Jeffrey Barron. Of the old gang only Silvio Caranchini was still with us. Sil had tried to escape several times, but I always got him back with the promise of more money. He believed me, showing how nine trips to Vietnam can soften the brain.

Most of our shows were done on the decks of U.S. ships on patrol in the Mediterranean and off the Lebanese coast, ships like the old battleship U.S.S. *New Jersey*. I had talked a great group of performers into coming along; they believed me when I told them we were going to entertain the croupiers at Monte Carlo. We had Cathy Lee Crosby, Ann Jillian, Brooke Shields, and the new Miss U.S.A. Some of the ships were too small to do a show on, so we just phoned in the act, although there's no way you could phone in what those gals had. If you could, the military could recruit a whole navy by promising each man a cordless phone.

The ships were packed with marines, all of them on alert. Most of them were kids who hadn't heard the jokes; it was a pleasure to get laughs with some lines older than the audience.

"It's great to be playing in front of marines. These guys are so tough they use barbed wire for dental floss. . . . I saw some marines eating a plate of nails. The sissies were the ones who had to put salt on them. . . . After chow the other night I said to one of them, 'Toothpick?' And he said, 'No, thank you. I'll use my bayonet. . . .' Discipline is very strict in the Marine Corps. They're not even allowed to turn their electric blankets above 'just friendly.' "

I began to hope this was the last generation I could use those jokes on. Or would have to.

In the Mediterranean, we played to the Navy, which occasionally did let the men out of their cages to go on shore leave. But not often enough. The jokes took a slightly different tack.

"You guys are really getting lonely, aren't you? This morning I saw a sailor swabbing the deck . . . with his tongue. . . . I saw one group of sailors playing poker and I said, 'What are the stakes?' And one of them said, 'The winner gets to sleep with the fire extinguisher. . . .' I've seen towns after you guys have had liberty. You make Attila the Hun look like the Avon lady. . . . That's some port you've got near here, Piraeus, Greece. Greece is really something. If I wanted to see guys dancing together, I could have stayed in Hollywood. . . . I hear you guys are pretty wild on liberty. Some of you bring back girls, some bring back goats, and it takes the shore patrol the rest of the night to sort 'em out."

Laughter doesn't solve anything, but then,

neither do battleships today. They certainly didn't solve what was going on in Lebanon. I wanted to take our whole group ashore to do a show for the marines in Beirut, or what was left of it, but I was told it was too risky. This war was not just soldier against soldier, but sometimes father against son, brother against brother. The terrorists on both sides drove trucks loaded with TNT to their targets, and only the cowards bothered to get out. Any American was a sitting duck.

There was no point risking valuable lives, so they let me go in alone.

I didn't quite know what to expect. We took off from a carrier on Christmas morning and landed at the shot-up marine compound, where the marines now lived in underground bunkers. After the big bomb went off, they'd learned their lesson. Don't sleep anyplace that has a driveway.

The marines issued me a flak jacket and a helmet. I guess my old movies play everywhere. I saw somebody else similarly dressed, and it turned out to be Johnny Grant, the L.A. radio personality who has played almost as many trouble spots as I have.

There was no time or place to do a show; we were there to see one they put on for *us*.

In a makeshift chapel, American marines

in combat dress sang Christmas hymns, and a minister delivered a prayer. And then all the marines sang "Silent Night."

They couldn't forget it would always be silent night for 241 of their buddies.

I flew back to the ship and the Gypsies finished the tour and returned home. The mood in the States was like during the last days of the Vietnam War. President Reagan gave up trying to play M.P. to the whole nation of Lebanon and withdrew the Navy, the marines, and every American who wasn't chained to a bedpost. We pulled everything out of Beirut except one branch of our embassy.

This one was blown up by a station wagon. Trucks were no longer chic.

The Gypsies never went back to Beirut. Neither did the marines. I can't say any of us miss it.

Not everything that happened around that time was a disaster, depending on whether you were a Republican or a Democrat. The presidential campaign was between Ronnie Reagan and Walter Mondale. They scheduled a big TV debate, and it certainly stirred a lot of interest. And monologue jokes.

"Ronnie's advisers are afraid that Reagan will fall asleep while Mondale's talking. Or worse, while *he's* talking. . . . The two candidates have started fighting about who's more religious. Mondale got a little nervous when he saw skywriting that said: REAGAN IN '84. There was no plane. Just a giant finger. Reagan told his campaign manager, 'I've never let religion have any influence on my presidency. Make a note of that and give it to all my disciples.' "

Ronnie and George Bush won the election easily, which is something of an understatement. Mondale and his veep candidate, Geraldine Ferraro, only carried one state, Minnesota. Ronnie would have carried that one, too, but nobody told him it was there.

Reagan topped all my jokes that year, making up one of his own. Testing the microphone for his weekly radio broadcast, he said, "My fellow Americans, I'm pleased to tell you today that I've signed legislation that will outlaw Russia forever. We begin bombing in five minutes."

Somehow, the joke got on the air. If it had been Orson Welles who said it, it would have caused a national panic. But since it was Reagan, nobody took it seriously. They just figured Nancy had forgotten to make out his cue cards.

Reagan did much better in 1987, when he stood at the Brandenburg Gate with his back to the Berlin Wall, right near where

President Kennedy had gotten a standing ovation for saying, *"Ich bin ein Berliner."* Reagan relied on English for his ovation. He shouted, "Mr. Gorbachev, open this gate! Mr. Gorbachev, tear down this wall!" He was so startled when it actually happened in 1989, as predicted by Nancy's astrologer, that he called her and asked her to put two dollars for him on the Kentucky Derby.

Before he left office, Reagan was offered more than $5 million for his autobiography. Gorbachev had just written his own and was paid fourteen rubles for it. Gorby asked for a summit meeting with Reagan to find out the name of his literary agent.

Their meetings made history. Reagan was the actor, but Gorby upstaged him every time.

I went on the air with "Gorbachev started his visit by stopping his limo in Washington so he could shake hands with the spectators. He was the first leader of a country to hold out his hand in our nation's capital and not come away with foreign aid. . . . It was easy to spot Gorbachev. His limo had a bumper sticker saying, 'I brake for reporters. . . .' Everything Reagan does, Gorbachev does him one better. Reagan wears the flag of his country on his lapel. Gorby wears the map of his country on his forehead."

Glasnost came to mean considerably more than "openness." Gorbachev was the first disciple of Marx and Lenin to travel with a press agent.

We all felt this was truly the beginning of the end of the Cold War. This revolution, *everybody* would eat strawberries and cream. Things were looking so rosy, I even traded in my Kaopectate.

And then, in 1987, the Ayatollah Khomeini decided to close the Persian Gulf to oil shipments during Iran's war with Iraq. It was a national crisis. If America didn't get that oil, Reagan would have to comb his hair with the dry look. He ordered the Navy in. Things got pretty tense around November. When it looked like all the oil tanks in the Middle East would go up in flames, somebody in Washington with a sense of humor sent for the Gypsies to do our Christmas act again. After all, if everything blew up, the Air Force would only have to fly us one way.

We were sent by way of Hawaii, Manila, and Cape Espiritu Santo (I think the Defense Department was trying to confuse us) until we finally located the 6th Fleet. We did our final Christmas show December 1987, in the Persian Gulf, some forty-four years after our first one, in Europe. This time the villain had a Santa Claus beard instead of a Charlie

Chaplin moustache. I guess that's progress.

We called it "Bob Hope's U.S.O. Christmas Show from the Persian Gulf, or Around the World in Eight Days." We *had* to make it in eight days; that's as long as I can go now on tuna sandwiches.

We did one show from Bahrain, an Arab oil sultanate on some islands in the Persian Gulf where everyone was so rich, they hired Merv Griffin as garbage collector.

The U.S. had a busy Navy base there, and the strange customs of this strange country made for some strange jokes.

I told a huge audience of sailors and marines, "Here we are in Bahrain, the real land of brotherly love. . . . Everyone here looks like Danny Thomas. And that's just the women. . . . No show of public affection is allowed. In Bahrain, that's called the law. Back home it's called marriage. . . . Women here can't show any skin. I ordered a chicken breast and it was wearing a bra. . . . This is the kind of country where they cut off your hand for stealing. I don't even want to think about what they cut off if you steal someone's wife."

We left them laughing in Bahrain, flew out over the north Arabian Sea, and made a helicopter landing on the deck of the U.S.S. *Midway*. The flight deck was jammed with men who had come, as usual, to see our girls: Cathy Lee Crosby, Ann Jillian, Brooke Shields, Barbara Eden — who had brought her two daughters along — the Super Bowl Dancers, and Michelle Rogers, the new Miss U.S.A. Of course, the U.S. Navy now included women, but the men on the *Midway* outnumbered the females stationed aboard by three hundred to one. On this carrier, you didn't ask for a date; you called ahead for a starting time.

So we were doubly welcome, first for bringing them more females, but mainly for showing them they were not forgotten during their strange duty, playing tugboat in a floating shooting gallery, ten thousand miles from home at Christmas time with the thermometer at 106°. And that was at night. It was the only part of the world where Santa Claus arrived in a bikini.

I started my routine with "Here we are in the north Arabian Sea aboard the *Midway*. . . . I think this is appropriate, the oldest aircraft carrier meets the oldest operational comedian. . . . I knew this carrier was old when someone grabbed my Geritol and poured it into the fuel tanks."

In spite of the laughs and cheers and applause, we all began to feel a little uncomfortable on this hurried trip, as if we were being used as a Band-Aid on public opinion. Our Navy and marines were doing their dangerous job, but again this was no all-out military effort, and many people questioned its wisdom. Sure, we did need the oil in America. How else could Dolly Parton get into some of her dresses? But the Navy wasn't sure how best to carry out its mission in the Gulf. I told the men on the next ship, the U.S.S. *Kennedy,* "You ought to drain the sucker. Then it'll be the Army's problem."

Jokes couldn't make it go away, but we could do a little to help the men endure the heat and the boredom of another nonwar. The U.S.S. *Kennedy* was on station very close to Iran, the Disneyland for fanatics. Iran is where Santa makes three lists: Who's been naughty, who's been nice, and who's nuts. But before we laugh — or, preferably for me, *after* we laugh — we ought to consider how sane any nation was during the paranoid eighties.

We left the Gulf after doing our final Christmas show aboard the U.S.S. *Okinawa,* where everybody sang "Ave Maria" on the flight deck.

We had hardly finished the hymn when both sides in the Gulf began firing at each other again.

The insanity at home continued with another political campaign. Senator Gary Hart, running for the Democratic presidential nomination, was seen by the press coming out the backdoor of his girlfriend's house.

His wife was not amused.

I told it this way: "I don't know if the presidential candidates are running for the White House or Animal House. . . . As you all know, Gary Hart threw his hat into the ring for the second time. I guess he finally remembered where he left it. . . . And how about evangelist Pat Robertson? He's already tossed his halo into the ring. . . . He had his first child eight weeks after he was married. Poor Pat. Before he could say, 'I do,' he did."

In the end, George Bush ran on the Republican ticket against Mike Dukakis, who self-destructed during the campaign. Bush picked Dan Quayle as his running mate and there were a lot of questions about Quayle's youth and his intelligence. A story went around that he had missed Air Force One because he couldn't remember the flight number. But Bush and Quayle won the election, and Bush got off to a good start. Within two weeks, Rich Little was impersonating him.

Ronnie Reagan made headlines by going off to Tokyo to earn $2 million for two days' work. He said it was the minimum wage in Japan. Larry Gelbart wrote in the *New York Times* that when Reagan left the Oval Office for the last time, he looked back at the desk and said to himself, "The buck starts here."

Then came November of 1989, when East Berliners danced with West Berliners near the spot where I had swiped the swastika flag from Adolf Hitler's bunker. We hadn't seen so many happy Germans since the last Löwenbrau commercial. Three million East Germans danced through the wall, took one look at the prices, and danced back home.

I remembered all the shows we had done in the days when Berlin was in ashes, and later when it was sliced in half like a pumpernickel sandwich. And now, the Wall was coming down and being sold in little pieces in the doorstop section of K Mart.

And all the Communists voted themselves out of office and admitted they had been incompetent. This frightened the hell out of Congress; they were afraid democracy might spread to the United States.

Maybe all this means that the Gypsies are now obsolete. I hope so, but knowing the ingenuity of men when it comes to blowing each other up, I'm not going to unpack yet. It's the suspense that keeps me young.

Everything in my life seemed to come full

circle on October 2, 1989. I went back to where it all began: vaudeville. I had started out in Cleveland in 1923, doing that dance act with that girl named Mildred Rosequist. Mildred was about fifteen at the time and the act bombed, so I figured this time I'd go for a little more experience. Almost fourteen thousand people showed up at Madison Square Garden to see two guys whose ages added up to 179 years do a live act, which I guess a lot of the audience came to see if we could prove.

They needn't have worried. George Burns on a stage is as good as Mildred Rosequist ever was. And she couldn't dance and smoke a cigar at the same time. George is what vaudeville was all about. When he walked out in that spotlight, you could feel the electricity between him and the audience. Of course, when he first walked out on a vaudeville stage, only George and Benjamin Franklin knew what electricity was. When George walks into a restaurant today and orders a three-minute egg, they make him pay in advance.

Madison Square Garden would seem to be a pretty outrageous place for two guys to try to keep a crowd's attention, unless they were trying to beat each other's brains out with boxing gloves. But with microphones, a good sound system, and seats crowding right up to the stage, it proved to be sensational.

We both wanted to show as many people as possible what vaudeville used to be like. After all, we were only going to give one performance; it was a little late for us to turn it into a career.

And of course, we both needed the money. Those hormone shots are expensive.

Vaudeville in the old days was something different every night, because you never knew what to expect from the audience. If they got ugly, it was the performer's job to keep them from throwing overaged tomatoes. No laugh machine, no retakes. It was all as live as life itself.

As we stood out there, two lonely figures in the glare of the spotlights, I felt lucky to have the best ninety-three-year-old tap dancer in the business as my partner. We only had to look at each other to see all those years of one-night stands in places like Williamsport, Pennsylvania, and Hamtramck, Michigan, when we both learned to cook hash over a hotplate in our dressing room and wondered if we'd eat again tomorrow. We both knew it hadn't really changed for us since the days of the Gus Sun Time and the Balaban and Katz vaudeville circuit. This wasn't an audience that we faced in Madison Square Garden; it was a jury. These weren't G.I.'s grateful for any kind of free entertainment, but New Yorkers only half a mile from Broadway. Go ahead, we could almost hear them saying; lay an egg, with two old yolks.

This could be the flop heard 'round the world.

Of course, if it had been, I wouldn't be mentioning it here. We must have done pretty well, because we got offers to play the Miami Arena, the Detroit Dome, and Sun City right after we finished. In Sun City we'll be considered a kiddie act.

When it was my turn to get into the ring at Madison Square Garden, I pretended it was still Cleveland. I hit 'em with local jokes:

"I was surprised to see so many homeless people on the streets. The first one I met was Ed Koch. . . . He finally found out what it felt like to be mugged. . . . And I can't believe the ticket prices. When I was doing *Roberta* on Broadway if you paid that kind of money you owned a piece of the show . . . and the leading lady. I heard a mugger tell a tourist, 'Your *Phantom of the Opera* tickets or your life!' *Phantom of the Opera*. If I was charging those prices, I'd wear a mask, too. . . . Our tickets are nothing like that. George and I fig-

472

ured you should be able to take a tour of these two old monuments for about the same price they charge for the Statue of Liberty. . . ."

We go back a long way, George and I, not only in vaudeville, but in pictures, too. We made *College Swing* at Paramount in 1938, George and Gracie and I, and George didn't make another film until he won the Oscar for *Sunshine Boys* in 1975. George certainly knew how to wait for the right script.

We weren't foolish enough to think we could supply all the sex appeal by ourselves in the New York show, so we had added Dionne Warwick and Miss Universe and Miss U.S.A. to the bill. That's when I found out George still chases after girls. It's after he catches them that he's in trouble.

That reminds me of the joke about the George Burns doll — you wind it up and it takes a nap.

George came out all alone, and held the stage for almost an hour. After all the years of being Gracie's straight man, he's finally been recognized as one of our best stand-up comedians. Even though he had to sit down. He was playing in the round, with that big audience on every side, so he kept turning his chair around to give them all an equal chance at the jokes.

When the laughter died down, I walked out to join George for the first time on a stage. We did one of the old routines George had made famous in vaudeville with Gracie, I played Gracie under protest and a lady's hat, which we had somebody toss to us from the audience.

It was a strange feeling, being half of Burns and Allen, even in fun. The two of them had been the real vaudeville, and one of the true love stories of another generation. I wondered what George was thinking, but I couldn't see through the cigar smoke. But after we danced "Tea for Two" together, George said, "Say good night, Gracie," and I said "Good night, Gracie," and he smiled, and we walked offstage, arm in arm.

The team of Burns and Hope had finally made the Big Time.

The audience in the Garden stood up and cheered the way the crowd did when Joe Louis kayoed Max Schmeling at Yankee Stadium.

You don't remember that far back? It doesn't matter. George and I do.

It was only Yesterday.

CLOSING CREDITS

I don't want anyone who's had the courage to read down this far to get the impression that I'm the longest-running one-man show in history. Nothing could be further from the truth. I've had more help in my career than a starlet with a stuck zipper.

The road from Cleveland to Madison Square Garden was paved with good writers. But those brilliant guys — and a few equally brilliant gals — were more than just writers. I still spend more time with them than I do with my family, Dolores keeps reminding me. The writers and I have shouted at one another, laughed with one another, played golf with one another, and ducked into foxholes together.

Mort Lachman likes to tell the story of the time we were shooting a Christmas show someplace in 'Nam, and he kept directing me to move to the left. I kept objecting, and he kept insisting. When we got back to Hollywood and started editing the show, I saw that shot and finally found out why. When I moved over, the camera revealed flashes from a VC patrol in the jungle behind us, firing in our direction as I kept telling jokes. When I asked Mort why he didn't warn me — a guy could get killed — he said I wasn't getting really big laughs, anyway.

I don't know how to thank all the stars I've worked with over the years. Hollywood takes a lot of bum raps, but the biggest names in the business were always ready and eager to take the same chances, eat the same box lunches, and face the same scorpions as the rest of us. They were real Gypsies. And even at home and at peace, they were still willing to take the risk of appearing on my show. After the spiders, the lizards, and the VC, it must have been a vacation.

And to all the others, from the bit players and grips and cameramen and art directors and lighting men and makeup people (who had the toughest job of all) to the orchestra leaders and musicians, especially Les Brown and his band, and all the producers and directors and, yes, studio and network executives, I thank you, too.

There have been a lot of jokes about how young the executives are getting to be these days; in fact, Hal Kanter suggested that in its next negotiation, the Writers Guild insist that no network executive be allowed to take a meeting with a writer unless accompanied by an adult. But network executives play an important part in the creative processes on our show, they keep telling me.

In spite of them, I do love television. In fifty-one years, I've never missed a show because of illness. No matter how sick of me NBC gets, I show up.

Next, thanks to all the Presidents of the United States, from FDR to George Bush, who remained my friends even after what I said about them. They all laughed and told me they enjoyed every bit of it. Maybe they didn't understand the jokes.

Two of my closest friends aren't around to accept my gratitude. Bing Crosby, the Groaner, and Jerry Colonna, the Mad Professor. Bing left us suddenly on a golf course in France, and if he had to go, what better place to hit the Road to Heaven?

Jerry left us gradually, and that was even tougher.

Have I forgotten anyone? Only my family. And particularly the torch singer I met in that speakeasy off Broadway in 1936. Dolores. We're still together, and if you don't think that's making history in Hollywood, you don't get around much.

I always remember Satchel Paige's famous line: "Don't look back. Somethin' may be gainin' on you." I look ahead, it's safer.

I look ahead to more laughter, more audiences, and more jokes like "I love playing golf with Jerry Ford. If you beat him, he pardons you. . . . And golfing with Reagan when he was President was fun. But Nancy would always follow us around saying, 'It's my turn. . . .' "

People ask me why I don't retire and go fishing. I have one stock answer that sums it all up.

Fish don't applaud.

To be continued.

BOB HOPE
Toluca Lake, California, 1990